A TEXT BOOK OF
VEGETABLE CULTURE

Dr. PREM SINGH ARYA
Senior Vegetable Breeder
Department of Vegetable Science and Floriculture
Himachal Pradesh Agricultural University
Palampur-176 062 (H.P.), INDIA

KALYANI PUBLISHERS
LUDHIANA • NEW DELHI • NOIDA (U.P.) • HYDERABAD • CHENNAI
KOLKATA • CUTTACK • GUWAHATI • KOCHI • BENGALURU

KALYANI PUBLISHERS

Head Office

B-1/1292, Rajinder Nagar, **Ludhiana**-141 008 • Ph : 0161-2760031
E-mail : kalyanibooks@yahoo.co.in

Administration Office

4779/23, Ansari Road, Daryaganj, New Delhi-110 002
Ph : 011-23271469, 23274393, 23278688 **E-mail :** kalyani_delhi@yahoo.co.in

Works

B-16, Sector-8, **NOIDA** (U.P.)

Branches

1, Mahalakshmi Street, T. Nagar, **Chennai**-600 017 • Ph : 044-24344684
110/111, Bharatia Towers, Badambadi, **Cuttack**-753 009 (Odisha) • Ph : 0671-2311391
3-5-1108, Narayanaguda, **Hyderabad**-500 029 • Ph : 040-24750368
10/2B, Ramanath Mazumdar Street, **Kolkata**-700 009 • Ph : 033-22416024
Arunalaya, 1st Floor, Saraswati Road, Pan Bazar, **Guwahati**-781 001 • Ph : 0361-2731274
Koratti Parambil House, Convent Road, **Kochi**-682 035 • Ph : 0484-2367189
No. 24 & 25, 1st Floor, Hameed Shah Complex, Cubbonpet Main Road, **Bengaluru**-560 002

KPP K 16834 05

Re-typesetting, 2015

Laser Typesetting at
Elite-Art

ISBN 978-93-272-5013-8

PRINTED AT

B.B. Press, A-37, Sec-67, Noida-201301
and published by Mrs. Usha Raj Kumar for
Kalyani Publishers, New Delhi-110 002

Dedicated to

THE MEMORY OF

MY RESPECTED PARENTS

FOREWORD

Vegetables have a special significance in human diet by supplying protective nutrients and tone up energy and vigour of man. They have a vital role to play in the food front from the nutritive menu which make the food tasty, with specific flavour, aroma, and for making the health of better quality.

In India, vegetable growing is based on the basic principles their understanding and utilization for commercialisation and running several cottage industries and to generate employment opportunities for the unemployed youths and women folk. The role of vegetables in social, cultural and economic front is well known and are used daily in the family because of their nutritive value, change in the dietary habit and more intake in different forms besides their manifold medicinal properties.

These being environment specific are primarily confined to the areas suitable for their growing. The increase in area and production may depend on the domestic consumption and demand in the international market. India with a diverse agro-climatic conditions is congenial for growing vegetables and can take legitimate pride in potential pockets need to be explored as a specialised enterprise and contribute almost major share next only to China, in the world vegetable production. Moreover, India is the largest producer, consumer (domestic need) of most of the vegetables like bhindi, garden pea, etc. which holds a very coveted position as a leading vegetables in the international market and are exported to various countries in the world.

The book "A Text Book of Vegetable Culture" may be of great significance and intend to be a better guide to the students appearing in competitive examinations (UGC, ICAR, NET, etc.) farmers, learners, scientists, policy framers both public and private sector organisations and *vis-a-vis* all engaged in the vegetable industry.

The attempt made by Prof. Prem Singh Arya, Senior Vegetable Breeder, HPAU, Palampur to put together the information from various sources on the various applied aspects basic principles of vegetable culture in the form of a book is appreciable and I congratulate him for the same.

Palampur

PROF. PREM KUMAR KHOSLA
Vice-Chancellor,
HPAU, Palampur

PREFACE

The book entitled A Text Book of Vegetable Culture has been written keeping in view the typical conditions of the country. The information in the book has been distilled from various sources *viz.*, various reports, important reviews and research papers, personal communication books, monographs, periodicals, seminars and symposiums etc. from where the matter has been gathered and is based on the research work done by the author, his practical experience. It put together the applied aspects of vegetable culture with special reference to diverse conditions, more so, the information embodied does cut across the geo-ecological boundaries but most applicable in agro-climatic situations, akin to the length and breadth of the country.

However, a few books on the subject are available but have scattered information and efforts have been made to compile the consolidated latest and detail information in one script on the various aspects required by the farmers growing vegetables, students competing in different examinations and interviews (UGC, ICAR, NET, etc.), teachers teaching students, policy planners and all others engaged in vegetable industry. This is intended as a reference for all concerned with vegatable culture particularly, importance, classification, farming systems and sundries, economic role of vegetables, poly-house technology, bio-fertilizers, healthy nursery production, kitchen gardening and off-season vegetable production. It also includes, uses, nutritional and medicinal uses, taxonomy, cultivars grown and detail cultural practices *viz.*, climate, soil, manure and fertilizer, irrigation, plant protection, etc. for all the vegetable crops.

A unique feature of this book is that special attention has been given on importance of less important vegetables which are otherwise nutritive, growing in nature, easily available in their natural habitate and are consumed.

The book has been written for the benefit of all those who are interested in increasing their knowledge and understanding about detail valuable information of vegetable culture emanating from the above concerted efforts. I hope that the information contained in it will be of immense value to the farming community, especially those engaged in vegetable growing extension workers involved in promoting vegetable industry, the students interested in learning the basic principles of vegetable culture, scientists engaged in research, teaching and other extension work.

The author is extremely thankful to Dr. P.K. Khosla, Hon'ble Vice-Chancellor, HPAU, Palampur for writing the foreword.

Lastly I gratefully express my sincere feelings to my wife Smt. Savitri Arya, son Mr. Mahesh, and daughters Miss Kalpana and Leena for sparing me to complete this book at their personal comfort and against heavy odds.

Needless to say, errors and omissions are mine. In the end I request my readers to send their opinion on and about this work by writing back to the publisher or direct to the author. Truthful analysis and critical estimate will be the real record of this mammoth work.

Palampur

PROF. PREM SINGH ARYA

CONTENTS

CHAPTER 1

INTRODUCTION

Vegetables play a vital role in balancing human diet being nutritious and protective. It is highly essential to take vitamins and minerals in required quantities for sound health of human body to create resistance against diseases, as vegetables have become integral part of the daily diet of the all classes of society. Vegetables being rich source of vitamins and minerals besides having medicinal values. Indian Council of Medical Research recommends that an adult should consume about 300 g of vegetables daily. The per capita consumption is very low (about 120 g) as compared to the most advanced countries. Consumption of vegetables like greens help in easy digestion and proper bowl movement. Further, vegetables help to neutralise the acidity of intestine due to intake of meat items. No doubt India being a vegetarian country and there is a alarming challenge to planners, growers and others engaged in vegetable quality production in the country. Today, India prides itself as the second largest producer of vegetables in the world and has maintained a measured growth in production for meeting the growing-demands at home and abroad.

Vegetables are increasing in number all over the world and approximately 500 million tonnes produced with the annual growth rate of 2 per cent. In India, the annual production of 80.8 million tonnes of vegetables from an area of 6.2 million hectares having a share of 13.38 per cent in the world production. During 8th Plan both the production and productivity of vegetables recorded impressive growth. Adoption of high yielding cultivars and hybrids and suitable production technologies has largely contributed for higher production and productivity. Now per capita consumption has also increased from 95 to 175 g/capita/day.

Vegetables provide nutritional security for the increasing population of the country and help in reducing the malnutrition being faced by the underfed, down trodden masses through various required important nutrients carbohydrates, fats, vitamins, minerals especially digestive proteins. Malnutrition is a serious problem and leading to an imbalance diet. Moreover, increase in population, urbanisation and incomes accompanied by affluence and greater health awareness, change in dietary habit (more intake of vegetables) have contributed to rise in domestic consumption of vegetables. These vegetables produce more bio-mass which can be used to feed the increasing population, animals, poultry, etc. besides addition of organic matter in the soil to improve and maintain soil fertility and avoidance of use of chemical fertilizers, excess use of which produces polluted vegetables harmful to the consumers. These being short duration, produces higher quality yields and get well fitted in the cropping systems of a particular place with better cropping intensity. These also prove most suitable for growing as mixed, companion, relay and as inter-crop with many cereals, sugarcane, vegetables, spices, fruit and forest plantations, more specific in young orchards economically by generating additional income to the farmers heither to supplement the farmers in case of any natural hazards or failure of the crop/orchard in which these are inter-cropped.

Looking at the national scenario, vegetables have tremendous strength in terms of natural resources and biological assets especially genetic resources which have been exploited and need further attention to utilize and capitalize the same to solve the pressing problems of biotic and abiotic stresses effectively. Further concerted efforts are required to make use of the potential markets of vegetables in the country, cheap manpower especially labour and qualified scientific manpower, etc. which are the strength of the vegetable research and development. From all angles these vegetables are economical to grow in a particular area having appropriate suitable facilities and congenial agro-climatic conditions. In addition, the farmers are well equipped with latest growing techniques regarding the production technology of different vegetable(s). Therefore, resulting in maximum output and more income per unit area as compared to cereals, pulses, fruits and forest trees. Moreover, most vegetables *viz.* high value, off-season, European vegetables and their seed production helps in generating higher incomes to the poor and marginal farmers having small land holdings, more so their cultivation is quite suitable for small farmers who are hard working, honest and basically poor. When a number of vegetables (varieties and hybrids) are grown in a sequence on the same piece of land in a year, need intensive cultural operations, post-harvest management, effective transportation and marketing network in a well organised way enabling to make available fresh, attractive, nutritious and quality vegetables to the consumers at the earliest. This all helps in generating employment avenues to the unemployment masses, young youths and women-folk including labour, best utilisation of family members and all others engaged in vegetable trade.

While considering the trade point of view, vegetables occupy an important place in Indian economy. Apart from fresh vegetables, processed, canned vegetables are now exported to other countries especially to middle-East. Vegetable seed industry is an another profit earning venture in our country.

The plant protection measures need to be followed by the farmers judiciously to cause minimum harm to the useful pollinators (which helps in bringing about pollination in vegetables) to avoid chemical residual pressure and not to use the chemicals in the form of insecticides, fungicides, weedicides, for ripening and brightening, etc. which not only pollute the vegetables but make them hazardous to the human health leading to many dreaded diseases like AIDs and cancer, etc. More so, the surplus produce at peak season should either be processed in various forms acceptable to the military and paramilitary forces, civil masses and export purposes. Thus the various organisations both government and private need to plan and execute programmes on large scale to produce better quality vegetables which meet the standards and can compete in the international market and supply the same to the needy countries. Therefore, by exploiting the export potential for both fresh and processed vegetables products will not only avoid the wastage but help in disposing-off the surplus produce and help in earning the valuable foreign exchange beside boosting the economy of the farmers.

In order to supply the minimum requirements of the constantly increasing population of the country, the present requirement of vegetable and vegetable products has to be substantially increased to meet the demand of growing population, this can be done by exploiting the potential of vegetable production fully for which production technologies need to be strengthened. Among the technologies, integrated nutrient management is the foremost important one because of the introduction of new improved, high yielding varieties and hybrids. This necessitates heavy inputs of organic and inorganic forms of nutrients. The huge gap between present production and future requirements necessitates much higher vegetable production and wider availability to narrow down the same by adopting the vertical and possibly horizontal expansion in vegetable production by various means in order to ensure much greater availability and consumption level as well as income generation.

Vegetable production calls for strategic planning to ensure their round the year availability to the increasing population at reasonable prices while also safeguarding the interest of the farmers. There has been substantial increase in both the production and productivity of vegetables. However, productivity continues to be lower and post-harvest losses are higher than in most developed countries. To achieve higher production levels, productivity has to be increased through the adoption of high yielding varieties/hybrids and improved production technologies coupled with a more efficient system of post-harvest handling. However, the latest techniques of vegetable breeding, production and seed production are of dire need both in private and public sector to increase the required production level. In addition, use of various tools like biotechnology, poly/green-house technology, other protected production methods can help to a greater length.

Therefore, the major concerted emphasis need to be given on research and development efforts required to boost all the three major fields of vegetable breeding, production and seed production in general and transmission in particular are required to achieve the target by providing common platform and net working to the vegetable workers especially vegetable breeders, production and seed production scientists and extension workers in the country. However, efforts by the planners, funding agencies both in public and private sectors, more so the ICAR, IARI, PDVR/IIVR, IIHR, SAUs and others concerned with vegetable industry as a whole, covering all the aspects of teaching, research and extension etc. from seed sowing/planting to maturity to disposal of the produce and post-harvest handling and processing, etc. without putting the farmers in any type of loss and others involved in the vegetable trade. Also to make the vegetable industry on sound footing and up to the satisfaction of the organisers.

There are issues in vegetable research and development which warrant adequate attention with special reference to the problems of varied nature, which have been minimised by developing better varieties/hybrids, high yielding and resistant to biotic and abiotic stresses and also plant protection technology. However, this requires the application of modern bio-technological and genetic engineering tools. International collaborations among different countries may have a catalytic role in solving unsolved problems in vegetable research.

CHAPTER

2

CLASSIFICATION OF VEGETABLE CROPS

In the world there are about ten thousand species used as vegetables and nearly sixty vegetables are of commercial value in the country for ease these can be classified as :

Botanical Classification

Classification based on nature of pollination

Sl. No.	*Family*	*Botanical name*	*English name*	*Hindi name*
(*i*)	**Aizoaceae**	*Tetragonia expansa*	New Zealand spinach	New Zealand Palak
(*ii*)	**Amaranthaceae**	*Amaranthus blitum* *Amaranthus tricolor*	Amaranths Amaranths	Chhoti chauli Badi chauli
(*iii*)	**Amaryllidaceae** (Amaryllis family)	*Allium cepa* L. *Allium sativum* L.	Onion, Shallot Garlic	Piyaz Lahson
		Allium ampeloprasum L.	Leek/Kurrat/great headed garlic	Leek
		Allium schoenoprasum L. *Allium fistulosum* L.	Chive Welsh Onion/Japanese bunching onion	Chive —
		Allium cepa var. *viviparum*	Top Onion or Tree Onion	—
		Allium cepa var. *aggregatum* *Allium tuberosum* L.	Multiplier onion Chinese chive	— Zimmu
(*iv*)	**Araceae** (Arum family)	*Colocasia esculenta* L. Schott.	Colocasia	Kachalu, Ghuiyan, Arvi, Taro, Dasheen

		Amorphophallus companulatus Blume	Elephant's foot or yam	Zimikand, Suran
(*v*)	**Baellaceae**	*Basella alba* L.	Basella	Poi
(*vi*)	**Chenopodiaceae** (goose family)	*Beta vulgaris* L. *Beta vulgaris* var. *cicla* L. *Spinacia oleracea* L. *Beta vulgaris* var. *bengalensis* *Atriplex hortensis*	Garden Beet Swiss chard Spinach Beet leaf Mountain Spinach	Chukandar — Vilayati Palak Chakwat
(*vii*)	**Compositae**	*Cichorium intybus* L. *Lactuca sativa* L. *Cynara scolymus* L. *Helianthus tuberosum*	Chicory Lettuce Artichoke (Globe) Jerusalem Artichoke	Kasni Salad Hathichak Artichoke
(*viii*)	**Convolvulaceae**	*Ipomoea batatas Poir*	Sweet potato	Shakarkandi
(*ix*)	**Cruciferae** (Brassicaceae or mustard family)	*Brassica oleracea*var. *acephala* *B. oleracea* var. *gemmifera*	Kale Brussel's Sprouts	Karamsag Brussel sprout
		B. oleracea var. *capitata*	Cabbage	Bandh Gobhi
		B. oleracea var. *italica* *B. oleracea* var. *botrytis* *B. oleracea* var. *gongylodes/coularapa* L.	Sprouting Broccoli Cauliflower Knol-khol	Broccoli Phul Gobhi Ganth Gobhi
		Brassica rapa *Brassica napus* var. *napobrassica*	Turnip Rutabaga	Shalgam —
		B. pekinesis (*heading*)	Petesi/Chinese cabbage	Band China Gobhi
		B. chinensis (*non-heading*)	Pak-choi/Chinese cabbage	Klmli China sag.
		Raphanus sativus L. *R. sativus* var. *caudatus*	Radish Rat-tail radish	Muli Mungre, Sungre
		Armoracia rusticana	Horse-radish	—
(*x*)	**Cucurbitaceae** (gourd family)	*Cucurbita pepo* L. *C. moschata Poir* *C. maxima Dusch*	Summer squash Pumpkin Winter squash	Chappan Kaddu Sitaphal Vilayati kaddu
		Citrullus lanatus Schrad *Citrullus vulgaris* var. *fistulosus*	Watermelon Round gourd	Tarbuz Tinda

		Cucumis sativus L. *Cucumis melo* L. C. *melo* var. *utilissimus* *Momordica charantia*	Cucumber Muskmelon Longmelon Tar Bitter gourd	Khira Kharbuza Kakri Karela, Kareli
		Lagenaria siceraria (Molina) Stendl.	Bottle gourd	Lauki
		Trichosanthes dioica Roxb.	Pointed gourd	Parwal
		Trichosanthes anguina L.	Snake gourd	Pandole or Chichinda
		Luffa cylindrica Roem.	Sponge gourd	Ghiya Tori, Nenua
		Luffa acutangula Roxb. *Benincasa hispida* (Thumb). Cong. *Coccinia cordifolia/indica* *Sechium edule* *Cucumis melo momordica*	Ridge gourd Wax gourd Coccinia/Ivy-gourd Cho-cho or Chow-Show or Chayote Snapmelon	Kali Tori or Jhingli Tori Petha, Kumhra Kundru Launku Phut
(*xi*)	**Euphorbiaceae** (Spurge family)	*Manihot esculenta*	Tapioca	Manioc, Cassava, Yucca maravalli, Tikhoor
(*xii*)	**Graminae**	*Zea mays* var. *rugosa*	Sweet corn	Meothi, Makki
(*xiii*)	**Leguminosae** (Pulse or pea family)	*Pisum sativum* L. *Trigonella foenumgraecum* L. *T. corniculata* L. *Vicia faba* L. *Phaseolus vulgaris* L.	Garden pea Fenugreek Feenu greek Broad bean Kidney bean French bean	Matar Methi Kasuri or chana methi Bakla, Kaun Farash bean, Chhoti sem
		Dolichos lablab (Roxb. & L.) *Phaseolus coccineus/ multiflorus*	Hyacinth bean Multflora bean	Sem Bean
		Cyamopsis tetragonoloba (L. Taab)	Cluster bean	Guar
		Psophocarpus tetragonolobus *Phaseolus lunatus* L. *Vigna sinensis* Savi. *Vigna sinensis* var. *sesguipedalis*	Winged bean Lima bean Cowpea Asparagus or yard long bean	Goa bean or Fox tail bean — Lobia —
(*xiv*)	**Liliaceae**	*Asparagus officinalis* L.	Asparagus	Shatawar
(*xv*)	**Malvaceae**	*Abelmoschus esculentus* (L) Moench.	Okra/Lady's finger, Bhindi	Bhindi

(*xvi*)	**Polygonaceae**	*Rheum rhaponticum* *Rumex vesicarius*	Rhuberb, Sorrel Portulaca	— Khatta Palak
(*xvii*)	**Portulacaceae**	*Portulaca oleracea* L.		Kulfa
(*xviii*)	**Solanaceae**	*Solanum melongena* L. *Solanum tuberosum* L. *Lycopersicon esculentum* M. *Capsicum annum* *Capsicum frutscens* L.	Egg plant/Aubergine Potato Tomato Sweet-Pepper Chillies	Baingan Alu Tamatar, Vilayati baingan Simla Mirch Mirch
(*xix*)	**Umbelliferae**	*Daucus carota* L. *Apium graveolens* *Petroselimum hortense/crispum* L. *Pastinaca sativa* L. *Coriandrum sativum* L.	Carrot Celery Parsley Parsnip Coriander	Gajar Celery Parsley Parsnip Dhania
(*xx*)	**Zingiberaceae**	*Zingiber officinale* L. *Curcuma domestica longa*	Ginger Turmeric	Adrak Haldi

Growing vegetables is important to know which vegetable crops are self-pollinated and which are cross-pollinated. Below the vegetable crops are arranged to show how they are pollinated.

A. Highly cross-pollinated

(*i*) ***Wind-pollinated.*** Amaranths, beet-leaf, spinach, garden beet, sugar beet.

(*ii*) ***Insect-pollinated.*** All cucurbit, all Cole crops, radish, turnip, carrot and onion.

B. Often cross-pollinated. Lima bean, egg plant, okra, chilli, sweet pepper.

C. Highly self-pollinated. Asparagus bean, cluster bean, Dolichos bean, French bean, cow pea, garden pea, methi, lettuce, tomato.

In group B and C self-pollination occurs by reason of floral structures and any cross-pollination takes place is affected by insect-pollinators. The frequency of such cross-pollination is far greater in group B. It should be noted that cabbage, cauliflower, knol-khol, sprouting broccoli. Brussel's sprout and kale are all cultivars of *Brassica oleracea* and can freely cross with each other. Similarly both garden beet and palak, beet leaf, sugar beet, Swiss chard are cultivars of *Beta vulgaris* also crosses with each other. Hot pepper (chilli) and sweet pepper (Capsicum) are both cultivars of *Capsicum annuum* and Asparagus bean and cow pea are both cultivars of *Vigna sinensis.*

Grouping based on planting response

A. Easily survive transplanting. All Cole vegetables, Chinese cabbage, lettuce, tomato, brinjal, capsicum and chillies.

B. Needs care in transplanting. Onion, leek, celery, parsley, amaranths, cardamom.

C. Not suited to transplanting. Garden pea, turnip, radish, carrot, garden beet, spinach, gourds, bhindi, methi.

D. Suits both transplanting and direct seeding. Chinese cabbage, chillies, amaranths.

E. Poly pack planting. All cucurbit mostly, cucumber, bitter gourd, squashes, melons, pumpkins etc. tomato hybrids.

Classification based on nature of vegetable. The seed setting and production may occur in one season/year, two season/year or may live for many years with the help of under ground parts but behave as annual.

Annual	*Biennial*	*Perennial*
Tomato, brinjal, capsicum, chillies, garden pea, bhindi, methi, amaranths, all cucurbit, celery, parsley.	All Cole vegetables, Chinese cabbage, onion, leek radish, turnip, carrot, garden beet, beet leaf, spinach.	Asparagus, chayote, ginger, turmeric, colocasia, cardamom.

Classification based on area of seed production. Vegetables/varieties grown in temperate, sub-temperate and tropical areas for seed production as per their requirements.

Temperate	*Sub-temperate*	*Tropical*
Cabbage, knol-khol, kale Brussels sprout, sprouting broccoli, sugar beet, chicory, potato, amaranthus, temperate varieties of radish, turnip, carrot and garden beet.	Late cauliflower, beet leaf, spinach, celery, parsley asparagus, chayote, sub-temperate varieties of radish turnip and carrot.	Tomato, brinjal, bhindi, chillies capsicum all cucurbit, ginger, turmeric colocasia, cardamom sweet potato.

Grouping based on method of seed production

(*i*) **Seed to seed** *(In situ).* Garden pea, garlic, radish, spinach, methi, carrot, turnip, garden beet.

French bean, bhindi, tomato, brinjal, capsicum, chillies, cucurbit, cauliflower, cabbage etc.

(*ii*) **Replanting method (Stecklings/Head/curd/bulb to seed).** Turnip, radish, carrot, garden beet, cabbage, sprouting broccoli, Chinese cabbage, sugar beet and chicory.

(*iii*) **Both.** Carrot, parsley, celery, Chinese cabbage, turnip and radish.

Classification based on breeding systems

	Sexual		*Asexual*	
Predominantly self-pollinated	*Often cross-pollinate*	*Largely cross-pollinated*	*Dioecious*	*Vegetatively propagated*
Degree of selfing 90-100%	Adapted to self-pollination but degree of cross pollination more than 4%	Degree of crossing can be unto 100%	*i.e.* entirely cross pollinated	
Lettuce,	Bhindi,	Cole crops,	Spinach,	Colocasia

Garden pea, French bean, Tomato, Potato	Chillies, Capsicum, Brinjal, Lima bean	root vegeta-bles, onion, Cucurbit, Amaranths, Spinach beet	Asparagus, Parwal	Sweet potato Pointed-gourd, Ginger, garlic Turmeric

Classification based on mean growing temperature requirements (°C)

Narrow Range			*Middle Range*			*Wide Range*		
Species	*High*	*Low*	*Species*	*High*	*Low*	*Species*	*High*	*Low*
Artichoke	13-18	–5	Brinjal	18-30	–12	Broccoli	8-27	–19
Endive	15-23	–8	Pepper	18-30	–12	Broad bean	5-25	–20
Chicory	10-20	–10	Celery	10-22	–12	Brussels Sprout	10-20	–20
Parsnip	10-12	–10	Celeric	10-22	–12			
Garden pea	15-25	–10	Fennel	10-23	–13	Cabbage	10-30	–20
			Spinach	12-25	–13	Leek	10-30	–20
			Asparagus	15-30	–15	Onion	10-30	–20
			Cucumber	20-35	–15	Tomato	10-30	–20
			Parsley	15-30	–15	Garden beet	8-30	–22
			Pumpkin	15-30	–15	Carrot	9-30	–22
			Summer squash	15-30	–15			
			Sweet corn	15-30	–15			
			Radish	14-30	–16			
			Bhindi	18-35	–17			

Classification based on approximate seed size (ungraded) seed No./10g sample

0–500	700–2400	2500–4500	5000–15000	20,000 +
Broadbean-8	Salsify–700	Fennel–2500	Turnip–5000	Celery–25000
Limabean –8	Gardenbeet–750	Onion–2700	Parsley–5400	Watercress–38000
Pumpkin –30	Radish–1100	Cabbage–2800	Chicory–6000	
Comonbean –35	Pepper–1400	Knol-khol–3100	Endive –7500	
Sweet corn–50	Brinjal–2200	Tomato –3200	Lettuce–8600	
Garden pea–50	Broccoli–2300	Rutabaga–3300		
Squash–70	Parsnip–2300	Cauliflower–3500		
Watermelon –225		Leek–3600		
Bhindi–170		Cress–4000		
Artichoke –250		Bunching Onion–4500		
Mungbean–300				
Asparagus —500				
Cucumber-350				
Melon-350				

Classification based on growing season

Kharif vegetables. Beans, bhindi, brinjal, bitter-gourd, bottle gourd, cow pea, cucumber, muskmelon, chillies, capsicum, pumpkin, ridge gourd, summer squash, sweet potato, smooth gourd, snake gourd, tomato, watermelon and ginger.

Rabi vegetables. Garden beet, cabbage, cauliflower, carrot, garlic, knol-khol, lettuce, broad bean, methi, onion, spinach, beet leaf, turnip and radish, sprouting broccoli, Brussel's sprout.

Zaid vegetables. Dwarf beans, Dwarf tomato, cucumber (summer varieties) and summer squash.

Classification according to botanical parts used as food

Root. Garden beet, carrot, radish, turnip, parsnip, rutabaga.

Bulb. Onion, garlic.

Tuber. Potato, sweet potato.

Rhizome. Ginger, turmeric.

Corm. Colocasia, yam, elephant foot, cassava.

Stem and branches. Artichoke, knol-khol, asparagus, celery, parsley.

Petiole : Colocasia, celery, parsley, spinach.

Leaves. Cabbage, lettuce, spinach, beet leaf, fenugreek, leek, parsley, Celery, Chinese cabbage, kale, mustard, water cress, chard, sorrel, bathua, amaranth, coriander, zimmu, onion leaves, radish and turnip leaves.

Immature flower parts. Cauliflower, globe artichoke, sprouting broccoli, Rosalie.

Immature fruit/pods. Garden pea, French bean, guar, sem, okra, Lima bean, capsicum, chillies, cucumber, summer squash, parwal, snake gourd, bitter gourd, bottle gourd, round gourd.

Mature fruits. Tomato, brinjal, muskmelon, watermelon, pumpkin.

Classification based on method of culture

Vegetables belonging to the same group have the same general cultural requirements and subject to similar diseases, insects and weeds.

Leafy vegetables. Vegetables used mainly for their leaves whether consumed raw or cooked form, for example lettuce, mustard, amaranth, celery etc.

Cole vegetables. Cabbage, cauliflower, knol-khol, sprouting broccoli, Brussel's sprout, kale and Chinese cabbage.

Root vegetables. Garden beet, radish, turnip, carrot, parsnip, rutabaga, salsify.

Bulb vegetables. Onion, garlic, leek, shallot, zimmu.

Tuber vegetables. Potato, sweet potato.

Legume vegetables. Garden pea, French beans, broad bean, edible podded pea, cowpea.

Solanaceous vegetables. Tomato, brinjal, chillies, Shimla mirch, paprika.

Cucurbit. Cucumber, pumpkin, melons, gourds, etc.

Perennial vegetables. Asparagus, chayote, artichoke, Jerusalem artichoke, pointed gourd.

Others. Okra, colocasia.

Classification based on forcing

Cool forcing vegetables. Asparagus, garden pea, garden beet, carrot, late cauliflower, cabbage, celery, lettuce, onion, Spinach, beet leaf, radish, turnip, carrot.

Warm forcing vegetables. French bean, cucumber, brinjal, tomato, capsicum chillies, watermelon, muskmelon.

Moderately forced vegetables. Tropical cabbages, Indian varieties of radish, turnip, some cucurbit.

Classification based on relative rate of respiration of parts for fresh market

Very high	*High*	*Moderate*	*Low*	*Very low*
Asparagus Broccoli Garden pea Spinach Beetleaf Fenugreek	Beans Lettuce Lima bean	Garden beet Carrot Celery Cucumber Muskmelon Chillies Capsicum Tomato	Cabbage Turnip Sweet Patoto	Onion Potato Ginger Colocasia Turmeric Garlic

Classification based on soil reaction (pH)

Slightly tolerant (pH 6.8 - 6.0)	*Moderately tolerant (pH 6.8 - 5.5)*	*Very tolerant (pH 6.8 - 5.0)*
Asparagus, Garden beet, Broccoli, Cabbage, Leek, Chinese cabbage Cauliflower, Muskmelon Celery, Beet-leaf, New Zealand, Spinach, Okra, Lettuce, Spinach, Onion.	Bean, Brussel's sprout, Carrot, Cucumber, Brinjal, Garlic, Radish, Knol-khol, Parsley, Chillies, Garden pea, Capsicum, Pumpkin, Squash, Tomato, Turnip.	Potato, Sweet potato, Chicory, Endive, Rhubarb, Watermelon

Classification based on degree of tolerance to cold and frost

Hardy	*Half-hardy*	*Tender*	*Very tender*
Asparagus, Brussel's sprout, Cabbage, Kale, Garlic, Knol-khol, Leek, Onion, Parsley, Garden pea, Radish Spinach, Turnip, Sprouting broccoli.	Carrot, Chinese cabbage, Cauliflower, Garden beet, Globe artichoke, Celery, Lettuce, Endive, Parsnip, Spinach, Potato, Chicory.	Snap bean, Sweet corn, Tomato.	Amaranth, Okra, Brinjal, Capsicum, Yam, Chillies, Cluster bean, Colocasia, Cucurbit, Sweet potato, Cassava, Tapioca.

CHAPTER 3

FARMING SYSTEMS AND SUNDRY

The various farming systems prevalent and followed in different regions of the country for vegetable cultivation have a significant role to play in the increased production and productivity to meet the total requirement of the alarming population. However, the sundries which includes farm tools, implements and machinery are very important in growing vegetable crops without them the success in vegetable industry cannot be achieved. In this chapter their detail information is given for the benefit of the vegetable growers.

3.1. FARMING SYSTEMS

Farming systems used for growing vegetables, off-season vegetables, European vegetables and their seed production can be grouped into different types depending on the situations, topography, agro-climatic conditions and requirements of the farming community in a particular area. These may be terraced cultivation, flat land cultivation, shifting cultivation, cultivation in orchards, kitchen gardening and seed farms, etc.

Flat land cultivation. The fields/land is flat either a plateau type at the top of hill or in valley areas. The steepness is not much. The fields are large, uniform and fertile. The cultivation is very primitive, either these existed since old times or being developed later. The cultivation is mostly done with the help of bullocks or now-a-days tractors are also used where road facility exists. The farmers are rich and earns their livelihood from the agriculture.

(a) Upland. The fields are large, flat and land is in a open valley at the side or top of hills. The soils are fertile and well drained. The water do not accumulate in the fields. In most areas snowfall takes place and after its melting water gets either absorbed or drained.

(b) Low land. The situations of land are flat, located at the bottom or one side of hill. The soils are clay to clay-loam not well drained, mostly rain water or snow melted water get accumulated. In such areas underground drainage system need to be installed for proper draining of excess water for making fit for cultivation.

Terraced cultivation. Growing of vegetables in the terraced land or fields in the hills and the terraces may be wide, long, arranged on the hill side, looks from far as steps in some places where cultivation can be done with the help of bullocks. On the other hand these may be narrow, small or long and tilling is done mostly manually and the vegetables are grown accordingly. The terraces may be too steep or having gentle slope.

Shifting cultivation. Also called Jhoom cultivation mostly followed in the eastern-states. A piece of land is tilled by a particular community for some years and when it get exhausted then they shift to another site. There they put their temporary shelter and start tilling the land. The site may be any piece of land free from trees and bushes, etc. If trees and bushes, etc. are there then there will be cleaned. The cultivation of ginger, turmeric colocasia and root vegetables are mostly done successfully.

Mixed cultivation. Areas where farmers are engaged for mixed cultivation *i.e.* growing cereals, pulses, fruit and off-season vegetables including seed production for meeting their family's annual demand.

Cluster farming. The vegetables are grown in a area only one or two vegetables in cluster of fields in a large village or small hamlets located in clusters but the land-holdings are scattered which are needed to be managed accordingly.

Growing in orchards. Growing of vegetables in the orchards in all the agro-climatic and micro zones in the country. The orchards may be young or old. The growing of vegetables is done very easily in the young gardens in their early stages of development as the plants are small/young and cultural practices are also done very easily. Whereas in the well developed old orchards, the plants are widely spaced, the vegetables and shade loving crops like ginger, turmeric, and climbing vegetables including garden peas, beans and cucurbit are successfully grown. The orchards contained in low-hills/valley areas are of Citrus, Naspati etc. in mid-hills, plum, peach, pear, apple etc. and in high-hills (wet and dry zone) apple almond, apricot, etc.

Kitchen-gardening. Growing of vegetable crops either in the vicinity of houses or a piece of land developed into a kitchen-garden, a little far from the residence but close to the water source depending on the availability of farmers own piece of land, to meet the requirement of the family for most part of the year. The home or kitchen-garden is the most ancient type of garden and started when the human learnt tilling of field or lived in tribes or colonies and were of migratory nature. A single tribe tilled the land till it was productive and then shifted to another new virgin-land. Each tribe grew food/vegetables for its own consumption. The same practices is still continuing in the tribal and non-tribal areas, come what may be. Each farming family have their own individual small kitchen-garden and will grow all the vegetables including spice crops around the year depending on the agro-climatic conditions.

Specialised farming. A single farmer or group of farmers grow only one or two vegetables in a particular pocket on commercial scale and export the same to the markets in the plains. These farmers becomes specialised as they have the full knowledge of that specific vegetable(s). This type of farming may be called market gardening or truck gardening because the produce is carried to the big cities through trucks to the distant markets. The typical example is garden pea growing in; the Lahaul and Spiti, Kalpa and Pooh valleys, cabbage and cauliflower production in Shimla district etc. in Himachal Pradesh.

(*a*) ***Market gardening.*** The commercial growing of vegetables to meet the demand in the local markets or consumers *viz.*, villages, military and para-military forces and nearby cities.

(*b*) ***Truck gardening.*** The vegetables are sent to distant markets after proper packaging and transportation for maintaining their freshness.

Vegetable seed production farming. Vegetable seed production is a very specialised farming successfully done in the hills/plains because of congenial agro-climatic conditions suitable for quality seed production in all the different zones, especially temperate type of vegetable/varieties, their cultural (requirements, plant protection measures, seed production, their pre and post-harvest handling *i.e.* isolation, inspection, roguing, protection from birds, etc. optimum maturity stage, harvesting, curing threshing, cleaning, grading, drying, packaging in suitable container, marketing and storage are all specialised techniques. Thorough knowledge of vegetables and vegetable seed farming have exclusively meant for the production of quality vegetable seeds.

Green/poly-house vegetable production. Recently the green/poly-house structures have been possible to the progressive farmers in the country both in private and public sector especially in Himachal Pradesh on subsidised cost for growing vegetable and raising nursery/ cucurbit plants successfully in abnormal weather conditions. The main concept is to produce or grow vegetables/vegetable seedlings/plants in the poly-houses at a time when these can not be grown in the open. These need to be provided with some special devices for making these more effective by controlling optimum temperature and humidity for proper growth and development.

Vegetable forcing. Consists of growing vegetables other than their normal season by using special techniques or structures or by manipulating the time of sowing/planting either by advancing or delaying to make available for earning better lucrative prices. In the hills by using shelter of sarkanda or any other material etc. available for protecting from the northern chilly or cold winds are provided. To be commercially successful with vegetable forcing, the farmers should be able to produce vegetables at a time when the supply in the market is limited. Forcing the germination of melons or cucurbits in winter months by warmth of fresh cow dung manure may also be used as a forcing material. Hills can be called natural glass-house of the country.

Floating vegetable gardens. These type of gardens are found or seen in Dal Lake in Kashmir valley. Most of the vegetables grown in floating gardens are supplied to Srinagar and other parts of the valley. A floating base is first prepared from the roots of *Typha* grass which grows wild in the lake. Once this floating base is ready, seeds/seedlings of different vegetables are sown/transplanted on leaf compost made of the vegetation growing wild in the lake. The subsequent cultural practices are done from boats. These may be kept at one place or shifted. Harvesting is done and fresh vegetables are supplied to the local as well as distant consumers. This is a very specialised type of vegetable growing of its own type.

Subsistence farming. The cultivation of vegetables is done only to meet the family requirement or the farmer has the tendency to grow only those vegetables which his family needs from time to time.

Commercial off-season vegetable production. The off-season vegetables are produced in some pockets having congenial agro-climatic conditions on large scale. These may be supplied to the local or nearby markets or to distant markets. The typical examples are cabbage, garden pea, tomato, French bean, etc. Some of the varieties or hybrids in these vegetables have better shelf-life, transportability qualities and are carried to distant markets without any adverse affect on their freshness. However, there are other varieties which may not stay for more period and need to be disposed-off in the local markets at premium cost. In case of latter, the produce is sometimes carried in the baskets or bags depending on the nature of produce while in case of former, the produce in properly packed in suitable containers and sent to the distant markets where they are in great demand and brings better prices.

Processing. Some of the vegetables produced at peak season are in large quantities and the farmers always try to dispose-off vegetables in fresh form at premium cost but even then sometimes they are either over-mature or the prices in the market are considerably low, in such cases the surplus produce can be either processed locally or can be supplied to the processing units/plants and converted into various processed products and supplied to the local market, military and para-military forces or sometimes exported too if quality wise meets the international standards.

Growing vegetables in newly planted forests. In areas where forests land is being covered with new plantations, the land in the young plants can be used for planting most vegetables particularly the shade loving ones till the forest trees get full growth with additional incomes. In places where forests have been cut, the fertile area can be used for growing vegetables as the soil is very rich with leaf mould and humus which is quite suitable for growing these vegetables. By growing these vegetables not only the naked soils are covered and protected from soil erosion but additional income is also obtained. This also help in better utilisation of labour and employment to the young youths and women of the rural areas.

River bed cultivation. This is a very old practice to grow most vegetables in the river beds having fertile soil, and if not supplemented with organic manure and the vegetables particularly the cucurbit are grown under sub-normal conditions, literally in sand during winter months from November-February, in north and north-western India. When the water in the rivers get receded. The soil during day time is warm enough as compared to other areas and moreover these are protected with sarkanda or any other means from the northern chilly winds. The subsequent sowings are done and a regular harvests are taken. The markets are supplied with fresh vegetable produce at a time when there is no vegetable available in the market from February to May. The farmers get better prices for their produce. This system of vegetable production especially cucurbit cultivation is more economic than field crops because of low input requirement.

3.2. VEGETABLE FARMING SUNDRIES

The farm tools, equipments and farm machinery have a special significance in vegetable industry to carryout various operations *viz.* tilling of land, sowing, irrigation, hoeing and weeding, harvesting, processing, grading, spraying, etc. for overall maintenance of vegetables and their quality production. These all are required by the vegetable growers for the production of vegetable, varieties and hybrids at various stages.

The farm tools, implements, equipment and machinery constitute a number of diverse materials which are essential for cultivating land in different parts of the country in an efficient way. Therefore, the farmers interested in vegetable production should be well acquainted with different types of tools, implements, equipments and machinery and their uses. However, if these are used in other cereals/fruit crops can also be considered for use simultaneously in the vegetable production in various regions. Quite a varieties of these implements, tools, etc. are required for carrying out the various cultural operations, post-harvest handling, processing of vegetable crops like, digging, spading, tilling, breaking of soil clods, removal of weeds, levelling of fields, preparation of ridges, planting of seedlings/ stecklings, sowing of seed, mixing of manure and chemical fertilizer, ploughing, spraying or dusting of insecticides etc. harvesting, cleaning, grading, packaging, etc. The different types of farm tools and implements, etc. commonly used for vegetable growing are briefly described here under.

Hand Tools. Manual tools used are most primitive and simple form but variable and normally use of human muscles as the source of power. The vegetable producers do not have a choice but sometimes have to depend on these hand tools of various shape size are used depending on the nature of the crop. The digging farm tools are phawra, spade, hand hoe, pickaxes, crowbar (short.or long), kudali, khilana, khurpi etc. suited for working on different types of land/soils for cutting the soil clods, digging, breaking the clods into smaller particles, thus serving the function of ploughing and harrowing at the same time, khilana, kudali and crowbars are useful in transplanting of cabbage, cauliflower, tomato etc. and sowing of seeds of most vegetables. The spade and kudali is best suited for working with loamy soils where deep tillage is desired. The phawra and spade is normally used for preparing beds while the rake is used for levelling. However, the various farm tools are used for making channels, pits, holes, ridges etc. for sowing/transplanting and replanting the different vegetables. For handling and maintenance of vegetable crops, it is always better to select good quality and 'ISI' mark farm tools which can be used for many seasons rather than below standard quality or poorly designed or cheaply manufactured farm tools. The farmers with limited resources and small land holdings needs mostly locally prepared by the reputed iron smith in the village itself but should be of superior type of farm tools which may last for many seasons.

Animal drawn implements. Vegetable farming in hilly areas is done mostly by bullocks but in some areas, buffalo and horses are also used depending on their availability. However, in high temperate hills where churu (yak) are easily available are used or if not then the small stature bullocks are adapted for cultivation. The farm implements in use are, desi (small and large) plough with Junara (bullock teader), leveler (suhaga), spike tooth harrow; mould board, seed drill, hand plough with seeding pipe, potato digger cum grader, hand or bullock drawn cultivator and seeder. The size, shape, weight and number of farm implements usually depends on the topography of the land, size of land holding, status of the farmer, size of field, terraced or flat and the price and stature of bullock pair used for ploughing land. Where the fields are flat, the medium to large sized plough can be in use.

Maintenance and Manufacturing. All the farm tools, and implements are either locally manufactured or purchased from the local market. Traditionally in each village there is a small work-shop owned and maintained by a community called Lohar (Iron-smith). They not only help in maintenance (sharpening, repair etc.) of farm tools and implements but also manufacture the same. In token, the family is either paid in cash or kind at the time of harvesting season depending on the quantum of work done by him/family during the 6 month crop season. Mostly a fixed quantity of grains/pulses/vegetables etc. is given to the lohar or sometimes variable. There is at least one or two families for 10-20 villages for doing the job. The tools and implements purchased from the market also need regular maintenance and is always carried by the iron-smith of the village/area and he is obliged by the farmers of the villages. The number and type of farm tools/implements will depend on the family size its working members and size of land holding. Over and above in each case 2-3 extra items are maintained by each farming family in case of breaking or becoming blunt etc. for immediate and timely replacement so that the work do not suffer at peak season.

However, vegetable raising needs intensive care and for that the use of farm tools and implements is very much required. The help and assistance/services of village carpenter is also needed to manufacture the wooden implements and parts there of *viz.* desi plough (small and big), suhaga (soil leveller and compactor), wooden structure for teading bullocks, wooden handles for various farm tools and implements etc. The payment to the carpenter is also made in the same way as to the iron-smith. Normally the wood for these farm tools/implements is easily available with almost every farmer family and at times supplies to the carpenter and only manufacturing charges are paid to him.

The farm tools and implements should be cleaned properly before these are stored in a dry and clean place meant for the same after each use. Possibly a thin film of oil smeared on spade, shovels, hoes and sickles etc. will provide rust protection. At the end of the season, the tools should be sharpened and any repair needed be made. The farm tools and implements are normally stored in hills in the cowshed, basement of the house or storage shed meant for these or any other suitable place. If such facilities are not available, a temporary shelter may be erected for the purpose.

Farm Equipments. Vegetable plants have more enemies than friends as these are grown in summer months because of mild climate. Numerous insects and diseases greatly damage the vegetable plants at any stage and may kill them if proper care is not taken to remove or destroy the enemies at the earliest opportunity. The harmful weeds also compete for food, light, water etc. and also acts as alternate host for many diseases and insects. Therefore effective chemicals (insecticides, fungicides and weedicides) in various concentration and trade names are now-a-days easily available in the market but application to all the stages and parts of the vegetable plants becomes a problem without proper equipment. The spray pumps ranging from small hand pumps to power operated pumps are in use. The type of pump to be purchased will depend on the area under vegetable crop with the farmer, topography of the area, status of the farmer and whether the equipment is available in the local market or the government agency is providing the same on subsidised rate.

Maintenance and washing of equipment. The various types of sprayers, dusters and the other containers used for spraying dusting and preparation of solution should not be used for any other purpose. These particularly nozzle should be thoroughly washed with clean water after every use. The buckets or any other containers used for carrying water and for preparing solution should be exclusively be used for this purpose and never use for domestic purposes. When the spraying is finished these spray pumps should be rinsed properly in the field itself, place the same upside down and allow to dry completely.

Farm Machinery. The role and importance of mechanisation in vegetable production is being felt very significantly. These shall need to be so used as to bring about the maximum interaction between the various inputs. The promise of the new vegetable production strategy seems real after years of trial on the farm front. The various types of farm machinery including tractor have proved to be an important and wholeheartedly acceptable input(s) for higher production of vegetables. The tractors small and medium have become now an important source of power on the Indian farms for carrying all types operations *viz.* cultural, post-harvest management, processing, transportation, lifting of water for irrigation, etc. Tractors of various makes are now-a-days available and in use and the tractor can plough larger area per unit time to a better tilth efficiently and economically. The tractors have different attachments *viz.* disc plough, harrow, cultivator, planker for ploughing all types of land for preparing into fine tilth suitable for raising vegetables. The reapers are also run with the help of tractors. The trolley attached with the tractor is also helpful to carry the manure from pits to the field, vegetable produce to the collection centre at a very cheap rate. The bullock ploughing has been replaced by tractor ploughing and the farmers are saved from the annual expenditure incurred for the maintenance of the bullocks pair. The small and marginal farmers are also benefited as their fields are also ploughed by the tractor owned by the neighbour at nominal cost beside carrying their produce. The pockets where irrigation water facility do not exist, a pumping set can be installed for lifting irrigation water for growing vegetables and can be run either by tractor/diesel engine or electricity motor both in public private sector.

Power tiller or Rotary tiller. These are of small size and can be used economically for ploughing, cultivating and braking the clods etc. into fine tilth. These can plough the land in between the rows of fruits plants *viz.* apple, pears, citrus etc. to keep the land clean-off-from weeds and prepare for raising vegetable crops economically, successfully with additional income.

Threshing machines. These are the machinery used for threshing seed crops on a large scale. Now-a-days various types of threshers, small to large having different capacity and makes are available and in use. These are run by generator, or electricity or sometimes tractor accordingly. These may be owned by individual farmers or group of farmers. These are also available on hire basis on nominal charges.

Grading Machine/MB_2 Grader. Now-a-days in India, different types of seed graders or grading-cum-cleaning machines of various capacities are manufactured by a large number of firms are made available and in use. The latter is more common. These may have variable graded seed output and are run on electricity, generator or tractor depending on the availability of each source and expenditure involved. Mostly, these are installed at a central place of the seed growing area enabling each grower to make its proper use and easily approachable.

Packing machines. The main function of this machine is to pack the graded seed after proper drying in different sized containers/packets to be sent to the vegetable growing areas or market directly. Other things are like that of grading machine.

Pumping set. At places, where rain-fall is scarce or not well distributed in a year and more than 80 per cent of the area is rain-fed, the pumping set/kuhls can help the vegetable growers. The former can be installed in areas where source of water is near-by may be spring, river/tributaries or nallah, perennial source. The pumping sets of various capacities are available now-a-days and can be used for lifting irrigation water.

Periodic maintenance of farm machinery. Proper maintenance of the farm machinery including tractor, tillers, pumping sets, threshing machine, cleaning, cum grading machines etc. not only increased the life of these but also reduces a large investment on their up keep. However, these should be properly cleaned-off dust etc. and store in a dry and clean place after each use. A light film of oil on the exposed parts will provide rust protection. The farm power machinery with engine, motor, generator etc. be winterised according to the manufacturer's recommendations. Cleaning and lubricating of oil pipes, other axil etc. both internally and externally be done periodically before use. Farm machinery during slack season should be kept safely and protected from rain, dust in a shed or workshop. If such arrangement is not available then these should be covered with tarpaulin or polythene sheets during the slack season especially rainy season.

Miscellaneous. The miscellaneous articles in use for carrying various operations are seed dressers, buckets, water cane, tubs, tanks, staking or supporting material, tying material, packing material, storage material, baskets, pahari basket (kilta), tarpaulin, cloth sheets etc. These articles may also be properly maintained for proper use and to enhance their shelf-life.

Vegetable production is a very delicate proposition for changing and improving the social set up of the growers. The role and importance of various tools, implements (locally made or from the market), equipments and farm machinery is now well understood. Their proper use for vegetable growing is of utmost need. These may also be properly used and maintained for getting better results.

CHAPTER

4

NURSERY MANAGEMENT IN VETGETABLE CROPS

4.1. NURSERY PRODUCTION

Nursery management indeed is a very important operation in successful growing of vegetables especially those which are raised through seedlings in properly managed nursery beds. On the basis of nature of vegetable crop raised and transplanted in the field for production can be grouped as :

(*a*) **Direct seeding.** Okra, radish, turnip, carrot, garden beet, garden peas, beans, spinach, cucurbit, sugar beet, chicory, beet leaf and asparagus.

(*b*) **Nursery raising.** Tomato, brinjal, capsicum, chillies, Cole vegetables, onion, lettuce, celery, parsley, Chinese cabbage, amaranths, asparagus and potato (TPS).

(*c*) **Both direct seeding and nursery raising.** Lettuce, amaranths, celery, parsley, Chinese cabbage and asparagus.

(*d*) **Steckling raising.** Radish, turnip, carrot, garden beet, sugar beet and chicory.

(*e*) **Vegetatively propagated.** Asparagus (crown), ginger and turmeric *(Rhizomes)*, colocasia (corms) and potato (tubers).

Raising nursery from seed provide an easy and convenient way to nourish tender young seedlings in a well managed small and compact area for better germination of small and costly seed. A small area can be easily provided with favourable conditions in the open area specified for the purpose or glass/poly-house or any other protected area which is used for raising the healthy seedling. The nursery area can be conveniently protected from natural hazards, designated seed borne diseases and insect/pests and well managed economically. Some of the vegetable seeds are very costly and is necessary to raise nursery in the most optimum conditions. In areas (hills) where land holdings are small, nursery raising helps in making economic use of land for about one to one and half month and provides enough time for proper maturity of the previous crop, harvesting, threshing etc. and land preparation. The vegetables subjected for nursery raising easily tolerate transplanting shocks. The major advantages of nursery raising are :

1. Judicious use of small costly vegetable seeds.
2. Ease of controlling designated seed borne diseases, insect-pests effectively in the initial growth period of seedlings.
3. Ease of providing intensive care like frequent irrigation, weeding, protection against inclement weather conditions, etc.
4. Availability of sufficient time for field preparation, manure and fertilizer mixing after harvesting the previous crop, then nursery raising helps in planting the crop at proper time.

The site selected for nursery production should be safe, sunny, free from shade, soil borne diseases and insect-pests and natural hazards. The soil should be fertile and well drained. Possibly nursery bed should be established near water source and close to house for frequent visit and effective supervision. The nursery area should be well prepared into a better tilth. Mix the basic organic manure and fertilizers in balanced form. The surface of bed should be smooth to facilitate proper watering. The soil if virgin need not to treat. The area previously used should be treated indigenously by burning straw or plant remains or any other material locally available. It is cheap, easy to do and economical. The chemical treatment can also be done with formalin (1:10) solution in water applied @ 5 liters per square meter area saturated up to a depth of 15 cm and then covered with gunny bags, polythene sheet or tarpaulin for 48 or 72 hours to kill all harmful fungi and insects. The bed is uncovered and tilled to allow the formalin to evaporate/disappear. The recommended size of each bed may be 3 × 1 × 0.15 m and at least 60 cm space may be left between two beds for doing cultural operations easily. Add well rotten farmyard manure @ 20-25 kg in each bed. In addition, 150-200 g of single super phosphate 50-60 g muriate of potash and 50 g of BHC or Aldrin powder may be thoroughly mixed in the soil. The sides and corners of beds should be pressed firmly so that these are not easily eroded during irrigation or heavy rainfall. The surface of the beds should be smooth and levelled so that irrigation/rain water do not accumulate at one place.

Preferably use certified or foundation seed from a reliable source as the whole vegetable production programme is based on quality seed, the seedlings of which are raised in a properly managed nursery beds. On the smooth surface of nursery beds, U-shaped furrows are prepared with the help of a narrow row or wooden stick or finger 5 cm apart and one and half to two cm deep. Seed sowing is done in the U-shape furrows with a vibrating motion of fingers in such a way to avoid over-crowding of seeds. The very small seeds can be first mixed with sand or soil before sowing to avoid over-crowding. In case of costly hybrid seeds, proper spacing may be followed avoiding over-crowding. Now-a-days green/poly-houses are available and these may be used for raising healthy seedlings. Immediately after sowing, cover the furrows with fine soil or farm yard manure or leaf mould powder with the help of convenient motion of fingers or a small wooden leveller to make proper covering and uniform slope in the sown bed. Seed rate per hectare, depends on seed quality, germination percentage, size, vegetable/variety and existing conditions, etc. The sowing time, number of beds per hectare and seed rate for each vegetable is given in Table 4.1. Time of sowing should be adjusted according to the nature of vegetable, varieties, crop season, elevation (zone), etc. at least 28-35 days in low-hills (plains), 35-40 days in mid-hills and 40-45 days in high-hills prior to transplanting.

Covering of nursery beds (sown) should be done with 2-3 cm thick straw or dried grass, tree leaves locally available or use gunny bags, polythene sheet which helps to maintain optimum moisture. The micro-climate, protection from direct sun, rain, high and low temperatures, natural hazards, to create darkness and prevents seed displacement by beating drops of rain water and irrigation. Use of poly-house available now-a-days will be helpful in solving these problems. The covering should be immediately removed at the first appearance of cotyledonary leaves.

A temporary or permanent thatch on the nursery beds may be installed 60 cm high either of local material grasses, straw and leaves or gunny bags or polythene sheet readily available in the local market. The thatch helps in protecting the nursery from heavy rains, direct sun, chilling winds of the north, frost, etc. and also provides sunlight, easily from the side. However, in hills there is a common practice to cover the beds in the evening and reopens in the morning. At locations in the hills where there is a little or no difference in day and night temperature if poly-house facilities are used then there is no need of thatching. During winter season, the tender and delicate seedlings, thatching protects from frost and chilly winds of the north. The micro-climate of the nursery bed is also properly maintained by using thatch/poly-house.

Irrigation. Irrigation water should be provided early in the morning and late in the evening daily after seed sowing until the seedlings are transplanted. Careful and even watering should be done with the help of water cane or by keeping a grass bundle on the bed while irrigating. There should not be any packing or washing away of soil at the time of watering. However, the number of watering are adjusted according to day temperature, sunshine, rain, elevation, soil type and cloudy weather. Never irrigate the nursery during mid-day. When the seedlings are 3-4 weeks old in low-hills (plains), 4-5 weeks in mid-hills and 5-7 weeks in high-hills, either reduce or a stop irrigation to make the seedlings stocky, hard, short and resistant to bear the shock of transplanting better prior to uprooting.

Pricking of seedlings in the hills is a common practice especially with very small costly vegetable seeds in case of high density sowing. In case of onion, tomato, brinjal, capsicum, etc. may be pricked at their first pair of true leaves develop and by providing 5-10 cm spacing between and within rows.

The nursery bed should be checked daily for the appearance of diseases, insect-pests and any physiological problem/deficiency symptoms. Moreover, the seedlings showing poor growth apply urea @ 0.1 to 0.2%, and Indofil M-45 @ 0.25% or Sevin @ 1 ml/L of water. Pulverise the surface soil and eradicate the weeds as they appear. Some times the starter solution prepared from the farmyard manure/cow dung/or dilute solution of fertilizer is applied in the nursery bed or transplanted seedlings. It helps in boosting the initial growth of the young seedlings both in the nursery bed or field. It should be applied in the soil @ 250 ml per plant and never the plants were basal fertilizers has already been added as the overdose of nutrients may kill the tender seedlings/plants.

The nursery raised in an area of 20 × 18 sq. meter is enough for an hectare area depending on the vegetable/variety/hybrid to be grown. In most vegetable crops, the seedlings are raised on the higher side in the open or poly-houses and carried to the areas where vegetable crop is grown. Normally the seedlings are raised at least 30-35 days in advance and in most of the areas especially mid-hills, after transplanting a life saving dose of water is given where irrigation water is a limitation and then pre-monsoons are received for proper growth and development of the vegetable crop. The time of seed sowing/transplanting varies from pocket to pocket at different zones because of existence of varied micro-climatic conditions (Table 4.1).

TABLE 4.1. Sowing time, seed rate, number of beds ha^{-1} in different zones raised through seedlings for vegetable production

Vegetables	*Zones/Sowing time*				*Seed rate per bed 3 × 1 × 0.15 m size (g)*	*Number of beds/ ha/12½ bigha/25 kanal*
	Low-hills	*Mid-hill*	*High-hills*			
			Wet	*Dry*		
Cauliflower						
Early varieties	June-July	—	—	—	150	5
Mid	Aug.-Sept.	—	—	—	150	5
Late	—	Oct.-Nov.	—	—	150	5
Cabbage	—	—	April-June	April-June	150	5
Knol-khol	—	Sept.-Oct.	March-April	March-April	200	6
Broccoli	—	Sept.-Oct.	-do-	-do-	150	5
Brussel's Sprout	—	Sept.-Oct	-do-	-do-	150	5
Lettuce	Oct.-Nov.	Sept.-Oct.	March-July	March-July	150	5
Celery	Sept.-Oct.	Oct.-Nov.	April-May	April-May	150	5
Parsley	Sept.-Oct.	Sept.-Oct.	March-April	April-May	250	6
Chinese cabbage	Sept.-Oct.	July-Oct.	April-May	April-May	180	5
Asparagus	Aug -Sept.	March-June	April-May	April-May	150	5
Onion (Bulb)	Nov.-Dec.	Oct.-Nov.	April	April	200	10
Leek	Sept.-Oct.	Sept.-Oct.	March-May	March-May	200	5
Tomato	Nov. & Feb.	Feb.-March	April-May	April-May	100	8
Brinjal	May-June	May-June	-do-	-do-	200	5
Capsicum	—	May-June	April-May	April-May	150	5
	June	May-June	-do-	April-May	150	5

Transplanting. Generally transplanting is pulling of living plants where by these become established in new place. Usually this violent operation in most vegetable crops is performed when the plant is young and in an actively growing condition. However, a portion of the root system is damaged considerably, the plant attachment to the soil is disturbed and the progressive vital activities are checked, the transplanting becomes more successful in-spite of all this in the well prepared soil having better tilth. Though involvement of labour is more but even then in some vegetable crops, it is helpful in root pruning, better care of high value vegetables and hybrids and also extend the growing period of already growing crop. The healthy seedlings tolerate the unfavourable weather conditions in the open fields, either 4-10 weeks old or 10-15 cm tall are ready for transplanting in the well prepared fields in such a way that the soil come in contact of roots by pressing the soil around the seedling gently. However, the uprooting of seedlings need to be done with the help of wooden peg or khurpi where the nursery bed is moist which can be irrigated at least one hour prior to uprooting. Uproot only the required number of seedlings carefully preferably in the afternoon without causing any

TABLE 4.2. Spacing between and within plants, plant population ha. seeds/g and nature of variety in transplanted vegetables for vegetable production

Vegetable	*Nature of Varieties*	*Number of seeds/g*	*Spacing* in *cm*		*Seedlings needed/ha*	*Temperature range* °C
			Row	*Plant*		
Cauliflower	Early	250	45	30	74074	20-30
	Mid	355	45	45	49332	20-25
	Late	360	60	45	37037	15-20
Cabbage	Early	280	45	30	74074	15-20
	Mid	290	45	45	49332	15-20
	Late	300	60	45	37037	15-20
Knol-khol		310	30	20	166666	15-20
Broccoli		230	45	45	49332	15-20
Brussel's Sprout		240	60	45	37074	15-20
Lettuce		860	45	30	74074	15-24
Celery		2500	60	20	83333	15-20
Parsley		540	45	10	222222	15-22
Chinese Cabbage		305	45	30	74074	15-25
Asparagus		5010	15	45	14814	18-28
Onion		270	15	10	666666	12-22
Leek		360	45	30	74074	14-20
Tomato	Dwarf	320	60	45	37037	21-27
	Tall	320	90	30	37037	18-27
Brinjal		220	60	45	37037	13-21
Capsicum		140	60	45	37037	20-25
Chillies		140	45	45	49332	20-25
Potato (TPS)		225	50	15	150000	18-24

injury. Always transplant in the evening hours followed by irrigation. Keep some seedlings reserved for gap filling. Repeat irrigation till the seedlings are well established. Add insecticides like Folidol @ 20-25 kg/ha against cutworms, etc. at the time of land preparation.

Precautions

1. Treat seeds with fungicides like Captan/Bevistein @ 2-3 g/kg of seed before sowing.
2. Sow the seeds in lines 5 cm apart thinly avoiding overcrowding.
3. Cover the seeds with a thin layer of either soil or fine powder of farm yard manure.
4. Then cover the sown bed with dry grass layer or polythene sheet or gunny bags.
5. Water the sown beds with the help of water-cane with spreader once in winter and twice in summer either in the morning or evening and both times.
6. Water the beds till seedling are ready for transplanting or established in the field.
7. Remove the covering when seeds have germinated but during winter cover the bed during night and uncover in the morning.
8. In case of damping-off disease spray the seedlings with 0.25% Indofil M-45.
9. In case the seedlings are weak/deficient in nitrogen spray urea @ 0.3% for proper growth of the seedlings.
10. Remove the weeds and unwanted plants etc. as and when appear.
11. Depending on elevation, the seedlings become ready in 4-7 weeks or attains a height of 12-15 cm.
12. Stop irrigation for hardening-off the seedlings.
13. Digging (uprooting) of seedlings should be preceded by ample watering.
14. Uproot the seedlings from the nursery bed with a little or no injury.
15. Do not uproot more than the required number of seedlings.
16. Keep the reserve seedlings in shade or moist substrata.
17. Press the soil firmly in such a way the roots come in contact well with soil and prevent the air pockets near the roots.
18. Never remove the leaves or any portion of leaves from the seedlings.
19. Transplanting should be completed quickly after uprooting of seedlings from the beds.
20. To avoid disappointment, it is a good plan to raise a little more seedlings than actually required.
21. Uproot only that much seedlings which can be transplanted on that day.
22. Dipping seedlings, just before transplanting, in plant protection formulations may avoid pest or disease attack in the initial stage of establishment.
23. Irrigation water must be applied soon after transplanting .
24. Never transplant in the morning or mid day except cloudy days. Always prefer evening hours for transplanting.
25. Gap filling must be followed immediately to maintain plant population.
26. Irrigation water must be arranged well before transplanting.

27. Attack of insect-pests and diseases may be checked well before these spread throughout the field.
28. The spray pump, insecticides and fungicides etc. should be arranged well in advance.

4.2 RAISING VEGETABLES CROPS THROUGH DIRECT SEEDING

There are some vegetable crops usually suffer a serious set back in case these are transplanted as their root system is disturbed, therefore, their seed is sown directly in the well prepared soil *e.g.,* garden pea, French bean, bhindi, carrot, radish, turnip, cucurbits, etc. However, cucurbits commonly can be seeded first in poly-tubes and then replanted in the field. The fields are prepared to better tilth by the farmers at various zones accordingly because the land holdings are very small to marginal and a very few have large holdings. The following methods are followed :

(*a*) **Manually.** Mostly digging of land is done by family members and labour. Normally in tribal areas, the farmers have very small land holdings, fields are small, narrow terraced, very steep and undulating, manual digging is done. In eastern states shifting cultivation is mainly practised.

(*b*) **Plough tilling.** Land preparation is done with both small to medium desi plough or mould board plough depending on the land situations and availability of plough type. The ploughing with desi plough is normally done with small statured bullock pair always along the contour.

(*c*) **Both Manual and Desi plough.** In some places/land situations both the methods are practised depending upon the facilities available.

(*d*) **Tractor ploughing.** Usually it is done in flat lands or valley areas where the land holdings are large and linked with road.

The detail of spacings, seed rate plants/hectare and temperature requirement for directly sown vegetables is given in Table 4.3.

TABLE 4.3. Spacing between and within plants, seeds/g, plant population and temperature range of directly seeded vegetables

Vegetable	*Spacing (cm)*		*Seeds/g*	*Plants/ha*	*Temperature range °C*
	Row	*Plant*			
Coriander	25	15	60	266666	10-20
Parsnip	30	30	230	111111	10-20
Broad-bean	45	10	0.8	222222	5-25
Lima bean	90	15	0.8	74074	15-25
Pumpkin	150	45	3	14815	15-30
Dwarf bean	45	10	3.5	222222	15-30
Sweet corn	30	15	5	222222	15-30
Garden Pea (Dwarf)	30	5	5	666666	15-25

(Tall)	60	10	5	166666	15-25
Squash	90	60	7	18519	15-30
Bhindi	45	15	17	148148	18-35
Water Melon	150	50	22.5	13333	15-30
Artichoke	60	45	25	37037	13-18
Cucumber	125	50	32	16000	20-35
Sarda Melon	150	30	35	22222	18-30
Asparagu (crown)	150	30	35	22222	18-30
Salsify	45	45	70	49383	15-25
Garden beet	20	10	75	500000	8-30
Radish	30	10	11	333333	14-30
Turnip	30	10	500	333333	14-30
Parsley	30	30	540	111111	15-30
Chicory	45	10	600	222222	10-20
Endive	45	10	750	222222	15-23
Lettuce	45	30	860	74075	12-25
Fennel	45	30	250	74075	10-22
Beet leaf	30	5	75	666666	12-30
Spinach	30	5	90	666666	12-25
Cardamom	150	90	—	7407	13-35
Carrot	30	10	230	333333	8-30
Rutabaga	20	10	450	500000	15-25
Bitter Gourd	90	45	2.5	24691	15-30
Bottle Gourd	150	60	2.0	11111	15-30
Colocasia	45	45	1 (50-60 g)	49382	14-35
Ginger	20	15	1 (25-50 g)	333333	15-35
Turmeric	30	20	1 (20-40 g)	166666	15-35
Chinese cabbage	45	30	305	74075	10-5
Garlic	20	10	1 (5-10 g)	500000	10-30
Methi common	30	5	10-12	100000	10-25
Kasuri methi	20	5	20-25	100000	10-25
Sugar-beet	45	10	80	222222	8-30
Potato (tuber)	50	15	1-20	133333	18-24

Weight of seeds/g depends on variety.

CHAPTER

5

KITCHEN/HOME GARDEN

It is an art of growing vegetables including fruit plants continuously on a small piece of land in a planned way in the vicinity of living/residential house to meet the needs of family with fresh produce all the year around regularly. It is better to have a nutrition garden developed to grow fresh vegetables and fruits in the house compound in order to obtain requisite quantity and kind of these everyday to the family of their taste. Fruits and vegetables purchased from the market lack freshness and food value besides their exhorbitant price. Thus, the best quality of fresh produce can be had from one's own kitchen garden as the time interval between harvest and consumption becomes the least.

Objectives

(*i*) Raising fresh vegetables and fruits rich in nutrients to supply to the family.

(*ii*) Proper utilization of land in the vicinity of the house.

(*iii*) Best utilization of the time of the family members in a pleasure way exercising an efficient and effective training to the childern.

(*iv*) Utilization of kitchen water and waste.

(*v*) Keeping surroundings neat and clean beautifying by growing fruits, vegetables and ornamental flowers.

(*vi*) Economising the food cost.

(*vii*) Useful for utilizing the spare time in a profitable way.

The kitchen garden should aim at providing a continuous supply of vegetables to the family throughout the year according to the season, family members taste and the special features of a particular place. Kitchen garden should be part of home and hobby irrespective of the fact whether it is developed in the hills, plains, villages or cities. The idea of kitchen garden should be spread among masses especially women folk and house wives. Therefore, it can contribute substantially to the health, happiness and economy of the family life.

Types of kitchen garden

(*i*) Exclusively vegetable garden,

(*ii*) Vegetable and fruits garden,

(*iii*) Vegetable and flower garden, and

(*iv*) Combined vegetable, fruit and flower garden.

Principles of kitchen gardening. Developing and planning of a kitchen garden is very important and highly technical for securing proper and regular harvest. It needs a good scientific and planned experiences of various production operations like cultural and management practices including harvesting and processing. The basic principles to be considered while planning a suitable home or kitchen garden which need pre-thought are :

(*i*) Appropriate size and shape will depend on the family size. It is better to have a small well maintained garden than a poorly maintained large one.

(*ii*) Location is the fundamental principle and it should be close to the house as mostly the work is done by the family members.

(*iii*) Suitable and convenient layout.

(*iv*) Open and sunny site as sunlight is very important for proper growth of the plants and exposed to it for a good number of hours in a day.

(*v*) The site should be free from shade trees, etc.

(*vi*) Close to the well, water tap, natural source or any other source of irrigation including kitchen water which can be profitably utilized. If the kitchen garden is away from the source, necessary arrangement of irrigation may be made.

(*vii*) The ideal kitchen garden be established in a fairly highly level area preferably on the southern site of the house, which can be protected by a live fence from stray animals.

(*viii*) Shape of land influences, time of planting as well as the manner of making the rows.

(*ix*) Suitable and effective rotations should be followed to make best use of available land.

(*x*) Efficient and convenient plots adjustment be done for proper management and getting maximum output.

Lay Out. The kitchen garden may be established either near the house or at a distance so that odd hours could be utilized conveniently of the self labour to be invested, on a small piece of land which is converted into a kitchen garden or near a irrigation source. The size will depend on the land available and the individual family and their requirement utilized for fresh, storage and preservation in the form of pickles, sauces and dried vegetables. In new construction, it is wise to plan kitchen garden well in advance. Permanent plants should be planted at a right place that they do not obstruct sun-rays and ensure that your garden spot gets plenty of light as otherwise in the shade the vegetables will grow pale and sickly.

Layout plan of a kitchen garden. Layout plan for a model kitchen garden of about 200 square meter suitable for a specific location should be drawn well in advance on a diary, keeping in view the maximum output and a regular supply of fresh vegetables throughout the year. Therefore a better planning is very important and essential for successful management of a kitchen garden. Thus proper guidance may be sought from an experienced gardener to make a plan on a paper and to economize the efforts well before the season begins, vegetable cultivars or fruit plants their seed/seedlings or plants availability proper balanced distribution, experiences involved, etc. may be decided. The layout plan will vary in size and shape depending on the availability of space, likes and dislikes of the family members, etc. The following criteria should be considered while planning a kitchen garden :

(*i*) Prepare a clear sketch plan of a planned kitchen garden on a notebook before planting.

(*ii*) The plan should indicate the layout of plots, paths channels, perennial plants permanent spots, etc. and their dimensions.

(*iii*) The layout plan should look attractive and each bed or sopt is easily accessible.

(*iv*) The plots are always laid out along the path and water channel so that slope is given to each plot for proper irrigation.

(*v*) In between Iwo plots a path of about 50-60 cm wide should be kept for performing intercultural operations and harvesting.

(*vi*) Plots should be rectangular or square in shape to facilitate easy intercultural operations.

(*vii*) The size and shape of plots will depend on the slope of land and normally in 200 square meter kitchen garden sub-plots of convenient size are most ideal.

(*viii*) The allotment of area for each unit *viz.* vegetables, flowers and fruits will depend on the choice of individual's taste and requirement.

(*ix*) Sowing/planting of vegetable, flower and fruit plants be systematically planned.

(*x*) Choice of each component to be grown will depend on the season (round the year), region, area available, nutritive value/importance and preference of the family members.

(*xi*) Vegetables required in small quantities like lettuce, mint and coriander should not be grown in large area and instead be adjusted on ridges, along the path and water channels.

(*xii*) Vegetables required in large quantities like potatoes, onion, garden peas, dwarf beans, etc. should be allowed to occupy more area.

(*xiii*) Temperate vegetables like radish, turnip, carrot, etc. required for salad should bè accommodated on ridges and sown continuously at intervals to make available daily.

(*xiv*) Pole type vegetable varieties like cucurbits, French bean during summer/rainy season and garden peas in winter be planted along the fence on three sides along the boundary wall or roof so that maximum space can be provided for their optimum spread.

(*xv*) Taking into consideration the direction of sunlight, tall vegetable varieties should always follow medium and then dwarf ones so as every plot gets maximum sunlight.

(*xvi*) Perennial vegetables like asparagus, cho-cho, etc. should always be planted in corner plots so that they do not interfere with the preparation of land, annual beds, more so to avoid shade, they don't compete with for nutrition and disturb the normal rotation.

(*xvii*) Follow principles of crop-rotation based on the agro-climatic situations. (Table 5.1).

TABLE 5.1. Cropping pattern followed in kitchen garden

Plot No.	*Vegetable*	*Sowing lime*	*Availability*
SP_1	Cauliflower/Lettuce-Bush bean-Brinjal (long)	Oct.-Mar.-June	Feb.-May-Sept.
SP_2	Cabbage/Knol-khol-Onion (bulb)-Okra	Sept.-Jan.-June.	Dec- May-Aug.-Sept
SP_3	Broccoli/Leek-Summ-er squash (bush)-Capsicum	Oct.-Mar.-June	May-Sept.-Jan.
SP_4	Beet leaf/Fenugreek-Cucumber-Chillies	Sept.-Feb.-June	Jan.-May-Aug.-Sept.
SP_5	Garden peas-Potato-Amaranths	Sept.-Jan.- June	Dec.-May-Aug.
SP_6	Carrot-Cabbage (summer crop)-Pole bean	Sept.-March-June	Feb.-May-Aug.-Sept.
SP_7	Spinach/Coriander-Potato-Brinjal	Oct.-Jan.- June	Dec.-May.-Sept.
SP_8	Broadbcan/Garlic-Tomato (indeterminate)	Oct.-June	May-Sept.

Ridge:			Perennial-Lime	Asparagus
	A	Turnip		
	B	Radish	Papaya	Cho-cho
	C	Garden beet	Citrus	Mint
	D	Lettuce/Radish	Peach	
	E	Radish/Celery	Plum	
	F	Ginger	Amla	
	G	Turmeric	Almond	

SP = Sub-plot (The crop rotations will vary from region to region and may be framed accordingly).

(*xviii*) Several sowings or succession of plantings of one particular vegetable at short interval should be done to ensure a regular supply of fresh vegetable, using a continuous crop pattern in the form of succession and companion cropping.

(*xix*) Leguminous vegetables like garden peas, French bean, broad bean methi, etc. should be included in the rotation to maintain the soil fertility.

(*xx*) Ridges should always be used to grow root vegetables and sides of the path or channels must be used for growing tomato, amaranths and other leafy vegetables.

(*xxi*) Early maturing vegetable varieties should be planted together in continuous rows so that the areas may be available at once for planting late varieties.

(*xxii*) In interspace of vegetables which are slow growing and take long duration to mature like cabbage, brinjal, etc. must be used for quick growing vegetable/varieties like radish, turnip, spinach, lettuce, etc.

(*xviii*) Crops like ginger, turmeric, etc. which tolerate shade can be grown under tall crops and fruit plants while water-loving vegetables can easily be grown in drainage ditches.

(*xxiv*) Vegetables which are easily grown with minimum efforts, less expensive and of family member's choice be included.

(*xv*) A small pit in a corner of the kitchen garden may be dug and the kitchen/house waste and the plant refuse, etc. can be put their for preparing organic matter, which can be camouflaged by growing cucurbits or tall bean or garden peas. This helps in providing self-sufficiency in manure for the kitchen garden.

Perennial and seasonal flowers. The perennial ornamental plants may be established in their permanent spots where these give good and attractive look either along the approach path or boundary wall but these should not shade or disturb or compete with vegetables. The beds for seasonal flowers may be prepared preferably along the path, approach road, around the house and the arrangement of the flowers may be done according the taste of family members. However, those flowers may be sown according to season, canopy of plants, tall or dwarf, flower colour, weather these provide mass effect or look attractive individually, etc.

Fruit plants. The fast growing fruit plants which can be easily grown in that particular area or region should be given preference depending on the choice of the family members. Mostly various fruit plants chosen should be k-lime, peach, plum, banana, papaya, etc. depending on the agro-climatic conditions, hail, frost, etc. These trees are permanent asset and should be planted at place where these grows well but do not disturb the vegetable growing and also do not have shading effect on the plants growing in the kitchen garden. These should not be grown close to the house.

Harvesting/picking of vegetables. The major utility of a kitchen garden is to get fresh vegetables daily throughout the year without any loss in nutritional value. Therefore, these should be harvested at the optimum stage just before cooking otherwise over maturity will lower the quality and make unfit for consumption and the very purpose of the kitchen is forfeited. During summer, the growth rate of okra fruit is so fast that even one day overstay would produce fibrous fruits. Similarly in case of other vegetables like French bean, garden peas, radish, etc. become unfit for consumption if harvesting is delayed. Some vegetables grow during night to a large extent, for example okra should be picked in the morning while in other vegetables maximum fruit development takes place during day time and the harvesting should be done in the evening or next morning. The vegetables like squash, okra, etc. should be picked at very tender stage and others like tomato, brinjal, etc. need to be picked at ripe stage.

Storage. Mostly the kitchen garden supplies fresh vegetables according to the requirement of the family but in case of surplus production and supply the produce can be stored or processed successfully for future use or otherwise the neighbouring families can be obliged. There are different ways or storing or processing surplus produce for example, wax gourd (petha), pumpkin can be stored for 5-6 months and the former by cutting into pieces and put in sugar solution. Some other vegetables like garden peas, cauliflower, bean, onion, garlic, etc. can be dried and stored while carrot, turnip, chillies can be converted into pickles and tomato ketchup, sauce and carrot murraba can also be made.

Tools and implements. In farmer's kitchen garden, there is no specific need for tools, implements and equipments as he can utilize these available on the farm for the purpose. In town and city kitchen gardens it is necessary to have a suitable set of implements, hand tools and small equipments. The set contains all these that are normally needed in kitchen garden. However, the following list is given as below which can be purchased from the local market. Water cane, spade, khurpa, khilana, garden hoe, sickle, rubber or plastic 2.5 cm diameter (30 m) and hand sprayer.

The preparatory tillage and other cultural requirements, cultivars, nursery production, post-harvest handling, plant protection, etc. are given in different chapters.

TABLE 5.2. Vegetable, seed/seedling required/25 m^2 and approximate yield kg/plot

Vegetable	*Seed required g/25 m^2 plot*	*Seedlings required/m^2*	*Approximate yield kg/plot*
Cauliflower	—	75-150	20-35
Cabbage	—	75-150	30-35
Knol-khol	—	250-300	18-20
Chinese cabbage		180-200	30-40
Lettuce	5	150-180	18-20
Broccoli	—	75-150	30-35
Radish	20	—	40-50
Coriander	50	—	18-20
Turnip	10	—	40-50
Carrot	20	—	25-30
Garden beet	50	—	5-10 (40-45 roots)
Onion	20	41666	50-60 (green)
Garlic	1,500	—	30-40
Beet leaf	70	—	20-25
Spinach	60	—	18-20
Fenugreek (methi)	50-100	—	10-15
Garden peas	120-140	—	20-25
Potato	4-5 (tubers)	—	40-50
Broad bean	200-250	—	20-35
Brussel's sprout	—	175	20-25
Asparagus	30	200 or (crowns)	10-15
Celery	20	175	20-25
Parsley	20	150-200	10-12
Leek	15	125-200	20-30
Tomato	—	75-100	25-30
Brinjal	—	75-100	30-35
Shimla mirch	—	75-100	10-15
Chillies	15	75-100	15-20
Okra	40-50	—	25-30
French bean	200-250	—	18-20
Cucumber	10-15	—	20-25
Bitter gourd	20-25	—	30-35
Pumpkin	15-20	—	30-35
Summer squash	15-20	—	30-35
Bottle gourd	15-20	—	35-40
Colocasia (Arvi)	3-4	—	40-50
Ginger	4-5	—	35-40
Turmeric	3-4	—	35-40
Cho-cho	3 fruits	—	10-12
Amaranths	10-20	100-200	30-45
Mint (podina)	—	20-30 cuttings	3-5

Total yield per year = 1290 kg

Total yield per day = 1290 divided by 30 = 3.6 or 3-4 kg

(The cultivars, spacing and other information regarding cultural requirements have been given in each vegetable in this text)

However, there are certain limitations and problems like poor seed/seedling availability, lack of technical know-how and demonstration, no suitable literature available, inadequate water supply, lack of association with some organisations, that is needed to be tackled for encouraging better kitchen gardening. The government and other agencies should take up steps to lay demonstrations, hold healthy competition, encourage kitchen garden associtations, provide suitable facilities, technical knowledge, sufficient inputs for making this venture a economical and regular enterprise with all the families that have space around the house.

CHAPTER

6

ECONOMIC ROLE OF VEGETABLES

The economical status of farmers is normally based on mainly on agriculture and majority of the rural population depends on farming for their livelihood. In some states like Himachal Pradesh, Jammu & Kashmir, hilly areas of Uttar Pradesh, etc., the farmers have taken up vegetable, off-season vegetable and quality seed production as a primary programme while a substantial number of farmers grow vegetables/seed crops as a secondary business. The most part of the country, therefore bestowed with a wide range of congenial agro-climatic conditions, enabling the farmers to grow vegetable in one pocket or the other in each zone. This, besides maintaining a continuous supply of vegetables having typical flavour, better taste, attractive colour and appeal and better quality seeds with lucrative returns to the farmers, also provides scope for producing exotic vegetables which are in great demand both in the domestic market as well as in the neighbouring/Gulf countries. Therefore, vegetable/off-season/seed production has the potential of improving the living standard of the population are generally economically poor, and include small, marginal and even land less farmers. Because of limited resources at their command and they are not in a position to make use of the new technology required and plagued by their backwardness as have no other source of income, more so they are not aware about the vegetables/varieties to be grown, use of inputs like fertilizers, pesticides, weedicides etc. Production and consumption of vegetables is directly related to the improvement of the socio-economic status of the people. The following are the impact benefits of vegetable growing to improve the socio-economical status of the people.

Source of rich protective food. Vegetables have better food value, and their role in the daily diet of human beings as a protective food is well recognised. These are source of specific chemical substances needed in the human body for proper growth and development and maintenance of health. Since time immemorial, vegetarianism has been a way of life in our country, therefore, the intake of vegetables is very important for eliminating most dreaded diseases in the modern era and help in increasing vitality to have perfect health of the country's increasing population.

Helpful in solving food problem. More vegetable production and consumption will not only improve the health of population but it will also help to solve the food problem to a great extent, both quantitatively and qualitatively. The consumption of vegetables can only be increased by changing the dietary habits of the masses by including more vegetables, both raw or cooked form in each meal. At present, majority of the population is vegetarian but per capita consumption of vegetables is estimated to be hardly about 135 g against the requirement of about 285 g for a balanced diet. This intake need to be increased.

Off-season vegetable production. The off-season vegetables are raised is a monopoly of some pockets in the hills and are made available to the consumers in the plains at the time when these can not be grown there because of very hot climatic conditions. These not only play an important role in the improvement of economy of hill people by bringing higher returns but are delicious, attractive, fresh and keep the markets in the plains flooded. Moreover, the new technology, seasonal barriers are being broken and off-season production of vegetables have become popular, varied agro-climatic conditions also contribute to produce different kinds of vegetables in one or the other zone in the hills. Thus most vegetables can be grown and seen in the market during any season.

More consumption. With the large scale production of vegetables and rise in the living standards of the population are or have started consuming optimum to higher quantities of vegetables per capita per day as both the growers and the consumers are better understood about the protective food value of vegetables grown in various zones in the country.

More yield per unit area. The higher tonnage of vegetables are produced per unit area and time as compared to the conventional cereals and fruit crops being grown in the country, besides better food values and comparatively more income from each vegetable. Moreover, these vegetables grown very fast and are available to the consumers easily.

Vegetables are source of income. Some vegetable growing areas provide better conditions and act as a natural glass-house of the country for raising vegetables at one location or the other all the year round. The vegetables produced are tasty, flavoured, attractive and of better quality which are sold at a higher rate in the big metropolitan cities of the country. However, at the peak season, if sold at cheap rate particulary during rainy season, the returns per unit area are compensated by high tonnage. More returns can be earned by regulating the sowing timings either by advancing or delayed sowings of some vegetables will bring better prices in the market because of their early or delayed availability to the consumers. In hilly areas, vegetables like garden peas, tomato, bell pepper, beans, cucumbers, cauliflower, cabbage, radish, turnip, carrot and garden beet are the more paying crops which are more commonly grown. The farmers earn very lucrative returns. The incomes are much higher than the conventional cereal crops and equally compete with the fruit crops, therefore, the area is constantly increasing.

Better employment generation. Vegetable industry being labour intensive, offers better employment opportunities and because of difficult terrain, small and scattered land holdings, all the operations need to be done manually right from ploughing to harvesting, transport (head loads) to marketing etc. particularly in the hills. Therefore, production of vegetables create a number of jobs opportunities to the young woman folk and young youths in the complementary fields of vegetable trade that also involves packaging, transportation, processing, marketing and finally distribution in different parts of the country.

Proper utilisation of services of family members. The services of all the family members can be properly utilised for raising vegetables. Women in developing and potential areas play a major role in vegetable production in addition to their primary responsibility to the family, women also tend fields, harvest and sell the produce and prepare meals for the whole family.

Foreign exchange earners. Most of the vegetables grown in different parts of the country have become foreign exchange earners and help in improving the social set up of the vegetable growers including the state and country as a whole and save the foreign exchange. For *e.g.* pea crop pods raised in the hills have a better keeping quality and shelf-life and more so are available almost through out the year are being exported to the Gulf countries to the tune of crores of rupees annually.

Better utilisation of farm resources. Vegetables are more efficient converters of farm resources than other crops in terms of yield per unit area per time since they grow very fast. In hills, an hectare of potato can yield from two to two and half times as many calories as a hectare of rice or wheat. Yield of amaranths can be as high 10 tonnes of edible tender leaves in 20-30 days.

Better utilisation of land under young orchards. The space in between fruit plants and rows in young orchards of apple, peach, plum, walnut, almond and citrus can/are being used for raising vegetables like cabbage, radish, turnip, leafy vegetables and earned income till the orchards start bearing fruits, with additional income.

Aesthetic values of vegetables. The vegetables grown on small or commercial scale provides income besides satisfaction to the grower and his family members. Cultivation of vegetables right from seed sowing, sprouting, flowering, fruit formation, picking, packaging and marketing provides joy and aesthetic value to all besides supply of fresh vegetables.

More vegetables can be raised in a year. Some vegetables as compared to cereals or fruit plants can be raised throughout the year. More so most of the vegetables/varieties are of short duration, season bound and grow quickly can fit in cropping pattern of the area. The lead given by these hilly areas especially Himachal Pradesh in developing vegetable industry can be a source of inspiration to vegetable growers of other hilly/plain areas and will help the nation to tide-over the food shortage. Besides exotic vegetables, seeds can also be exported to earn more foreign exchange as potential venture which needs to be tapped.

CHAPTER

7

OFF-SEASON VEGETABLE PRODUCTION

Traditional agriculture is not economical for the hill areas of the country because not only are the yields low but the crop also takes longer time to mature. The prevailing agro-climatic conditions on the other hand, are very congenial for vegetable, off-season vegetable cultivation and temperate vegetable seed production. Both these propositions are very paying and can go a long way in improving the economy of the hill farmers.

The hilly areas of the country comprise of warm valleys (low-hills) mid-hills and high-hills both temperate wet and temperate dry. During summers in the valleys, the temperature goes up while in mid-hills, it is mildly, cool and in high-hills only one season is there which starts from March-April and lasts up to September-October. Both summer and winter vegetables are successfully grown after one another or side by side in the same season. Due to these reasons, varied agro-climatic conditions prevail in different parts of the hills. In some places the micro-climate changes after every 15-20 km. Even with in each agro-climatic zone, there is slight variation in the temperature and other conditions.

Mostly the land holdings in the hills are small, scattered, undulating, terraced in some places, very steep and marginal and only 18-20 per cent of the area is under assured irrigation. Rest area is rain-fed where also a few off-season vegetables are cultivated by the hard working farmers. The seedlings are raised under protected conditions by using indigenous methods or poly-house and transplanted in the months of April-May or seed production done. The transplanted seedlings or plants are given life saving dose of about half litre water once in the evening or twice in morning and evening for sometime till the pre-monsoons are received followed by monsoons particularly tomato. Shimla mirch, cucurbits, etc. The cultural practices recommended for the normal crop are followed for the off-season crop also. The productivity may vary at places/pockets. There are certain suitable pockets where two or three harvests of the same vegetable are taken in a year because of mild climate *e.g.* Kullu valley of Himachal Pradesh where three crops of cabbage are grown in a sequence.

Mostly hill people are dependent on agriculture and cereals/fruits crops grown takes more time to mature and yields are very low. At present, the appearance and infestation of fruit orchards with various notified diseases and pests and costly chemicals needed for controlling them, fear of residues on the fruits, etc. has forced the farmers to shift for vegetable growing. As a result the traditional agriculture and horticulture is not economical although most of the hills folk are engaged in diversified farming for their survival. The agro-climatic conditions and eco-systems prevailing in various parts of the hill zone, on the other hand are quite suitable for vegetable/off-season growing and temperate vegetable seed production. Therefore, these propositions are very remunerative and can help in the improvement of over all socio-economic status of the poor hill vegetable growers.

Vegetable cultivation is also labour intensive and needs skilled labour for carrying various operations, hence, provides, suitable employment to the members of the family and other unemployed youths/women-folk and also land-less persons. Moreover, varied agro-climatic conditions permit to grow some of the vegetables in various pockets almost throughout the year and make available from one part or the other to ensure regular and static flow of off-season vegetables without creating a glut in the market. These vegetables have earned name, fame as a **"pahari sabjeya"** in the plain markets because of better taste, flavour, prolonged keeping quality and brings very lucrative returns to the farmers.

As compared to one/two cereal and fruit crops per year, 3-4 different or same vegetable can be raised in a year as they are of short duration, better get fitted in the cropping system as an inter-crop in the orchards by making best use of the land/space which is unutilized with additional income to the farmers. At places where the orchards have become non-profitable are being replaced by off-season vegetables also produce much higher yields per unit of land as compared to cereals/fruit crops.

Majority of the Indians are vegetarian and their diet is ill-balanced. Vegetables from hills being very tasty, nutritious, play a vital role in making the food palatable (both raw and after cooking) and balanced by their proper substitution. Moreover, these vegetables are less prone to various diseases and pests because of mild/cool climate resulting in less or no expenditure on chemicals and no residual impact, leading to no health hazards. Also the growers are dependent on organic manure and do not add or use the chemical fertilisers which helps in improving the quality of off-season vegetable produce and expenditure on chemical fertilisers is skipped. At present, more and more people are becoming aware of their useful role in human nutrition with the result that their consumption is gradually increasing thereby more demand in the market. The consumers do not mind to pay a little more while purchasing these vegetables because of their better quality. However, the per capita consumption of vegetables is still low as compared to the most advanced countries. There is need to educate the masses about the usefulness of vegetable consumption by changing the food habits which consists mainly of cereals. Vegetable residues also form rich diet for the domestic animals in the form of leaves, tender stems and left-out un-utilised vegetables and parts thereof at a time when green fodder is not available.

Therefore, under such situations the hill farmers have been able to earn substantial profits by growing vegetables in the off-season in the hill zone of the country particularly Jammu & Kashmir, Himachal Pradesh, Uttarakhand, part of West Bengal, Tamil Nadu, other seven eastern states and Karnataka. Many reputed organisations both in public and private sector are already undertaking/helping off-season vegetable production in a big way in the hills. All short of help is rendered in the form of inputs like quality seeds, fertilizer, etc. and technical know-how from time to time. More such areas/pockets may be explored to meet the increasing demand of quality off-season vegetables.

Conditions favourable for off-season vegetable production in the hills

Soils. Soils in general are shallow, fertile, rich in organic matter, potassium, slightly acidic, well drained free from any residual effect if supplemented with chemical fertilizer, becomes more suitable for growing quality off-season vegetable production.

Land situations. The belts/valleys with good arable soil, terraced fields, undulating topography, slope fields, well drained soils can produce almost all types of vegetables with better returns.

Climatic conditions. The varied climatic conditions available in the different hill zones especially in valley areas or pockets or hill tops are quite congenial for growing off-season vegetable varieties/hybrids. The temperature is mild and quite suitable and optimum humidity is maintained by receiving well distributed rains/snow. The cultural operations are for these vegetable crops are conveniently carried without any disturbance.

Isolation distance and pollinators. The hill tops, forest areas, and river catchment area, provides natural barriers between the valley, pockets or off-season growing areas for obtaining better quality uniform produce with high yields. The pollinating agents (pollinators) especially bees and other bee flora are available in plenty naturally in the hills which plays a significant role in bringing about cross-pollination and by producing better quality product.

Irrigation facilities. Irrigation water which is of prime importance in the production of quality vegetables is available in plenty from various sources *viz.,* perennial rivers and their tributaries, springs, kuhl, tube-well well distributed rainfall/snowfall etc.

Identification of vegetable varieties/hybrids. The off-season vegetable production programme of only those vegetables varieties/hybrids should be taken up after thorough thought of which is successfully done and no problem crops up later, keeping in view the economics of production and their demand in the domestic markets with in the stale, country and its export potential outside.

Quality seed. The quality seed available from reliable sources *viz.,* the agencies and organisations like NSC, State Department of Agriculture/SAUs and other reputed seed companies and preference should be given to certified seed as the whole off-season vegetable industry depends on quality seed.

Sowing/planting. This is very important operation and sowing/planting at appropriate time can be worked out on the basis of the altitude, latitude, slop, aspects, etc. It need to be worked out for each pocket/valleys either by early or delaying this operation enabling the farmer to earn more returns from his produce.

Technical know-how. The proper knowledge of growing technology of vegetable varieties, hybrids in off-season may be imparted to the farmers well in advance through personal contact, by organising training camps, literature, newspapers, radios, television, etc.

Less loss due to pests. Because of mild climate and other factors being favourable, there is less or no attack of diseases, insects and other weeds etc. and thus saving of expenditure on chemicals and harvest residue free produce.

Post-harvest handling. A good harvest of these vegetables can be obtained economically and the post-harvest handling operations are done easily because of the prolonged shelf-life of vegetable varieties considered for the purpose at proper maturity and method of harvesting, etc.

Availability of cheap labour. Labour needed from time to time is easily, available throughout the year to carryout the various operations at cheap rate. Moreover, in some places the joint family system is prevalent and the services of the family labour is efficiently utilised.

Women's role. In the hills the women number exceeds men and they are engaged in all types of agriculture work in addition to social domestic, child rearing etc. Thus woman plays a significant role from land preparation, up to marketing of vegetable produce.

Means of communication. Almost all the interior parts of the hill zone have been linked by national high ways, main roads or link roads. Where road is not possible the bridal path and rope ways and jhulas are used. Thus the produce is being taken to the various markets from these areas which used to be most difficult areas. Green vegetables like cabbage, peas, cauliflower etc. produced deep in Himalayas *e.g.,* Kinnaur and Lahaul & Spiti Districts of Himachal Pradesh is either supplied to the army and other para-military forces and local government employees or sent to the markets in Delhi, Mumbai, Kolkata, Chennai or even exported to the Gulf countries fresh or processed.

Improved economic status. At present, the economic condition of the people/farmers in hills has improved with passage of time with their own efforts and also concerted efforts of various organisations and the economy now is far better than it was a few years back.

Short duration nature of vegetables. Almost all the vegetables grown are of short duration for example radish variety. White Icicle, French Break Fast, etc. get ready in 30-40 days, pea varieties Arkel in 60-65 days and Azad pea in 60-70 days. Thus because of mild climate 2-3 or more crops in a year can be raised from the same piece of land.

Better fit in the cropping system. Almost all vegetables because of small stature, short duration and shallow rooted some of them leguminous get better fitted in the prevalent cropping pattern of the area. More, so, these are/can be raised in the young and well established orchards as a inter-crop with additional income.

Small land holdings. Major population in the hills have small and marginal land holdings, therefore, production of vegetables in off-season is easy and economical for them.

High productivity. All the vegetables grown in off-season produces higher yields of better quality product as compared to cereals or fruit crops and the cost of production is less and makes best use of small land holdings and space in between orchards, thus more remunerative returns per unit area.

Development schemes/agencies. Now a days there are various development schemes/ agencies both short and long term nature operating in each district/state *viz.,* Indo-German,

Indo-Dutch, Small Farmers. Development Scheme, MAFAL, Tribal Development and Improvement Project, various Agricultural/Horticultural projects in each state funded by State/Central/World Bank and other funding organisations. Recently, Central Government has extended help to the hill states in the form of various Pilot projects *viz.*, ATAMA NATP, etc.

Loans and subsidies. The Central/State Governments are assisting the hill farmers by providing loans at nominal interest and subsidies etc. through banks and other agencies. The various organisations particularly in public sector, the Government through Stale Department/Universities and NSC have made provision to make available all inputs including seeds at subsidised rates.

Poly-house Technology. During the present decade the poly-house technology has been extended to the interested farmers, and the cost of installation and inputs are arranged at subsidised rates up to 50% subsidy. There is awareness among the farmers about its use particularly in those areas where snow-fall/heavy rain-fall and natural hazards like hails, frost, etc. is a regular feature, these poly-houses are profitably used for raising vegetable seedlings, cucurbits in poly-tubes and high value vegetables including rare vegetables.

Co-operative societies. Various small farmers co-operative societies/units are being created and formed at village/block/district and state level to handle the off-season vegetable produce in a efficient and systematic manner. At places, it is wholly their responsibility to collect, transport and market the produce at appropriate time to fetch better prices in various markets.

Improved socio-economic status of hill farmers. The economic status of the hill farmers have greatly improved by diversified farming. They have gained the technical know-how of off-season vegetable production and are fully aware about their utility and significance.

Insurance cover. The inseparable loss caused to the tender and delicate vegetables grown in off-season are subjected to vagaries of weather at any stage and time during the life span of vegetable crop. Like other crops in some states an insurance cover have been provided which will provide security to the poor, honest and hardworking farmers with small limited land holdings.

Marketing structure. The transportation marketing and distribution system is now well established in a systematic manner. After harvesting it is very important to pack properly in appropriate containers, with less damage or injury etc. during transit and follow better marketing system/channel which helps in bringing better returns and immediate carrying of these perishable commodities for proper distribution as otherwise if not marketed properly and in time will affect the quality, price and get rotted soon.

Impact on the socio-economic status of hill population. It has been observed that there is a drastic improvement and change in the socio-economic status of the hill people particularly in those areas where the pockets and valleys have been exploited. More so, the hill farmers being hardworking, honest, capable and acceptable to adopt new production technology imparted by various extension agencies from time to time have started growing off-season vegetables in their small, scattered land-holdings with slope, undulating and terraced fields. Rich in organic matter where rain/snow water do not accumulate make suitable for proper growth and development. Some of the progressive farmers have started raising 2-3 vegetable crops on the same piece of land, better suits in the particular rotation in the eco-system which helps in maintaining fertility and balance with better yield potential in a year as compared to cereals and fruit crops, more so they have altogether stopped cereal growing as it earns remunerative returns to the farmers engaged in the production of high value off-season vegetables. Moreover, these vegetable being short duration fit well in the croping systems as a catch crop (Arkal-Maize) and as an inter-crop either with other vegetable crops (French bean in tomato) Peas in wheat or orchards. In addition, the leftout vegetables, leaves, tender plant remains, stubble, etc. makes nutritious and balanced fodder to the domestic livestock. Therefore, the marketing structure is also functioning well as the vegetable growing areas which have been linked with national, state highways and bridal paths which are mostly metalled for smooth plying of small and big vehicles, transporting tonnes of fresh vegetables to the distant markets either by the farmers himself or jointly by farmers of the village or area and many other organisations both in public and private sector at nominal carriage changes almost daily at the peak harvest season. The contractors or middlemen enter into the trade and help the small and marginal farmers in this direction. In some places, the young educated graduates have taken up the programme in an efficient way who were otherwise unemployed. In the recent past, the poly-house technology has contributed a lot at least in seedling/poly tube plants raising in odd or off-season in the hills. Therefore, the hill agriculture scenario has almost changed by the diversified farming systems and the main component of which is the off-season vegetable production. Thus, the socio-economic status of the hill farmers have greatly improved and have become well to do.

CHAPTER

8

POLY-HOUSE TECHNOLOGY IN VEGETABLE PRODUCTION

The recent advent of plastic has been a unique gift to the modern agriculture and its manifold uses in the form of green or plastic commonly known as poly-house. In most advanced countries, there is a sizeable area under poly-houses and tonnes of vegetables are produced. In India, poly-house technology was adopted late but owing to its merits and incentives given by the Central and State Governments, a notable increase in the poly-house area has occurred in the recent years. The vegetable crops can be grown under a framed structure with transparent or translucent material under partially controlled environmental conditions (light, temperature, air composition and a rooting medium). This system of vegetable cultivation can be considered as green-house cultivation.

In addition, some high value vegetables/varieties and valuable ornamental plants also need protection from frost during winter and excessive rains during rainy season, and other natural hazards like hails, gales etc. provides congenial conditions for their quick propagation, over all in the situations a poly or green-house structure has a great role to play as seedlings/ plant can not be grown outside due to prevailing unfavourable weather conditions in different pockets. This helps in saving the valuable time and vegetable crop growth which can be advanced at least 1-2 months in the field. Also disease and insect free seedlings/plant are made available in off-season. Poly/green-houses are easy to manage and useful in areas prone to hailing, storm, heavy snow, rain and strong warm winds.

Advantages of poly-house cultivation

(*i*) Off-season nursery period.

(*ii*) Shortening of the nursery period.

(*iii*) Off-season production of high value vegetables.

(*iv*) Higher productivity.

(*v*) Superior quality of the produce.

(*vi*) Effective utilization of different resources like seeds, fertilizers, water, labour, etc.

(*vii*) Easy to perform plant protection measures *viz.*, to control diseases and insect-pests.

(*viii*) Protection of vegetable crops against hails, extreme weather conditions, birds, rodents, animals, etc.

(*ix*) The produce harvested is neat and clean.

Poly/green-house. Wood, bamboo, G.I. pipe, conduit pipe, angle iron and aluminium are the common materials used for the framework of a poly-house. A green-house is a framed or inflated structure covered with transparent or translucent material either glass (fibre-glass) or ultra violet stable polythene film in which vegetables/crops can be grown under controlled environment. Durability of the structure depends on the type of the material used. Ultra violet resistant plastic film of 150-200 micron thickness is the commonly used covering material. The common shapes are gable, quenset and gothic. For small farmers single span green-houses are good but for large scale economical production gutter connected multispan green-houses are economical. Based on the type of glazing material used in covering the installed structures, green-house can be broadly grouped into the following :

(*i*) Fibre-glass green-house,

(*ii*) Single or double polythene films (poly-house),

(*iii*) Ordinary glass-house,

(*iv*) Poly-carbonate houses, and

(*v*) Ultraviolet stable polythene film house.

Each one of these green-house have specific uses and are meant for specific locations in the hills. A green-house must be cost effective structure with desired level of climatic control. It should be large enough to allow a person to walk in them to carryout various cultural operations and where vegetables could be grown under completely controlled or at least partially controlled environment. Green-house enable us to regulate the growing conditions for exploiting the full potential of any plant species at any time of the year. The size and type of poly/green-house varies from place to place and depends on the following factors-requirement of the farmer for seedlings raising or commercial vegetable growing, economic status of the farmer, material cost and availability, simple, partially and completely controlled environment and financial assistance received from the government or any other organisation by way of subsidy, loans etc. for their installation. Also the technology made available to the farmers.

Environmental control. Depending upon the need to control environment, green-house may be installed with full, partial or without any control mechanism. Based on the degree of control over the environmental factors like temperature, light, humidity and air circulation, poly-houses are categorised as high cost, medium cost and low cost.

High cost poly-house. In the high cost poly-houses, there is a complete control over the environment using sophisticated equipments and the system may be fully automated and computerised. The green-house with full regulating mechanism though costly is the best to grow crops/vegetables throughout the year.

Medium cost poly-house. In medium cost poly-houses there is a provision of cooler (usually fan-pad system) shading and misting which keep a check over the rising temperature during summer, while hot air blowers may be used to maintain higher temperature during winters. The medium cost green-house could have double layer of plastic or poly-ethylene film for covering and cooling and heating arrangements.

Low cost poly-house. In the low cost poly-house no equipment is installed to control the environment artificially. At higher altitudes such poly-houses are/may have year round utility but in plain areas having cool winters and warm summers, their utility is primarily restricted only to winter months.

A plastic film or fibre glass covering over a green-house acts like selective radiation filter which allows solar radiation to pass through it but help in trapping thermal radiation emitted by the objectives/material in side the green-house. Carbon dioxide released by plants at night was also trapped inside the green-house. This helps in raising the level of Carbon dioxide available to plants during the day by five to ten times thus enhancing photosynthetic activity in the plants body growing inside the green-house. In view of the fact that the environmental conditions plays a crucial role in vegetable crop damage caused by unfavourable weather conditions, to modify the local climatic conditions, to improve productivity and quality of vegetable crops and help to eliminate weed growth. These structures also protect the vegetable plants from extreme temperature, rain, high velocity winds, insects and diseases, with the result the vegetable plants are able to grow unchecked.

Choice of vegetable crops. The choice of the vegetable crop/variety to be grown in a green-house is normally made on the basis of the physical size of the structure and economics of vegetable production. Generally, high value vegetables are preferred for poly-house growing. The selection of crops also depends upon the altitude, size and structure of the poly-house and the market demand. While it may be possible to grow any crop at any time in a high cost poly-house, selection of crops is more critical in case of ordinary low cost poly-houses. In plains and lower hills cucumber, bottle gourd, bitter gourd, French bean, tomato, capsicum, okra, etc. during winter and cabbage, broccoli, tropical cauliflower, beet leaf, coriander, etc. during summer/rainy season are found more suitable. At higher altitudes leafy vegetables, salad crops and temperate cultivars of root vegetables have been found good during winter with greater choice available during summer season. However, green-house have a tremendous potential in raising production and productivity of vegetable crops including rare vegetables and medicinal/ornamental plants especially under adverse agro-climatic conditions. Moreover, local experience showed that the use of green-houses for commercial vegetable production was lacking, moreover, the green-house technology for vegetable production, is still in a infancy stage and need to be exploited fully at least in the hills where these are of great need and significance.

Size of green-house and cost involved. In case if indigenous types where local material is used for the frames and for covering transparent or translucent films are considered. These structures are comparatively quite cheap but their life is short. These can be installed by the local carpenter. There is no provision of environment regulating mechanism. The other better green-houses, the conduit pipes properly shaped are installed on a RCC base and covered with transparent or translucent films. These are specially installed with environment control mechanism especially for proper temperature, humidity etc. are regulated according to the wish of the farmer and specific requirement of the vegetable crop and purpose for which raised. Heavy inputs are required for the installation of such type of green-houses which comes in the way of propagation of this type of technology. The technology could be successful if it was made cheap and cost effective.

Green-houses in Hills. In most of the areas including hilly areas of the country having mild agro-ecological situations existing naturally and both summer and winter vegetables are successfully grown side by side from March-April to September. Under such situations poly-house has to play a significant role in vegetable production in different zones starting from the Shivalik hills 300 m.a.s.l. to deep in Himalayas up to 3500 m.a.s.l. Therefore, the hilly areas are gifted with varied agro-climatic conditions for growing array of vegetables in different zones more particularly during summer months. Hill regions of our country are mostly situated in North Western Himalayas, comprising of J & K, H.P., Kumaon and Garhwal in Uttarakhand, Darjeeling hills in West Bengal and some hilly regions in North-Eastern states to about 15% of geographic area and only 5% population of the country. These areas possess vast potential for growing various vegetables in normal and off-season.

In low-hills, the seedlings for tomato, brinjal, capsicum, chillies, seasonal annuals and plants of cucurbit *viz.,* cucumber, bitter gourd, muskmelon, watermelon, bottle gourd, pumpkin, summer squash, etc. are raised under protected conditions during December, January-February and these can be transplanted/planted outside in the main field from February onward as and when the risk of frost, coldness is over, enables to catch early markets for getting better lucrative returns.

In mid-hill areas vegetables are grown under protected conditions (poly-house) during February-March and transplanted outside in April prove more remunerative. In areas having high rainfall, seedlings of winter-vegetable like cabbage, cauliflower, knol-khol, Chinese cabbage, tomatoes, etc. for off-season crop can be raised under protected conditions during July-August for timely transplanting in the main field. In high-hill areas where there is only one growing period during summer and is short. In these areas, also seedlings of vegetables like tomato, capsicum, cauliflower, cabbage, knol-khol, Chinese cabbage and plants of cucumber and Sarda-melon and all type of seasonal flowers (annuals) can be grown under protected conditions for timely plantation outside.

The approximate cost of a green-house of 40 square metres in dimension is about ₹ 22,000 in Himachal Pradesh. This cost may vary from state to state and zones/pockets. These structures are being installed by both State Departments of Agriculture/Horticulture under different schemes being financed by the Central/State Governments. This programme has been launched in a big way and the state governments are providing liberal financial assistance in the form of subsidy ranging 30 to 50 per cent at different times to the interested farmers. There is a special facility for advancement of loans by the banks for installing these special structures costing ₹ One Lakh or more. The green-houses are in various stages of construction in all parts of the state. This facility can also be extended or being extended to other hill states of the country enabling to grow exotic, off-season vegetables, high value vegetables, temperate vegetables, high value rare vegetables, fruits and flowers. In these green-houses, the desired temperature and humidity can be maintained, which can be raised or brought down by heating and cooling system. Normally, there is a difference of about 10°C in temperature inside the green-house as compared to outside, However, these climatic conditions are low throughout the year. These green-houses will prove boon to the vegetable industry in the hilly regions.

Nursery raising in poly-house. Seed germination and rearing of nursery in early stages is a difficult task being faced by the vegetable growers in those vegetables which are transplanted through seedlings. This problem is solved if the seed are sown in small poly-houses. Generally, the seedlings of tomato, capsicum, chillies takes more time to get ready in the open while in poly-house these are ready in half or 1/3 time with greater unit area population. Seedlings of early cauliflower cultivars exposed to intense sun heat and saturated soil conditions during rainy season show high mortality due to damping-off diseases. A properly ventilated poly-house can ensure greater survival.

TABLE 8.1. Utility of poly-houses for growing vegetables and vegetable seedlings

Zone	*Vegetables*	*Sowingtime*	*Transplanting time*
A. For Nursery	**Raising**		
Low-hills	Tomato, capsicum brinjal, chillies, cucumber, summer squash in poly-bags	Mid-Dec. to Mid-Jan.	Mid-Feb. to Mid-March
Mid-hills	-do- + Broccoli	Mid-Jan. to Mid-Feb.	Mid-March to Mid-April
High-hills	Cabbage, cauliflower, broccoli	Mid-Feb. to Mid-March	Mid-April to Mid-May
Dry temperate	Cabbage, cauliflower broccoli, tomato, capsicum	Mid-March to Mid-April	Mid-May to Mid-June
B. Vegetable Growing			
Low-hills	Tomato, brinjal, capsicum, chillies, cucumber and squash	Mid-Oct. (in open)	Dec. (in poly-house)
Mid-hills	Tomato, brinjal, capsicum, cucumber and squash	Mid-Oct. to Mid Nov.-Dec. (in poly-tunnels)	Mid-Nov.-Dec.
High-hills	Tomato, capsicum, cucumber	Mid Feb.-Mid-March March-Mid-April	Early April to Mid-May
Dry temperate	Tomato/capsicum and brinjal	Mid-March-Mid-April	Late April to May

The timings may vary according to climatic fluctuations outside.

Off-season production of vegetable. In high rainfall areas of the country, the yield of some vegetables like tomato are considerably high under poly rain shelter. Similarly other vegetables-capsicum, cucumber, bitter gourd, bottle gourd, etc. have been grown in off-season during winter under sub-tropical climates producing high yields. In such areas where no vegetable can be grown during winter months in open, successful crops of lettuce, beet leaf mustard, radish, turnip and garden beet have been found suitable to grow in the poly-house.

Raising plants through root cutting. The green-houses are also used for rapid rooting of cuttings of different ornamental plants.

Multiplication of elite material. The green-house are also used effectively for raising/multiplying the elite material of vegetables, flowers and horticultural plants.

Precautions. When raising seedlings or vegetable plants in the poly/green-houses the following precautions may be taken care of :

(*i*) During hot months especially May to August for raising nursery of vegetables, arrangement may be made for proper ventilation *viz.,* electric fans may be installed for maintaining the cool environment inside by sprinkling water regularly and using exhaust fan(s).

(*ii*) In hail prone areas, provision of wire-netting above the poly-ethylene sheet will prove effective, economical and enhance the life of the sheet/film used.

(*iii*) Normally the poly-house seedlings/plants get very good congenial conditions and if they are transplanted/shifted to outside environment in the main field directly the survival rate will be affected because of warm/different/unfavourable climatic conditions outside. Therefore, it is very important to make them withstand the harsh climatic field conditions by adopting the following procedure. Before uprooting the seedlings/plants in the green-house, stop irrigating them prior to uprooting at least 5-7 days for their hardening. After uprooting these, expose them to outer conditions, by keeping the trays/polythene bags outside in shade either in veranda or under tree or any other temporary shelter. At the time of uprooting the seedlings, water them well and transplant the seedlings. In the field always in the evening hours. Similarly prepare pits at appropriate spots in the main-field for transplanting of cucurbit plants. Tear the poly-bags before planting and irrigate them immediately after planting. Irrigate the plants. regularly for 3-4 days till they get established well.

Major constraints

(*i*) Initial high cost is involved in the installation of poly-house structures which is beyond the reach of poor farmers. However, use of local material like bamboo/wood instead of conduit steel pipes can help in reducing the initial cost of poly-house to some extent.

(*ii*) In simple poly-house, there is no proper devices for controlling/regulating optimum required temperature and humidity.

(*iii*) Prevalence of more harsh conditions like high rainfall, high incidence of hail-storm in mid-hill areas, extreme low temperature, heavy-snowfall and high strong velocity winds in high-hills and use of poly-house may not be possible until and unless it is covered with wire netting.

(*iv*) In addition, inadequate knowledge of farmers about the optimum growth conditions of vegetables in the green-houses and lack of green-house technology are the major constraints which is being made available gradually to the farmers.

(*v*) In hilly areas, where the poly-houses are installed by the progressive farmers are mostly used for raising healthy seedlings only because of the fact that these areas are quite suitable for growing most vegetables on a commercial scale in the open because of mild climate.

(*vi*) In other places, where early harvests are to be taken in cucurbit, the plants are raised in the poly-tubes in their early stages *i.e.,* up to two or four leaf stage and the germination and growth is very fast because of higher temperature insided as compared to outside the poly-house. These poly-tubes are planted in the main field at the appropriate time.

Suggestions. To make poly-house a successful enterprise the following points may be kept in mind to increase their popularity in the hills :

(*i*) To reduce the cost of poly-house installation by using only the local material.

(*ii*) For regulating the temperature and humidity in such cheap poly-houses, open the poly-ethylene sheet on one side manually when the temperature increases inside and irrigate or sprinkle the beds with water to increase humidity and reduce the temperature.

(*iii*) To make it more popular among the poor and marginal farmers the rate of subsidy already given may be increased so that more farmers can make its use.

(*iv*) The amount of loan extended to the interested farmers may be increased and the rate of interest may be lowered so that all progressive farmers can get these installed in their land holding.

(*v*) At places, where the natural hazards like hails, gales, strong winds, heavy rains etc. are the regular feature, a wirenetting may be fixed on the polythene sheet to protect the same from blowing or tearing and thus its life will increase for a pretty long time.

(*vi*) The farmers can have their co-operative societies to make best use of the poly-house jointly in arranging materials at cheap rate for their installation and further taking the produce to the market at premium prices for earning lucrative returns.

(*vii*) The appropriate technology developed at the university or department level for growing vegetables, high value vegetables flowers and their seedlings and rooting of cuttings of both ornamental and horticultural plants should be imparted to all those immature farmers in the initial stages. They should be given the latest technical know how by training them.

(*viii*) To popularise the poly-house technology in other areas, the Directorate of Extension Education of respective SAU's/Department of Agriculture/Horticulture or any other agency should take lead to extend the programme among the masses.

(*ix*) A suitable situation or place may be selected for installing a poly-house which is near the living house, site is sunny, free from shade residual impact of chemicals, diseases, insects and weeds, soil should be fertile and well drained with irrigation facility.

Thus, success of green-house lies in the use of cheaper material like bamboos in place of conduit pipe and use of smoke to reduce effect of frost/fog, arrangement of subsidies, specific loans from the bank or Govt. agencies and imparting training to the farmers about the green-house technology. Further studies are in progress for making the green-houses cost effective.

CHAPTER 9

ROLE OF BIO-FERTILIZERS INVEGETABLE PRODUCTION

Vegetables play a significant role in the nutritional food security for the increasing population of the country. To increase the vegetable production in terms of productivity per unit area and to maintain long term productivity it is essential to maintain soil fertility level through judicious application of chemical fertilizers, organic manures and bio-fertilizers. At the same time, it is also necessary to ensure balanced nutrients for the normal growth of the vegetable crops without affecting the eco-system. But the extensive application of chemical fertilizers has reduced soil fertility, deteriorated the soil structure, destroyed water bodies and created the problem of environment pollution. Self sustainability of soil has been lost through the continuous application of chemical fertilizers alone. A serious situation has arisen by the excessive use of these chemical fertilizers which are not fully utilized by the plants and there are problems of losses of applied chemical nutrients through leaching, volatilisation and fixation to an unavailable form. The progressive farmers use the highest quantity of nitrogen based fertilizers and are now getting diminishing returns from their fields even after using any amount of fertilizers. The soil fertility has declined because of reduced soil microbial activity and reduced soil organic matter. Since increase in the cost of petroleum products due to oil crisis which is the feed stock of fertilizers production, all over the world efforts are being made to look for alternative renewable sources of nutrient supply. Over the years soil test results have shown that bulk of the Indian soils are poor in nitrogen. However, Punjab's farmers are the leaders in the use of the highest quantity of nitrogenous fertilizer per hectare. This implies that the nitrogen deficit cannot be met only through chemical fertilizers which are costly, pollution-causing, affecting the eco-system and destroying the water bodies. Moreover, the judicious use of chemical fertilizers in vegetable production is not only the solution as still many people of our country are not meeting the minimum demand of per capita consumption of calories and also vegetables produced by the use of chemical fertilizers alone are of poor taste and flavour and their keeping quality is very low.

Considerable research efforts were made to identify effective strains of biological fixation sources which could be profitably used for making nitrogen available to the vegetable crops. Moreover, with ever increasing cost of chemical fertilizers and widening gap between demand and supply, utilization of bio-fertilizers offers an opportunity to introduce renewable nutrient source. Realising the importance of the bio-fertilizers, the Government of India sanctioned a National Project on Development and Use of Biofertilizers. The progressive use of bio-fertilizers world over offers the best alternative to intensive chemical fertilizers. Moreover, the bio-fertilizers are an economically viable, ecologically sound, partial substitute to costly and pollution causing chemical fertilizers.

Definition. Bio-ferlilizers are living cells of different types of micro-organisms (bacteria, algae and fungi) which have the ability to mobilise nutritionally important elements from non-usable to usable form. Bio-fertilizers are cultures of microbes which are capable of fixing atmospheric nitrogen where suitable vegetables/crops are inoculated with them. These micro-organisms require organic matter for their growth and activity in soil and provide valuable nutrients to the plants in the soil.

Bio-fertilizers as the name indicate, are the fertilizers of biological origin. Recent use of the term encompasses all the organic manures including green manures. However, in restricted scope bio-fertilizers are the preparation of living micro-organisms used to improve vegetable plant nourishment and soil fertility and thereby achieving enhanced and sustainable vegetable crop production.

The use of bio-fertilizers by growing legumes with non-legumes in the cropping system is an old agronomic practice, although the scientific reasoning for this practice came to be known over a decade.

Bio-fertilizers which are organic contains micro-organisms are capable of decomposing organic matter in the soil. Organic manures will help to retain soil fertility. Hence and integrated approach should be made.

Advantages of use of bio-fertilizers

(*i*) Bio-fertilizers are biologically active products containing five bacteria or fungi as single or composite cultures and thus improve soil health and fertility.

(*ii*) They are less expensive, eco-friendly and renewable source of nutrients particularly nitrogen.

(*iii*) Easy to use and pollution free.

(*iv*) Best suited for marginal and small farmers as they are cheap.

(*v*) They are highly cost effective.

Micro-organisms in bio-fertilizers make the soil living and dynamic and thus influence the soil fertility and productivity by solubilization of insoluble phosphorus through N fixation breaking down of organic material and nutrient release and improvement of soil structure.

The symbiosis is affected by many biotic and abiotic factors like type of legumes, rhizobial strain, different soil factors and strain competition, etc.

For effective inoculation, there is specificity between *Rhizobium* species and legume vegetable crops. This particular group of vegetable crops being infected by particular species of *Rhizobium* are termed as *"Cross inoculation group"*.

Classification. Depending on the physiological activity, the bio-fertilizers may be classified as (*i*) nitrogenous, *(ii)* phosphatic or cellulolytic.

(*a*) **Nitrogenous bio-fertilizers (biological nitrogen fixers).** These are of diverse types such as symbiotic nitrogen fixing organisms which form associations with higher plants. *Rhizobium* and *bradyrhizobium* are well known bacteria which forms root nodules in the leguminous vegetables like garden peas and beans and this association meets most of the nitrogen requirement of these vegetable plants. Legumes are also known to leave behind some residual N in soil, besides increasing the crop yield. *Rhizobium* can survive at low temperature and tolerate temperature- upto 50°C for more than few hours. *Rhizobium* is more tolerant towards salt than its host legume and therefore survive in saline soils. The responses of rhizobia inoculation at the farmers field with respect to cowpea, urad and broadbean have been demonstrated. The azotobacter and azospirillum play a significant role in nitrogen nutrition of vegetables, cereals, etc. Field trials conducted in India revealed that inoculation of seedling roots of vegetables with azotobacter increases yield of onion (18-22%), brinjal (16-62%), cabbage (25-50%) and tomato (2-29%) as compared to uninoculated control. These also improved root length in carrot and radish, increased number of flowers in brinjal and chilli when treated with *A.chroococcum.* Azotobacter increase shoot length, number of leaves, bulb and bulb yield in garlic. Incidences of bacterial, viral and fungal diseases were reduced when crops were inoculated with *Azotobacter. Azospirillum* is recognised as a very ubiquitous soil organism capable of colonising effectively not only the roots of a wide variety of vegetable plants but also their above ground portions forming apparently an associate symbiosis. The particular bacteria has growth promoting effect on root and shoot parts of *Brassica chinesis* and *Cucumis sativus* when inoculated into root. *Azospirillum* promotes fruit and seed yield of pumpkin, cabbages, knol-khol and onion. Other quality parameters in onion such as T.S.S., anthocyanin and pyruvic acid were also improved. Seed inoculation with *Rhizobium* and *Azospirillum* in combination has increased the nodulation and yield of soybean, clover, lucerne and chickpea.

(*b*) **Phosphatic or cellulolytic.** Phosphate is second major element in plant nutritions but when water soluble fertilizers are applied in the soil get converted into an unavailable form due to chemical fixation in soil. In such situations the phosphate solubilizing bacteia have also been identified belonging to genera of *Pseudomonas* and *Bacillus* help in rendering insoluble phosphates available to plants. Some new promising phosphorus solubilising bacteria and fungi are *Pseudomonas striata, Bacillus megaterium, Bacillus polymxa, Aspergilus awamori, Penicillium digitatum* and *Penicillium,* etc. can produce several organic acid (Butyric acid, Citric acid, Formic acid, etc.) and convert unavailable phosphorus into available form known as phosphorus solubilization. The use of such cultures have definitely increased the phosphorus availability and crop yield (soybean and potato). These cultures are being multiplied and prepared as carrier based 'Microphos cultures' for field trials and for supplying to farmers.

(*c*) **Mycorrhizae.** The importance of Vesicular Arbuscular Mycorrhizal (VAM) fungi in vegetables is well known. They improve nutrient uptake, disease resistance, nitrogen fixation, hormone production and drought resistance. Increase in nodulation, growth and yield was noticed in garden pea, pigeon pea, cowpea and mungbean. Economics of VAM inoculation have shown that 25 to 50% of P could be saved due to VAM inoculation in chilli and okra. Mycorrhizal tomato plants were found more resistant to damping-off and nematode infection. This is one of the recent bio-fertilizers which to help uptake of several nutrients (P, Zn, Cu, Fe, etc.).

Method of application

Bio-fertilizers are applied to seed, seedling, seed material or soil. These improve the quality of produce. They are cheap and economical — the cost benefit ratio is more than 1 : 10. It is an eco-friendly practice and improves natural character of soil.

Tips for improving efficiency of Bio-fertilizers

A good quality inoculant means high population of genetically effective strains of bacteria. Apart from the available of genetically potential strains indigenous to soil, there is a great scope to improve N_2 fixing capacity by using bio-technological manipulation. Some genetic determinants like genes for bacteria in production, for nodulation specificity and efficiency and for extra cellular polysaccharides production have been identified. Manipulation of these genes to construct competitive strains appears to be an elegant proposition. Some extra cellular proteins are also implicated to play role in strains competition. More recently some chemical inhibiting flavonoids induction of nod genes in *Rhizobium* and *Bradyrhizobium* have been identified. These chemicals can be used strategically used with inoculant strain having flavonoid independent nod D gene. These inhibitors, will present nod gene induction of these indigenous strains. Thus inoculated strain only will have chance to nodulate while indigenous strains will loose capacity to nodulate in presence of inhibitors. However, it remains to be seen how effective these inhibitors remain in soil. Moreover, in nature there is a lot of variability among these nitrogenous strains with regard to effectiveness, competitiveness and adaptive adaptiveness. The numerical quality of inoculants depends on the quality of carrier, moisture content of the carrier, moisture content of the carrier based preparation, packing tin and storage conditions at laboratory and retail ends.

Saprophytic effect of rhizospheric on biological N, fixer is well established and be exploited to increase efficiency of legume inoculants by co-inoculation. Co-inoculation with vascular arbuscular (V.A.) myccorrhizal fungi, phosphate solublizing microbes, PGPR have been found to increase nodulation and N_2 fixation. It may be advisable to prepare inoculants containing two synergetic microbes.

The important tips for using bio-fertilizers and storage at farmer's level :

(*i*) Prepare slurry of inoculant, pour on seed and mixed well till a thin coating of carrier is formed in each seed.

(*ii*) Sow the seed immediately without drying them and if drying is needed do it under shade.

(*iii*) Normally one packet of 100-200 g carrier based culture having inoculant population in the range of 10^8–10^{10} cells/g carrier be used for 10 kg seed.

(*iv*) Use more culture for problem soil.

(*v*) Don't store the culture packet near pesticide/fertilizer/herbicidc bag or container.

(*vi*) Purchase culture from reliable source and use it before expiry date.

CHAPTER 10

SOLANACEOUS VEGETABLES

10.1. TOMATO

Tomato is one of the most popular and world's largest fruit vegetable widely grown ranking second in importance to potato. In India, tomato is grown in 355 thousand hectare area with a production of 544 thousand tons and 15.32 t/ha productivity. (FAO, 1998). The area under tomato is constantly increasing to produce more quality yield because it is a major vegetable in the menu of human diet. Tomato is grown under varied agro-climatic conditions almost throughout the year in the country. The number of crops grown varies from region to region. In Northern India, generally, autumn and spring crops are grown and in hills, only one crop is taken. In recent years, interest in its production has increased rapidly because of its nutritional food requirements and its higher remunerative value.

Uses. It is consumed either raw a component of salad seasoning vegetables, curries to impart them special colour, flavour and taste or in the form of various processed products as juice, ketch-up and paste. It tops the list of processed (canned) vegetables and are used for soup, salad, pickles, ketchup, puree, sauces and many other ways. It is also one of the important raw materials for the fruit and vegetable industry.

Nutritive Value. Nutritive value varies in different cultivars and depends upon the agro-climatic conditions in which tomato is cultivated. Tomato is a rich source of vitamins, minerals and organic acids, sugars, ascorbic acid, titratable acidity, minerals and lycopene. Dried tomato juice retains vitamin C.

Medicinal uses. Tomato is rich in medicinal value. The pulp and juice are digestible, mild aperient, a promoter of gastric secretion and blood purifier.

Origin. Native of the Andean region of South America.

Taxonomy. Tomato belongs to the family *Nightshade* or *Solanaceous,* genus *Lycopersicon* and species *esculentum.* The genus comprises a few species of annual or short lived perennial herbaceous plants. Stems are round, soft, brittle and hairy when young but become angular, hard and almost woody when old. Leaves are alternate, odd-pinnate with 7-9 short-stemmed leaflets. Flowers are small borne in clusters, sepals lanceolate, small in initial stage and increase in size as the fruit mature, corolla deeply five-cleft, yellow, five stamen borne at the throat of corolla, large anthers borne on short filaments. Fruit is a many celled berry with fleshy plancentae and many small kidney-shaped seeds covered with short stiff hairs.

Cultivars. At present, there are a large number of cultivars and hybrids being developed in public and private sector, grown throughout the country which are of specific nature suitable for region or state. The cultivar can be grouped into determinate (are normally dwarf and early), indeterminate and intermediate.

Determinate cultivars (d). Roma (EC-13513), Rupali, MTH-15, Ptom-18, VL-1, VL-2, CO-3 (Marutham), Arka Ashish (IIHR 674 SBSB), Arka Alok (BWR-5), Pusa Early Dwarf, HS 101, HS 102, Hisar Arun (Sel 7), Hisar Lalit (NT 8).

Indeterminate cultivars (ind). Pusa Uphar, Solan Gola, Sioux, Marglobe, Naveen, Shalimar-1, Shalimar-2, Angurlata, Solan Bajr, Solan Shagun, CO-2, Pusa Ruby, Arka Vikas, Dhanashree.

Semi-determinate. Arka Saurab, Arka Ahuti (Sel. 11), Arka Abha (BWR-1), Pant T 3, Arka Shreshta, Arka Abhijit, Arka Ashish.

Other varieties. NT-3, Sel-18, Flora Dada, Hisar Arun, Sonali, Ajanta, Swarna, Century, Sakti, Arka Alok, PKM 1, HS 110, Arka Meghali.

Hybrids, (*a*) Public sector. Karnataka, Vaishali (d), Rashmi, Pant Hybrid-2, Pant Hybrid-10, Kt-1, Kt-2, Kt- 3, Kt-4, Pusa Hybrid-1, Pusa Hybrid-10, Pusa Hybrid-2, Pusa Hybrid-4, FM-1, FM-2, Arka Shreshta, Arka Vishal, Arka Vardan, Arka Abhijit, Palyur 1, Rajashree, Pusa Sadabahar.

***(b)* Private sector.** Apurba, Sheetal, Rupali (d), Mangla, Naveen (ind), MTH-2, MTH-6, Gulmohar (d), MTH-15, MTH-16, Sonali (d), Priti, Ratna, Sadabahar (d), Lerica, Vijay, Vipul, SC-9, GS-12, SH-18, Sutton Gram, Sutton Gram Sweet cluster, Sweet-Heart, Sutton Gram Prolific, Sutton Gram Wonders, Masuraj, Arth-3, Arth-4, ATH-1, NARF-101, Avinash-2, BSS-71, BSS-171, BSS-175, Madhuri (BSS-39), BSS-20 (Meenakashi), BSS-99 (Manisha), BSS-98 (Megha).

Suitable for processing. Punjab Chhuhara, Arka Ashish (IIHR 674 SBSB), Bhagyashree.

Resistant to Bacterial Wilt. Shakthi, Arka Abha (BWR-1), Hisar Lalit (resistant to root-knot nematode).

Climate. It is a warm season fruit crop sensitive to frost and requires an average temperature of 18-27°C for proper growth, development and fruiting. Fruit setting is adversely affected by extremes of temperature (both low and high) and low humidity. However, tomato plants are sensitive to temperature, light intensity and humidity and affect the fruit set, pigmentation and nutritive value of the fruits. The domesticated tomato is a delicate plant and is susceptible to a variety of diseases and insect-pests. The tomato crop thrives best when weather is clear and aerial temperatures are moderate which permits economic yields. However, the success depends upon climatic conditions, varietal character and the end use of fruit *viz.* fresh market or processing.

TABLE 10.1. Optimum temperature range and lower and higher limits for the development of tomato during various stages.

Stage of plant development	*Temperature (°C)*		
	Biological minimum	*Optimum*	*Biological maximum*
Germination	11	16-29	34
Vegetative growth	18	21-24	32
[Fruit set – night	10	17-21	22
– day	18	25-30	35
Red colour development – night	10	19	24
– day	20	30	35
Yellow colour development	10	25-33	> 40
Chilling damage	<6		
Frost damage	<1		
Lethal temperature	– 2		

Source : Prihar *et al.* 1992.

Soil. The soil should be fertile, well drained and free from residual impact of chemicals etc. Good texture of the soil is of primary importance. Tomatoes thrives best on well drained sandy loam to clay soil with pH between 6.0 to 7.0 and moderate to high moisture holding capacity is ideal. Deep fertile sandy loam is considered best for high yields. Winter crop thrives better on light to medium textured soils while the main season (February transplanted) crop perform well on medium to heavy soils.

Land preparation. The land may be given 2-3 ploughings to bring it into better tilth. Level the field to have better drainage. Prepare beds for transplanting the tomato seedlings in lines. In the northern plains of India, growing season for tomato is quite short. All spring plantings are almost killed in June due to low humidity and high temperature (Nandpuri, 1972). Tomato being sensitive to lack of soil aeration does well on raised beds which are prepared after application of basal dose of manure and fertilizer. Growing of tomato on beds avoids the direct contact of fruit with wet soil and thus reduces fruit rot.

Sowing Time. To raise a successful and virus-free tomato crop, sowing time is very important. The nursery sown in early October is more prone to the attack of virus carrying white fly under plains conditions. The nursery grown in late October and transplanted in the first week of December produces excellent crop. The plants should be protected from frost during winter. In plains, two crops are grown depending on weather conditions.

Crop	*Transplanting time*	*Harvest time**
Main season crop	February-March	May-June
Winter crop (determinate)	November end	April-June
Winter crop (indeterminate)	Mid-October	Feb.-June

*The winter crop takes 155 to 170 days for 85% ripening while the summer crop takes 90-120 days.

In South India, two crops are grown—last week of May and first week of December.

In low hills, the crop is transplanted in Oct.-Nov. up to 900 m.a.s.l. elevation while in other mid and high hills transplanting is mostly done in March-April for which seedlings are raised in February-March under protected conditions, especially by using poly/green-houses.

Seed Rate. It is normally propagated through seed but it can be propagated vegetatively also through tissue culture. Always use breeder or foundation seed from a reliable source for raising tomato crop and for one hectare crop a quality seed of 400-600 g in most varieties and 250 g in case of hybrids will be sufficient. The healthy and disease free plants should be transplanted without any injury to the root system.

Seed treatment. The seed is coated with rice kanji just to have a thin coating and then sprinkle 100-200 g of *Azospirillum* culture, stir with a stick thoroughly, dry in shade for 30 minutes and use for sowing.

Spacing. Depending on the nature of cultivar the spacing are followed *i.e.* 45 × 45 cm determinate varieties and 90 × 30 cm for indeterminate types, between and within rows be transplanted. In hills where rain-fed crops are grown, immediately after transplanting a life saving dose of irrigation is given in scarcity areas, followed by pre-monsoons/monsoon rain. In some places, spacing between the rows is adjusted to meet the intercultural requirements of the farmer through mechanical means.

Manures and Fertilizers. Tomato crop needs large quantities of readily available nutrients in the form of organic and inorganic commercial manure and fertilizers and their application varies with locality and soil tests. Fertilizer rates must be decided on the basis of soil test. Application of 15-20 tonnes of organic manure (FYM or leaf mould) and 100 kg N, 60 kg each P_2O_5 and K_2O will produce better yield per hectare. The whole quantity of organic manure, P_2O_5 and K_2O and l/3rd N be added at the time of land preparation and rest N in two splits be top dressed after 20-25 days of transplanting and rest N be added at pre-flowering stage. More addition of N will lead to more vegetative growth and less fruiting and thus optimum dose is advocated. However, foliar application of 35 kg of N through urea and 45 kg phosphate (triple super phosphate) per hectare in 4 or 5 sprays is recommended. Concentration of higher than one per cent may scorch the leaves.

Micro-nutrients. Apply 50 kg of zink sulphate per hectare as a basal dose when tomato follow an exhaustive crop rotation like wheat-paddy.

Nursery Production. A healthy and disease-free nursery is the first pre-requisite. Major advantage of producing seedlings in the nursery include saving of costly seed, (*e.g.* F_1 hybrid) and ease of management and controlling diseases and insect-pests. (Details given in nursery management chapter-5).

Direct seeded tomato crop. However, in most part of the world growing tomatoes is done by direct seeding in the field. Direct seeded plants develop better root system and have higher yield potential per hectare. Direct seeding requires good land levelling, precise bed making, a suitable soil tilth and good irrigation programme.

Transplanting. Before transplanting the seedlings adequate availability of water for the young transplants is to be ensured. Irrigate the field to its optimum moisture condition. Put one seedling in each hole made at a proper spacing, holding it from leaves. Lift the plant a little so that there is no bending of roots which may hinder proper development of root system. Press from the sides, so that no air-gap remains in the hole and plant roots come in contact with soil directly. Keep the rows perfectly straight to permit subsequent mechanical operations like hoeing, weeding, fertilization and spraying, with minimum damage to plants.

Just after transplanting, apply 200 ml of starter solution (or water) per plant. It will fill the air gaps in the hole and promote direct contact of roots with soil. Starter solution contains 0.5 per cent single super phosphate and 0.1 per cent urea or (0.2 per cent CAN). Apply controlled irrigation till the plants are well established and maintain optimum soil moisture.

Irrigation. The irrigation soon after transplanting is very important. The number of irrigation will depend on crop, season, soil type and stage of crop. The soil should be in its optimum moisture condition. Excess moisture leads to vegetative growth and less fruiting and rainy season may be regulated accordingly. In the initial stage, irrigate the plants if needed. The indeterminate types may be irrigated at an interval of 6-7 days while the determinate after every ten days. Cracking of fruits may result when the crop is heavily watered after a long dry spell particularly at fruiting stage.

Hoeing and weeding. Weeds are a serious problem in tomato cultivation. They compete with the crop for nutrients, moisture and light. Some weeds act as hosts for insect and disease organisms which attack tomato crop. Timely removal of harmful weeds and pulverising the soil be done for proper growth of the plants. However, use of weedicide(s) like metribuzin, trifluralin and paraquat can be helpful to destroy (either mechanically with a bed harrow or chemically with weedicides) the germinated weeds before transplanting and economise intercultural operation as the labour input is costly and non-available now-a-days.

Harvesting. Harvesting of tomato fields is best performed as a single, destructive operation beginning when 80-90 per cent of fruit is ripe. Harvesting should be done when the fruits are fully ripe and firm. Multiple harvests, and removing of ripe fruit several times, invariably lead to lower total yields. The tomato crop can be harvested by picking up at different stages depending on the purpose for which these are required and the market where to send, local or distant market. While harvesting give a vigorous jerk to remove the fruit without any injury to the plant. Put the fruits into boxes or crates. Picking up of green to pink, sound pink, yellow and fully ripe fruits separately. Keep these in shade in boxes in the warehouse to remove the field heat, storage and product heat. Select only the healthy fruits and reject all the rotten, insect damaged and diseased one.

Grading. Grading of tomatoes is done before packing for the market by the specialised persons. The Indian Standards Institution has specified four grades-Super A, Super, Fancy and Commercial.

Crop-residue disposal. Immediately following the harvest the remains of the tomato crop must be ploughed deeply into the fields to prevent the built up of insects, diseases and weeds. This is a very important operation which is often overlooked in new tomato production areas with very damaging long-term results.

Trellis system. Indeterminate tomato varieties do not exhibit uniform ripening, the plants set and mature one cluster after another over a period of several months. The first cluster matures 60-80 days after transplanting. Normally tree branches are used for providing support to these varieties which are easily available and cheap. But some private companies have designed a special trellis structure-2.10 m long bamboo sticks of 3.5-5 cm diameter having 3 mm hole 10 cm below the top are embedded (vertically) 20-30 cm into the ground and 1.40 m apart in the centre of the bed. 1.5 m long bamboo sticks of 2.5-3.5 cm diameter having 3 mm holes on both ends are fixed horizontally at the top of vertically fixed poles and tied to them with wire passing through holes provided in respective sticks. A total of 5350 sticks of 2.10 m length and 5250 of 1.5 m length are required per hectare. After fixing the vertical and horizontal structure, a plastic string is fixed horizontally just above the bed-top in the centre of the bed with the help of vertical poles. Thereafter, vertical strings are tied at the base with the horizontal string 35 cm apart. These are stretched vertically up and tied with the horizontal bamboo sticks. One vertical string is used for each plant.

Pruning, twisting and training. The main stem is allowed to grow but each auxiliary shoot is pruned as soon as it appears. The string tied vertically between the horizontal string at the base and horizontal stick at the top is twisted around the plant clock wise such that it keeps the plant straight. Knot at the top end is loosened when string gets tight; the string is twisted around the plant and tied again. When the plant grows up to a height of 1.50-1.80 m and its growing point touches the horizontal stick at the top, the plants are lowered gently so as to avoid the breaking up the main stem. At one go plant should be lowered down by 45 cm. All the leaves below the cluster to be picked up should be removed.

Handling and marketing. The quality of raw tomato cannot be improved after harvest, but could be lost to some degree depending upon the method of harvesting and handling of raw produce during transit *i.e.,* field to warehouse, preparation, packaging, packaging material used, transport to the local or distant market or the processing factory. Harvesting for fresh market is done as soon as the fruit colour changes to pink but for processing fruits are picked when the whole cluster becomes red. In case any fruit in that cluster is not ready it is left on the plant till next harvest, usually done at a week's interval. Tomatoes are transported from field to the warehouse on head loads or tractor trolleys or in trucks either in plastic crates or in bulk. Each crate holds 20-25 kg fruit. To reduce damage to fruit during handling adopt the following procedure. Minimise the period between harvesting and unloading in the warehouse or factory. Discard the unripe, less coloured and damaged fruits before packaging or sending for processing. For bulk loading, keep the thickness of fruit-layer in the truck or the trolley less than 70 cm. otherwise use braces (supporting planks) for loading boxes or crates in layers for safe transport to distant markets. Ensure good communication between field, factory, marketers and others involved in the trade and fall-back arrangements for any breakdown in the transit. Supply fruit according to the demand in the market or capacity of the processing factory at regular intervals. Restrict bulk handling to shorter distances and to metal roads and use plastic crates for distant fields and kacha roads. Wooden or plastic or iron boxes/crates should be used to transport the produce to the big metropolitan cities. Handle the loading and unloading of the produce carefully at the field, warehouse, transit, market, processing factory and the consumer's corner. To avoid direct contact of fruit with any metal during transport spread tarpaulin or polyethylene sheet before loading. Partitioning of truck or trolley in 2-3 compartments can reduce fruit damage during handling and transport. Transportation of fruit should be done preferably during evening, night or early morning. Vehicles waiting for unloading in the mandies or factory should be parked under shade. Large heap of fruit should be discouraged at farmer's field and should be kept under shade.

Storage. The best storage temperature ranges from 12-15°C. If stored at freezing-point, the fruits show low temperature injury. Mature green fruits can be kept for as long as 30 days at 10-15°C. Ripe tomatoes can be kept for ten days at 43°C. The recommended relative humidity is 85-90 per cent.

Yield. The fruit yield varies from variety to variety and hybrid. It ranges from 15-35 tonnes/ha in case of varieties and 60-80 tonnes/ha in case of F_1 hybrids.

10.2. BRINJAL

Brinjal is extensively cultivated round the year as a commercial crop in the country covering 4.34 lakh hectare area and produce 64.43 lakh tonnes of fruits with an average productivity of 14.84 t/ha. It is popular and a warm season fruit vegetable commonly grown widely from tropical to sub-temperate regions of the country.

Uses. The brinjal fruits are consumed as vegetable in various ways as mixed, in curries, in sambhar and for the preparation delicacies (pakoras, etc.)

Nutritive value. The brinjal fruits contains protein, fat, fibre, carbohydrates, minerals, calcium, magnesium, oxalic acid, phosphorus, iron, sodium, potassium, copper, sulphur, chlorine, vitamin A, nicotinic acid and vitamin. For processing purposes the fruit should have dry matter content and a low level of phenolics.

Medicinal properties. The fruits of brinjal are an excellent remedy for those suffering from liver troubles. The green leaves of brinjal plant are the main source of supply of antiscorbutic vitamin C. Its seeds are used as a stimulant. It has got Ayurvedic medicinal properties and white brinjal is said to be good for diabetic patients.

Origin. India is known for its centre of origin.

Taxonomy. It belongs to the family *Solanaceae,* genus *Solanum* and species *melongena.* Many cultivars grown in India which differ in shape, size and colour of fruits and the growth habit of the plant. The round or egg shaped fruited cultivars are considered under var. *esculentum,* long slender tubes are put under var. *serpentinum* and the dwarf early ones under var. *depressum.* Brinjal behave as a strong annual in temperate zones and as a weak,perennial in tropics.

Cultivars. There are cultivar patterns and forms as regional preferences are predominant. The brinjal fruits may be white, yellow, brown, green, black, pink, purple and striped in colour, and in shape they may be round, long, elongated, pear shaped and oblong depending upon the cultivars. The long green varieties are preferred in Bihar and Karnataka and round green in Orissa. In north India pinkish-purple or violet and black colour varieties are preferred and the yellow, brown and white-coloured brinjal fruits are not very popular. Since the ultimate aim of the farmer is to get maximum return for his produce, judicious selection of the type with reference to market demand and consumer need is very important in this crop.

(*i*) **Long fruited cultivars.** Azad B-3, Pusa Purple Long, Pusa Purple Cluster, ARU-2C, ARU-10, ARU-20, Pusa Anupam (Kt-4), Shalimar Improved, Arka Nidhi, Arka Keshav, Arka Neelkanth, Surya, PH-4, Arka Kusumkar, Arka Sheel, Arka Shirish, Punjab Barsati, Sada Bahar Baingan, Punjab Neelam, Cluster White, CO-1, MDU 1, PKM 1, SM 609, Annamalai, Pattabiram, Krishnanagar Green Long, Muktakeshi, Nurki Long, PLR 1, APAU Gulabi, APATJ Shyamala, APAU Baghyamathi, Pusa Ankur.

(*ii*) **Round fruited cultivars.** Pusa Purple Round, Pusa Bhairav, Pusa Uttam, Pusa Upkar, Pusa Bindu, Pant Rituraj, Hisar Syamal (H-8), Dilruba, Black Beauty, Pant Samrat, Punjab Bahar, Aru-2, T-3, Jamuni Gola, BPr-7, Punjab Neelam, Aruna, Pb. 8, Makra, Elokeshi, Krishnanagar Purple Round, Nurki Round, Banjari, Banaras Giant, Muktakeshi, Ramnagar Giant, Muktakeski 1, Manjari Gota, Vashaili, Pragati, RHR B-9-1-1.

Oblong types. Pusa Kranti, Azad Kranti.

Hybrids, (*a*) **Public sector.** Arka Navneeth (R), Azad Hybrid (R), Vijay, Pusa Hybrid-5, Pusa Hybrid-6 (R), Suphal, Pant Hybrid-1 (L), Pusa Hybrid-9, Pusa Anmol, Krishna (R).

(*b*) **Private sector.** MHB-1 (L), MHB-2, MHB-3, MHB-9, MHB-10 (Kalpataru), MHB-39 (Ravaiyya), AHB-2, AHB-4, ARBR-216, Sumex-9, Sumex-19, HOE-404, Nemabakar, NDB-1, (R), NDBH-6 (Narendra Hybrid Brinjal-2), NDBH-1, ARBH-201.

Bacterial wilt resistant varieties. Pant Samrat.

Climate. Brinjal is a warm season crop, though it can be grown almost throughout the year but it flourishes best during a long and warm growing periods. It is susceptible to severe frost and low temperature during the cool season causes deformation of fruits. A daily mean temperature of 13.2°C is most favourable for proper growth and yield. The brinjal seeds germinate at 25°C.

Soil. Brinjal can be grown in all types of soils varying from light sandy to heavy clay. Light soils are good for an early crops, while clay-loam and silt-loam are well suited for high yield. Generally, silt-loam and lay-loam soils are preferred for brinjal growing. The soil should be deep, fertile and well drained with soil pH not more than 5.5. to 6.0.

Land preparation. Since the crop remain in the field for a number of months, the soil should be thoroughly prepared by ploughing 4-5 times before transplanting the seedlings. Proper drainage is essential for brinjal cultivation.

Seed rate. About 400-500 g of seed are required for raising one hectare crop as there are 200-250 seeds per gram depending on cultivar.

Sowing time. In Northern India

— June-July, (rainy season crop is the best)

— November (spring-summer crop) and

— March-April.

In East and South India–all round the year (main sowing done in July-August).

In hills-March-April-May. (The sowings can be advanced by raising the seedlings under protected conditions (poly-house or carrying seedlings from lower hills).

Transplanting. The seedlings are transplanted like that of tomato.

Spacing. Bushy, non-spreading type-50-60 cm and

Spreading cultivars-75-90 × 60-70 cm between plants and rows.

Manure and fertilizers. The brinjal being a long duration crop requires a good balanced quantity of organic manure and fertilizers, which are mixed with the soil at the time of its preparation. This all will depend on soil tests and availability of these inputs, however, apply farmyard manure @ 20-25 t, 100 kg N, and 50 kg each of P_2O_5 and K_2O/ha. Full dose of farmyard manure, P_2O_5, K_2O and half dose of N should be applied before transplanting and rest dose of N should be top-dressed in two splits after 40 and 80 days of transplanting. In case of ratoon crop, add the same nutrients after harvest of the first crop.

Irrigation. Irrigation should be given according to local need and rainfall received. In plains, irrigation should be applied every 3rd-4th day during hot weather and 10-15 days during winter. About 100-110 cm of irrigation water are needed for a successful crop. Timely irrigation is very important for obtaining higher yields in brinjal. The brinjal fields should be regularly irrigated to keep the soil moist during frosty days.

Hoeing and weeding. The weeds should be controlled as soon as they are seen, either by hand weeding and hoeing or by application of herbicides. Frequent shallow cultivation should be done at regular intervals so as to keep the field free from weeds and to facilitate soil aeration and proper root development. The field should be sprayed with a pre-emergent weedicide such as Fluchloralin 1 L *a.i.* (Basalin 2L, dissolved in 500 L water)/ha or Trifluralin at 1 kg/ha gave the best yield and helps in controlling most weeds.

Mulching. Mulching brinjal plants with crop residues or black polythene film reduces the growth of weeds, increase crop growth, maintain optimum soil moisture, improve earliness and increase yield.

Earthing-up. In some areas, the brinjal plants are earthed-up at each top-dressing which helps to make the plant more stable.

Growth regulators. There are four types of flowers found in brinjal *viz.* long-styled, medium-styled, pseudo short-styled and true short-styled and only the first and second types marked by a swollen ovary at the base, bear fruits. The last two types having rudimentary ovary do not bear any fruits. The use of growth regulators by treating seed or whole plant spray have given better results. Parachlorophenoxyacetic acid (4-CPA), 2, 4-dichlorophenoxy acetic acid (2,4-D), seed treatment with 4-5 ppm for 24 hours or spraying whole plant with 2 ppm at flowering produced 50 per cent higher yield and early harvest.

Harvesting. The first starts from 55-60 days after transplanting. The brinjal fruits are harvested when they are developed a good colour and marketable size, are still immature and tender and have not lost culinary qualities. Although the fruit is harvested before it fully ripens, it should be allowed to attain a good size and colour. The surface should be attractive bright and glossy shine in appearance having freshness and optimum size of fruit are qualities for good market price. When the fruit looks dull, it is an indication of over maturity and loss of quality. The fruits are edible from the time they are quarter-grown, until they are near-ripe. The fruit should be severed from the plant by cutting with a small pruning shears or a sharp knife with stalk at joint where they are attached to the branch. The fleshy calyx and a short piece of the stem are left attached with the fruit. Fruits of round varieties are usually heavy and should be handled with care. Care is taken in avoiding injury to the plants.

Grading. The Indian Standards Institution has recommended three grades of brinjal *viz.* Super, Fancy and Commercial.

Packaging and marketing. The fruits should be handled with care in transit. Before transporting, the fruits should be wrapped in paper and packed in cartons or any packing material locally available. However, they are packed loose in bulk or in containers like loosely-woven gunny bags or net bags or plastic/wooden crates for trading and transport.

Storage. The brinjal fruits can be stored for a day or two in summer and 3-4 days in winter season provided they are kept in shade. The fruits can be kept for 7-10 days in a fairly good condition at 8-10°C and 85-95 per cent relative humidity. Waxing (in 3 per cent concentration) helped to reduce weight loss and retard in change in acidity and starch, sugar and ascorbic acid contents. The storage life at room temperature (25°-45°C) was extended by 30-40 per cent wax emulsion. Waxing also reduced microbiological spoilage.

Yield. The yield ranges from 20-35 t/ha, depending upon the cultivar.

10.3. CAPSICUM

Capsicum (Bell pepper) commonly known as "Simla Mirch" in northern India is an important summer/off-season crop grown extensively in mid-hill areas ranging from 800 to 1800 m amsl. Bell pepper is a tender perennials in tropics and sub-tropics and as an annual in temperate regions. Sweet pepper known as Kudamilagal in south India, the fruit of which are of large size with less biting taste and pungency. In India, it is cultivated commercially in Tamil Nadu, Karnataka, Himachal Pradesh and some parts of West Bengal (Darjeeling District), Uttar Padesh, Jammu & Kashmir, Haryana and Punjab.

Uses. Bell pepper forms an enjoyable dish when stuffed and gives a delightful soft pungency when added to the salad and tend to increase with maturity. This is mainly used as a vegetable.

Nutritive value. Bell pepper is highly rich in vitamin A and C and is superior to that of other Solanaceous vegetables.

Medicinal value. Capsicum preparations are used to counter irritants, in lumbago, neuralgia and rheumatic disorders. It has tonic and carminative action especially in dyspepsia.

Origin. The common cultivated pepper is native of Mexico with secondary centre of origin Goutemala.

Taxonomy. Capsicum or Shimla mirch belongs to the family *Solanaceae,* genus *Capsicum* and species *annuum*. All the green, pickle type and bell pepper belongs to this group. These are less or non-pungent, mild, thick fleshed and consumed as vegetable or pickle.

Cultivars. The bell pepper type produce large blocky sweet fruits about 8 cm wide and 10 cm long. The active principle is mildly present and is not located in all parts of the fruit, and cultivar differ widely in shape and colour. The cultivars are Yolo Wonder, California Wonder, Kt-1, Chinese Giant, Giant Bullnose, Anupum, Arka Basant, Arka Gaurav, Arka Mohini.

Hybrids. Bharath, KT-1, Pusa Dipti, Early Bounty, Sutton Gram Giant, Indira, Larie, Swarup, Hira, Green Gold, Anupum Solan Hybrid-1, Solan Hybrid-2.

Climate. Capsicum is a warm season crop and is sensitive to cool wet weather. Fruit set does not occur below and above the range of 16-32°C. The optimum temperature for pepper growth and development is higher than that of tomato. Relatively low night temperature (10°C) affect fruit size, shape, seed yield and Shimla mirch produce parthenocarpic fruits containing less seed as compared to high night temperature. Fruit set does not occur below or above the range of 16-32°C and the optimum range is between 16-21°C. High temperature and RH favour development of foliage diseases. Hot dry winds cause blossoms drop.

Soil. Fertile soils-sandy to sandy-loam or loam soils with pH 7.0, rich in humus and well drained are the best for growing Shimla mirch as it is susceptible to water logging. The seed does not germinate until soil has warmed up (22°C).

Land preparation. The land should be ploughed deep as it has a tap root system. The land should be ploughed 4-5 times before preparing the beds.

Seed rate. Standard cultivar-750-900 g/ha
Hybrid-250 g/ha.

Sowing Time. In hills, time of sowing varies from location to location. Seedlings are raised in green/poly-houses, hot beds or in mild climates in out-door seed beds. In plains, August for autumn crop and November for spring-summer crop. In Banglore, from July to February, West Bengal from September-October and mid-hills of north February-March under cover and April to June (outside). Nursery raising, transplanting and other culture, in general, resembles that of the tomato crop.

Transplanting. The healthy seedlings should be transplanted in the evening hours to avoid excessive transpiration and have proper crop stand followed by a light irrigation.

Spacing. The plant spacing should be kept at 60 cm between rows and 45 cm between the plants.

Manure and fertilizers. Apply 20 t FYM, 100 kg N, 75 kg P_2O_5 and 50 kg K_2O/ha like that of tomato. At the time of transplanting, the seedlings may be treated with *azospirillum* for better establishment and growth in the field. The seedlings are dipped in a solution of 2 kg of *azospirillum* culture in 10L of water for 20-30 minutes.

Irrigation. Most of the roots of capsicum plant occur in top 3-3.5 cm of the soil and insufficient soil moisture greatly affects the yields. In hot weather frequent irrigation at intervals of one week may be given, but in rainy season may be regulated accordingly. The soil should be kept moist to avoid water deficit in the plants as it results in blossom drop.

Hoeing and weeding. After one month of transplanting one hoeing and weeding is done to remove the weeds and pulverise the soil followed by earthing-up.

Harvesting. The fruits are ready from 75 to 90 days of transplanting for harvest depending on cultivar, soil and management. The fruits are picked when fully developed green (mature green) but before the colour begins to change. The fruit should be firm and crisp in texture. Fully matured green fruits should be harvested before ripening. Very tender and immature fruits should not be harvested. Harvesting is done by hand for fresh market while for processing may be hand picked or harvested mechanically in a single lot. After harvesting, the fruits should be kept in shade to remove the field or product heat.

Grading and marketing. Bell pepper fruits are wiped, cleaned in fresh water, graded in size, and packed in wooden boxes, paper cartons or plastic/iron crates before marketing. The glossiness of the fruits is a big factor for its disposal. The growers should sell the produce soon after harvest in fresh form for better returns.

Storage. The fruits can be maintained in good condition for up to two weeks at 7-10°C and high RH of 90-95 per cent. Temperature lower than 7°C will result in surface breakdown (chilling injury) shortly after exposure.

Yield. 150 q/ha

Crop protection. As in case of chillies.

10.4. CHILLIES

Chillies is an important vegetable cum condiment, an active ingredient in Indian cookery. It is grown throughout over tropical and sub-tropical conditions due to its wide range of adaptability. The total area in India is 575160 ha (Asian Seeds, 2000). The crop can withstand heat and moderate cold but is highly susceptible to frost. A fruit crop essentially requires a dry, warm climate at the ripening fruit stage of the crop. India's production of chillies is equal to 50% of the totai world production and major portion of this is consumed domestically. The productivity for open-pollinated cultivars and hybrids is 3.75-4.25 t/ha and 6-7 t/ha, respectively.

Nutritive value. In hot pepper (chillies), the pungent principle is called "Capsaicin" which is mainly present in the central placenta of the fruit, as well as seed and to some extent in the ovary wall also. Generally the content of capsaicin varies from 0.2-0.4 per cent. In green stage, the chilli fruit are rich source of vitamins, especially in vitamin A, C and E.

Uses. Various cultivars are grown for green, spices, condiments, sauces and pickles. The fruit at green stage are used for garnishing. It occupies an important place in the Indian dietary. Chillies impart peculiar beauty, taste and flavour to the cooked vegetables and other dishes. It is also an important valuable export-earner.

Origin. The probable origin is South Central America and it was domesticated in Mexico from ancient times.

Taxonomy. Chillies belongs to the family *Solanaceae,* genus *Capsicum* and species *frutescens.* The other species under commercial cultivation are *pendulum* and *pubescens.* These are small fruited, highly pungent, plants having erect or pendent bearing habit and the size (1-30), shape (long thin to tomato shape) and colour is variable and colour ranges from red to yellow.

Cultivars. In south India, chillies of types are cultivated *viz.* 'Samba' having long pods and Gundu type with round and short pods. The latter one are more pungent than the former and adapted to rain-fed culture.

NP-46, Solan Yellow, Pachhad Yellow, Hot Portugal, Hungarian Wax, Sweet Banana, Pb. Lal, Shalimar Long, Pusa Sadabahar, Surajmukhi, Hybrid-1, Chamatkar, Agni, HOE-808, Tejasvani, ARCH-236, BSS-141, BSS-138 (Gayatri), Musalwadi, Phule Jyoti, Phule Surajmukhi, Phule Sai, RHR-CPMR-50-1, X-235.

Samba type. K-2, Co-1, Co-3 (CA-586) G-4 (Bhagyalakshmi), Arka Lohit (Sel-1).

Gundu type. Co-2, G-5 (Andra Jyothi), PMK-1 (Paramukudi 1), PLR-1 (Palur-1).

Hybrids. Hybrid Chilli, K-l (Kovllpati), Pusa Jwala, Pant C-l, PKM-1, G-5 (Andra Jyothi), PMK-1 (Paramukudi), Agnirekha.

Export varieties. Bird Eye Chilli, Mundu, Rari, Sindhur, Byadagi, Tomatu, Sannum.

Climate. In our country it is cultivated both as a rain-fed and as an irrigated crop in tropical and sub-tropical regions requiring a warm humid climate. Its cultivation can be done from sea-level to 2100 m elevation successfully. It can tolerate extremes of climate better than tomato and brinjal. The crop is susceptible to frost and dies at freezing temperature. The chilli plant grows well in a temperature range of 20-25 OC and areas having moderate rainfall of 60-120 cm. Unfavourable temperature, water supply, excessive rainfall and dry winds (at flowering) are the basic cause for bud, blossom, fruit drops, defoliation and rotting of the plant.

Soil. Chillies is grown on almost all types of soils with adequate drainage facilities as it is very susceptible to water stagnation. Chilli plant is not very sensitive to soil pH but highly susceptible, to oxygen deficiency in the soil. The crop grown in heavier soils suffers from blossom-end-rot.

Soil preparation. The field is ploughed 4-5 times to bring it to better tilth and ridges and furrows are formed at a spacing of 45 or 60 cm depending on the variety. The field can also be divided into small plots for convenience of transplanting/sowing and irrigation.

Seed rate. Direct sowing-1-2 kg seed/ha
Through seedlings-750-900 g/ha
Hybrid-350-400 g/ha.

Sowing time. Sowing should be done as soon as the weather warms up.

Central and south India — Middle of May-mid-July.

Gangetic valley—June.

North India (Punjab and Rajasthan) —April-May.

Hilly areas — March-April.

It is possible to take two crops of chilli under north Indian conditions. One is a spring-summer crop and another is a rainy season autumn crop. Sown in the month of June and transplanted in the last week of July, the crop starts bearing by end of September. Fruits start ripening by October and give a continuous supply of fruits for three to four months.

Transplanting. It is directly sown in northern plains during March. In case the crop is to be raised through nursery, the seed is sown in November and nursery is transplanted in the end of February. The seedlings 3-4 weeks old are most suitable because these are vigorous in vegetative growth particularly top growth, and come in flower and fruiting earlier than those transplanted at 5, 6 and 7 weeks after seeding. Total yield of fruits of the younger transplant was also higher.

For direct sowing, the seed is sown on the ridges 0.5 to 1 cm deep and 20 cm apart in lumps of 6-7 seeds followed by irrigation.

Spacing. The ideal spacing for a chilli crop is 45 × 30 cm. In the south, the seedlings are planted @ 2 seedlings per hill at a spacing of 30 cm along the side of the ridge in which the fertilizer have been placed.

Rotation. Chilli should be rotated with other vegetables and field crops but do not rotate with other Solanaceous crops. It can also be inter-cropped with ginger, cucurbit, onion and okra.

Manure and fertilizers. Application of FYM @ 20 t/ha increases yield 100 kg N, 50 kg P_2O_5 and 50 kg K_2O level/ha is for a good crop. A rate of 50 kg/ha of nitrogen application is most economic under rain-fed conditions. The whole of FYM, P_2O_5 and K_2O and half N should be applied before transplanting and rest N in two split doses one and two months after transplanting. While applying the fertilizer in the standing crop, every care should be exercised that the fertilizer does not come into contact with the plants as it may kill the plant or adversely affect their growth.

Irrigation. Regular irrigation is an important factor in the successful production of the chilli crop. The first irrigation is given at the time of transplanting and the subsequent irrigation are given once in a week or 10 days depending on the soil moisture condition. Sprinkler irrigation increases fruit yield.

Hoeing and weeding. Inter-culture is necessary to keep the field free from weeds, which apart from robbing the crop of the nutrients serve to harbour insects and diseases. Tok-E-granule at 5 kg/ha or Stam F-34 or Eptam each @ 2.5 kg/ha is effective in controlling weeds in chilli plots. In south India, 2 L Basalin (Fluchlorlin 1 L a.i./ha) in 500 L of water, sprayed on the soil surface just before planting followed by irrigation controls the weeds.

Growth regulators. Three applications of Ethipon at 300 ppm increase yield of red fruits. Flower and fruit drop is a common problem in chillies which can be controlled by foliar spraying of NAA (Naphathaline Acetic Acid) @ 20-40 ppm (20-40 mg/1) twice or 2,4-D (Sodium salt) @ 2-4 ppm at bud stage.

Harvesting. The time and stage of harvesting chilli varies from place to place depending on variety/hybrid, summer or rainy season crop, agro-climatic conditions and is governed by the purpose for which it is grown. Green chillies (Fresh) are harvested when fruits have reached to full size, but before it begins to change colour. Pickings of green fruits should be done frequent interval and the produce is disposed-off in the local market for use as green. This practice not only supplements the net return to the farmer but also encourages plants to grow and produce further flowering and fruiting. When grown in the vicinity of the cities, the marketing of green chilli fruit is very remunerative. They are picked at frequent intervals and sent to the market promptly. The quality of green chilli fruit is mainly judged by the size, colour and the plumpness of the fruit. Long green, shining, smooth and moderately pungent fruits are preferred by the consumers. Therefore, fruit should be picked when they are fully developed and are still green. Cultivars used for pickles are picked either green or ripe and chillies used for drying are harvested red or yellow or brown when fully ripe.

Grading and marketing. Green chilli fruits are graded into different grades depending on the cultivar. The graded fruits are packed in baskets or cartons or plastic crates when they are fresh. These need to be marketed as soon as possible so as these reach to the consumers in the fresh form. The dried fruits are marketed in bags. The fruit drying is done in the sun by spreading on the thrashing floor or tarpaulin in thin layer. The chilli fruits lose 60-75 per cent of their weight during drying. The dried fruits can be transported or stored in gunny bags.

Storage. The dried chillies can be stored in dry place or ware houses or stores safely for 5-6 months or more.

Yield. Open-pollinated cultivars produce – 3.75-4.25 t/ha and
Hybrids – 6-7 t/ha.
Green chilli yields – 10-12 t/ha
Dry chilli – 1.8-2.2 t/ha

10.5. PAPRIKA

The commercial importance of paprika in the country and international market is increasing day by day as with world wide annual increase of around 30 per cent. At present, India has initiated steps to cultivate the prospective paprika crop to provide raw material for the oleoresin extracting units and grinding which has a great demand in the international trade. In India, it is commercially cultivated in Tamil Nadu, Karnataka, Himachal Pradesh and some parts of Uttar Pradesh, Haryana, Punjab and the frost free regions of some tropical and sub-tropical regions.

Uses. The various forms are widely used as vegetable, salad and valued for its red colour, aroma and different grades of mild pungency or non-pungent. It is commonly used as condiment to colour and flavour the food preparations. Paprika powder is used to flavour and garnish foods like cheese, eggs, fish dishes, salads, sauces and rice. The food processing industries use paprika powder and oleoresin in meats, sausages, ketchup, etc. where rich colour is desired.

Nutritive value. Paprika is very rich in vitamin C and the carotenoid pigments-capsaithin, carotene, xanthophyll, etc. Red ripened fruits when dried and ground after removing the seeds and pedicels, have more than 80,000 colour units as per EOA (Essential Oils Association) with a skin recovery of 16-17 per cent.

Medicinal value. Paprika has therapeutic, analgesic, anti-inflammatory, anti-asthrmatic and anti-oxident properties. It is being anti-obesity agent because of its cholesterol lowering property. Capsaicin protects the stomach from gastric irritation and ulcer and is used in pain-killing ointments.

Origin. Northern-south-central America, Mexico and the Islands.

Taxonomy. Paprika belongs to *Solanaceae* family, genus *Capsicum* and species *annuun var paprika.* The fruits vary from roughly cherry shape to long conical shaped. The ground dried product is available in sweet to mildly pungent forms with a wide range of colouring content capsaithin.

Nature of plant. Plants are annual upright (90-100 cm high) spreading habit with profuse branching, fruits with pendent bearing habit are mostly flattish anaheim shaped, two celled dark green when immature, turns to dark red at maturity. Fruits are long (13.5-16.8

cm), conical and 2.2-3.1 cm in diameter. Flesh thickness is less than 0.2 cm. Fruits are mostly tapering to slightly curved with pointed tips. On an average plant bears 55-59 fruits.

Cultivars. Ramillate, Trescsscos, Bola, Albar, Kt-PI-19, Arka Abir, SB-106, SB-104, SB-101.

Climate. Paprika requires a long and warm growing season which is frost free for 4-5 months. Optimum temperature range for seed germination is 18-24°C and foe plant growth 20-27°C with a maximum of 32°C.

Soil. Well drained sandy-loam or clay saline free soil is preferable. However, it can be grown on any fertile well drained soil suitable for chilli with pH 6.5-7.0.

Land preparation. Three to four ploughings are to be given to obtain tilth.

Seed rate. 600 g/ha is sufficient if germination is good (80-90%) for the transplanting crop.

Sowing time. In the plains of East, West and South, the crop can be planted in *Kharif* and *Rabi i.e.,* during May-June and September-November, but in hills there is only one planting season *i.e.,* during summer (April-May). In plains of North India, the crop can be sown in early October and transplanted in November. Sowing/planting time is more or less same as in chilli.

Transplanting. Seedlings are first hardened by gradually withholding the water 6-9 days before transplanting and exposing them to direct sunlight. Thoroughly water the nursery bed 12-14 hours before transplanting in the field. Healthy seedlings may be transplanted in the evening hours at the recommended spacing. Apply 3 g Furadan 1 g in each furrow by mixing well with the soil to avoid cut worm damage. Irrigate the field after transplanting.

Spacing. Paprika is preferably transplanted at a spacing of 45 × 45 cm between rows and plants, but in the plains 60 × 45 cm is also recommended.

Manure and fertilizer. Farmyard manure @ 20-25 t/ha is mixed with the soil at the time of land preparation. If FYM is not available well decomposed compost should be used. Apply total quantity of P_2O_5, half dose of N and K_2O as a basal dose and top dress 20 kg/ha each of N and K_2O after three weeks of transplanting. Top dress the rest quantity of 40 kg/ha each of N and K_2O after six weeks of transplanting. If the growth of the plants is poor give urea spray @ 2g/L of water after 30 days of transplanting.

Irrigation. Paprika loose a good deal of moisture via transpiration through the leaves, which keeps them cool. This water must be replaced regularly by timely irrigation. Excess water should always be drained out as this crop is very sensitive to wilt, waterlogging even for a shorter period is detrimental.

Hoeing and weeding. Crop should be kept weed-free. Weeding, hoeing, earthing-up and providing proper drainage should be attended to well in time.

Flower set. It is always beneficial to remove the first flower bud from the first dichotomus branching followed by pinching of two or more buds if possible from the nodes of the first stage branching as helps in producing high yield.

Harvesting. Biologically matured red fruits are ready for harvest after 70-80 days of planting. The fruits to be harvested three to four times and in the final, plants along with ripen fruits can be uprooted. Fruits are plucked by hand along with fruit stalk, however, machine harvesting has also been advocated in foreign countries. Ripened fruits after harvesting are stored in open, preferably in shade to avoid direct sun which may cause sun-scald. There is a common practice that after 2-3 days when the fruits are still flaceid, they are trampled or are rolled over to flatten them. Drying may take 3-15 days depending upon climate and drying percentage ranges from 15-19%. Its fruits are more fleshy and a incision on the fruit pericarp helps in early drying. The dried fruits after removing the seeds and pedicels are ground into paprika powder.

Grading and packing. Flattening of fruits by rolling enables a greater quantity of the dried fruits to be packed into gunny bags for storage and transport.

Marketing. The fruits after drying should be marketed to the demand centres or processing units or industries.

Storage. The dried product packed in gunny bags should be stored in a dry and safe place for months until send to the market or processing plant.

Yield. Average yield is about 25-35 t/ha.

Plant protection. Tomato crop is susceptible to various diseases and insect-pests that seriously reduce both yield and market value of the fruit. The loss can be avoided only if these are effectively controlled by following the integrated disease and insect-pests management programme. The plant protection measures need to be carried timely and by following appropriate methods keeping in view the crop stage.

Disease/Insect-pests	*Symptoms*	*Control*
	TOMATO	
Damping-off (*Pythium* spp., *Phytopthora* spp, *Fusarium* spp. *and Rhizoctonia* spp.)	Seedlings are killed both at pre- and post-emergence stages. Infested seedlings topple down on the ground.	Treat the nursery bed with formalin (1 part formalin and 10 part water). Drench the nursery beds with a mixture of Dithane M-45 (25 g) and Bavistin 50 WP (5 g)/10 L of water at the initiation of post-emergence symptoms.
Late blight (*Phytophthora infestans*)	Initially large irregular greenish, water soaked patches are produced on leaves and stem which later turn brown. Blighting of the entire foliage may occur during moist periods and the whole field can have extensive foliar and fruit damage. Fruit lesions are brown, irregular shaped, rough textured, with a slightly sunken but indefinite lesion margin.	Use disease-free nursery Eliminate all culled potato piles in the vicinity of tomato plantings. Destroy volunteer potato plants. Spray Dithane M-45 and Copper oxichloride each @ 3 g/L at an interval of 10-15 days. Spray Ridomil @ 2.5 g/L which has systemic, curative properties. Seed treatment with metalaxyl @ 0.25%. Four sprays of Ridomil at 7 days interval.

Early blight *(Alternaria solani)*	Spots appear first on older leaves as irregular, brown, dead areas with concentric black rings with a yellow halo, the leaf turns yellow and quickly dries up. Fruit lesions occur only while fruit is green.	Use treated seed and disease-free seedlings. Follow suitable crop rotations. Spray with Dithane M-45, Copper oxychloride each @ 3 g/L and Kavach @ 2 g/L.
Tomato leaf curl (TLV)	Curling, rolling twisting and puckering of leaves and deformation of flowers. Newly developed leaves show chlorosis and old become leathery and brittle.	Soil application of carbofuran @ 1.25 kg a.i./ha. Use disease free transplants. Rogue out virus-infected seedlings. Regulate planting to avoid periods when whitefly is high and control.
Bacterial spot *(Xanthomonas compestris* pv. *vesicatoria)*	Brown, water-soaked and circular spots are caused on leaves. Lesions less than 3 mm in diameter become angular and brown-black.	Plant crops in rotation. Treat seed and use disease-free seedlings. Spray with Copper oxychloride.
Buck-eye rot *(Phytophthora parasitica)*	Firm leathery rot with broad irregular concentric zones of light and brown colour.	Avoid conditions which promote fruit injury whether insect caused, natural or man made.
Phoma rot *(Phoma destructiva)*	Small sunken spots on the stem scar edge which develop into black leathery circular spots with small, black raised bodies and light margins.	Use cultural methods which keep fruit from coming in contact with wet soil to prevent many of the fruit rots. Use crack-resistant varieties.
Soil rot *(Rhizoctonia solani)*	Firm, brown sunken spots with narrow concentric zones of light and dark brown colour develop on fruit touching soil.	Fungicides, applied for late blight control assist in the control of buck-eye rot.
Blossom-end rot (*Calcium deficiency and drought*)	Blossom-end rot begin with light tan, water soaked lesions, which enlarge, turn dark brown to black and sunken at the blossom-end of the fruit. A black mould may grow on the surface of the lesion. Fruits affected by blossom-end rot ripen more rapidly than normal.	Use tolerant varieties. Elongated and pear-shaped tomatoes are more prone, to Blossom-end rot. Maintaining optimum soil moisture through mulch help to prevent this problem. Apply lime or Calcium amendments (*e.g.* gypsum) before planting to reduce the problem.
Bacterial wilt (*Pseudomonas solanacearum*)	Plants wilt without yellowing at any stage.	Grow resistant varieties. Follow 3 year crop rotation. Always use disease free seedlings.
Root-knot nematodes (*Meloidogyne* spp.)	Stunting, smalling of leaves and yellowing takes place due to gall formation on the roots. The symptoms appears in patches.	Grow resistant varieties. Crop rotation with rice crop. Deep ploughing during May-June reduce nematode population.

Insect-pests		
Shoot and Fruit borer *(Heliothis armigera)*	Polyphagus in nature and caterpillars damage leaves, flower buds, flowers and fruits. The caterpillars feeds on the fruits with its end portion outside, in the absence of fruits, they bore the tender stem.	Follow clean cultivation. Suitable crop rotations. Spray with Thiodan 35 EC (2L/ha) or Sevin/Hexavin 50 WP (2 kg/ha) or Ambush 50 EC (100 ml/ha) or Ripcord 10 EC (500 ml/ha) or Decis 2.8 EC (400 ml/ha). Use synthetic pyrethroids alternatively. Use commercial bacterial formulation containing spores of Bacillus thuringiensis in combination with synthetic insecticides to improve their efficiency.
Jassid *(Amrasca biguttula)* & Whitefly *(Bemisia tabaci)*	Suck the sap from leaves and stem resulting in yellowing and poor fruit set. Whitefly nymphs and adults act as carrier of leaf-curl virus.	At fruiting stage, fruits should be picked before spraying Malathion 50 EC @ lL/ha. At the pre-fruiting stage, spray with Dimecron 85 WSC @ 200 ml/ha.
Aphids (*Myzus persicae*)	Nymphs suck cell sap, attack the growing shoots and leaves, thus reducing plant vigour. They also spread virus resulting curling of leaves, reduction of leaf area and stem size.	At vegetative stage, spray the crop with Dimecron 85 WSC (250 ml/ha) or Rogor 30 EC or Metasystox 20 EC (750 ml/ha). At fruiting, spray with Malathion 50 EC @ lL/ha.
Leaf miner *(Liriomyza* spp.)	Larva make tunnel on the outer layer of leaf. Older leaves are attacked first followed by the younger ones and the mined leaves turn whitish yellow. Severity leads to more of sunscald.	Control measures are the same as for aphids.
Herbicide injury (2,4-D)	Severe leaf distortion and leaf rolling occurs. Leaves get narrow and stems and petioles get twisted. Excessive flowering and fruiting because of hormonal properties but flower drop, affected fruits get elongated. The younger plants are damaged more than the older plants at a given concentration.	The injury occurs mostly with the use of highly volatile ester formulations of the herbicide in the wheat fields nearby the tomato crop. -The use of 2,4-D and other salts be discouraged in the tomato growing areas.
Puff	Affected fruits are light in weight and when cut open large cavities are noticed. Fruits are some what angular in shape with flattened and a hollow core.	Grow only those varieties which do not have this problem.

Sun burn	During April to May, rapid warming up and high temperature cause sun burn to exposed fruits.	Cultural practices — good irrigation, varieties with good leaf coverage, good foliar disease control all help to minimise this problem.
Fruit cracking	Causes due to boron and calcium deficiency. Cracking appears all over the fruits.	Apply borax @ 20-30 kg/ha or spray 0.3-0.4% borax on seedlings plants. Spray 0.5% $CaCl_2$ solution at the time of fruit development.
Cat face	Fruits become distorted at the blossom end and have ridges, furrows, indentation and blotches. Blotchy ripening, Vascular browning, white and grey wall, etc. Causes due to the deficiencies of potassium and magnesium. Symptoms clearly defined as per their names.	Single spray of 0.5% $CaCl_2$ solution at the time of fruit development. Apply recommended dose of KC1 or spray 0.2% solution of K_2SO_4. Apply 1% solution of $MgSO_4$ as foliar spray.
Hail injury	Fruits hit by hails form hail spots which are small to medium, slightly sunken circular areas turning from white to yellowish green The underlying tissue becomes spongy in texture and whitish in colour.	Avoid growing tomato in hail prone areas. Use hail nets available now a days.
BRINJAL		
Diseases		
Damping-off *Phomosis* blight *(Phomosis vexans)*	As in tomato. Plant parts become brown, circular or oblong spots on the fruits becoming irregular with age.	As in tomato. Use of seed from disease free plants. Use only treated seed with fungicide/hot water at 50°C for 30 minutes. Grow resistant varieties. Long crop rotation. Spray fungicide in nursery and field weekly.
Fruit rot *(Phytophthora parasitica)*	Fruits start rotting from the apical portion.	Prophylactic spray with Ridomil MZ 250 g/100L water before onset of monsoon followed by spray of Bordeaux mixture (Copper sulphate 800 g + Lime 800 g + 100 L water) or Dithane M-45 (250 g/100L water). Repeat after 10 days.
Wilt *(Fusarium, Ozonium* or *Verticillium* spp.)	Lower leaves turn yellow & then brown between the veins. On cutting vascular tissue inside is dark. Plants become stunted and die.	Use of resistant varieties. Long crop rotations. Periodical spraying with some fungicide.

Sclerotinia wilt (Sclerotinia spp.)	Minute mustard-like structures adhere to the stem at ground level. These put mycelia which enter the stem and choke the vessels. Wilt spread is by irrigation.	Long crop rotations. Grow resistant varieties. Mixing some Copper fungicides in the soil before planting.
Bacterial wilt	As in tomato.	As in tomato.
Mosaic	Virus disease.	Roguing out the affected plants in the earlier stages. Maintain sanitary conditions. Grow resistant varieties.
Little leaf *(Mycoplasma)*	Affected plants highly stunted in growth and produce small dissected leaves and deformation of flower parts. Spread by *Cestius* leaf hopper.	Remove and burn the affected plants. Spray Rogor or Malathian to control the vector. Root dip of seedlings in 1000 ppm tetracycline followed by weekly sprays.
Insect pests		
Shoot and fruit borer *(Leucinodes arbonalis)*	Attack the terminal shoots and bores inside shoot and fruits in early stages.	When insect is seen, clip the terminal part along with the insect and destroy. Fruits with holes be destroyed. Spray Carbaryl 0.1% or Endosulfan 0.05% and repeat.
Hudda beetle *(Epilachna)*	Grubs and adults skeltonize the leaves which ultimately fall-off.	In initial stages pick up the affected leaves along with the insects and destroy. Dusting the field with 5% BHC @ 20 kg/ha. Spray Carbaryl 0.1% or Sevin 10% dust @ 25 kg/ha.
Jassids and aphids	Nymphs and adults suck sap from the underside of the leaves which curl upward along the tip and dry up.	As soon as attack is noticed spray 0.05% Malathion 50 EC or Endosulfan or Thiodan/Hildan/Endocel.
Red mites	Cause white specks and patches on the leaves affecting growth and vitality of plants.	Apply Temik granules. Irrigate the fields. Spray Endosulfan @ 1.5 ml/L of water and repeat.
Root knot nematode	Infected plants become stunted and leaves chlorotic. Some types cause nodule formation on the roots.	Rotation with resistant crops like marigold. Soil fumigation with nematicides like DD or Nemagon. Grow resistant varieties.
CAPSICUM AND CHILLIES		
Diseases		
Damping-off	As in tomato.	As in tomato.
Fusarium wilt	Wilting of plant, upward and inward rolling of leaves, turn yellow and plant die.	Soil treatment Grow wilt-resistant varieties Spraying with copper fungicides.

		Clean cultivation and long crop rotation.
Bacterial wilt	As in tomato.	As in tomato.
Furit rot and leaf blight (*Phytophthora nicotianae* var. *nicotianae*)	Appearance of water soaked spots on fruits and leaves which result rot and leaf blighting.	Use disease free seed. Treat seed with Dithane M-45 @ 2g/kg seed. Pick rotten fruits and burn Spray Ridomil MZ @ 0.25% onset of monsoon followed by Bordeaux Mixture.
Anthracnose or Die back (*Collectotrichum capsici*)	Branches show die back, fruits have sunken spots along with pink areas of fungal fructifications.	As above.
Powdery mildew	Powdery substance on the lower surface of leaves.	Spray wettable sulphur @ 2 g/L of water.
Mosaic complex	Chlorosis, mottling, green-vein banding, ring spotting, line pattern, thickening of leaf veins puckering and clustering of the infected leaves, stunting of plants, flower dropping and fruit deformities are observed.	Grow resistant cultivars. Plant barrier crops like maize or amaranths for reducing the incidence. Spray Malathian 50 EC @ 1 ml/L of water for vector (aphid) control.
Insect-pests		
Pod borer	Bore into pods and feed on seeds inside.	Spray Thiodan or Sevin @ 0.2%.
Whiteflies, aphids and thrips	Suck the sap from the foliage. Also act as vector for diseases.	Spray Malathion @ 0.05%, repeat at 15 days interval. (Do not harvest the fruit for one week after the spray)
Termites (deemak)	Feed on roots result in death of plant.	Mix 20-25 kg/ha Aldrin 5% or BHC in the soil before transplanting/ sowing.
	PAPRIKA	
Diseases		
Fruit rot	Fruits start rotting from the apical portion.	Spray the crop with Dithane M-45 @ 2 g/L of water.
Anthracnose	Similar to chillies.	Copper-oxy-chloride @ 2.5 g/L of water.
Powdery mildew	Similar to chillies.	Wettable sulphur (Sulfex 3%).
Damping-off, mosaic, root rot, leaf curl complex, viruses, bacterial leaf spot, root rot.	As in chillies.	Seed/seedling treatment fungicides. Spray Dithane M-45 0.2% and copper oxy-chloride 0.25% and Sulfex 3%.
Insect-pests		
Thrips, aphids, fruit borer, hairy caterpillar mites.	As in chillies.	Spray Endosulfan @ 1-2 ml/L of water.

Precautions. To reduce losses from diseases and insect-pests, take the following precautions:

(*i*) To avoid disease risk grow tomato in suitable rotation, *e.g.,* rice-maize-tomato, green manure-mustard (*toria*)-tomato. Tomato should not be grown on the same field for more than two consecutive years. Do not plant tomato where the previous crop had suffered from wilt.

(*ii*) In field testing positive in nematodes, grow only nematode resistant varieties.

(*iii*) Always use pathogen-free and chemically treated seed.

(*iv*) Take special care while growing nursery as losses from diseases are likely to be much less severe if disease-free seedlings are set in the field.

(*v*) Eradicate the alternate hosts and insect-vectors in the vicinity of the field.

(*vi*) Follow a preventive programme stringently for the identified problem.

(*vii*) Use right type of spray pump and nozzle as the leaf coverage with the chemical is as important as the actual chemical and concentration.

(*viii*) Do not spray when wind speed is high.

(*ix*) Stop spraying one week before harvesting.

CHAPTER

11

BEAN VEGETABLE CROPS

The bean group includes about 18 types *viz.,* French bean, Sem, Lobia, Guar and Broad bean. Except the last one which is grown in winter all others species are cultivated during *Kharif* season. Each type have specific requirements for growth and development but from seed production point of view these have similar needs.

11.1. FRENCH BEAN

French bean is extensively grown for its tender and flesh pods used as vegetable during spring-summer and rainy season. In hilly areas, it is an important off-season vegetable grown in mild summer. The area under French bean in India is 148 thousand ha with a production of 400 m.t.

Uses. The tender pods as well as fully matured shelled green seeds are used as vegetable and dry beans as pulse. It is used as a cover crop, fodder and vegetable.

Nutritive value. Cheap source of nursing food. French bean pods are a valuable source of protein, calcium, iron and vitamin A.

Medicinal value. Its use improves and maintain good health which helps to create resistance against many maladies.

Origin. South and Central America is the probable origin.

Taxonomy. It belong to the family *Leguminosae,* genus *Phaseolus* and species *vulgare.* Generally, there are three types of French or kidney beans are recognised by their growth habit. The dwarf bush type has a short, erect stem with the main axis consisting of 4-8 shortened internodes. The semi-pole or summer type has 4-8 internodes which are longer than those in the bush type. The pole type has longer internodes and their number is dependent upon the length of the growing season.

Cultivars : Dwarf. Contender, Arka Komal, Premier, VL Boni-1, Pusa Parvati, Pant Anupama, Pant Bean-2, Giant Stringless, YCD-1 (Yercaud-1) Phule Surekha and Jampa, VL-63, Pant Anupama.

Tall. Kentucky Wonder, SVM-1, Lakshmi (P-37) and Blank Queen, TKD-1.

Climate. Though beans are included under warm-season crops but they do not thrive well at extremely high temperature and frost. A monthly mean temperature of 18.3 to 23.9°C is best for the crop. Prevailing high temperature for few days at blossoming time result heavy losses in yield due to a dropping of blossoms. Cool, humid and rainy weather is also unfavourable. The plants are not tolerant to frost or to prolonged weather that is near freezing. Most varieties require a growing season of between 120 and 130 days for its seed production. However, some dwarf varieties may be harvested after 90 days. Beans are not resistant to drought, but some varieties are able to withstand short dry period and found comparatively better than others.

Soil. The soils for the crop should be fertile well drained, and of such nature that it will not interfere with the germination and emergence of the seedlings. The plants are sensitive to an alkaline or an acid conditions. Soils with a pH range of 5.5-6.0 are ideal for the best plant growth and pod development. Seed will not germinate in cold soil.

Seed rate. The seed rate used is 30 to 40 kg/ha for pole varieties and 80-90 kg/ha in bush varieties.

Inoculation. If beans are being sown in field for the first time, it is advisable to inoculate the seed with nitrogen fixing bacteria Rhizobium @ 20-25 g/kg seed using jaggery or rice kanji as an adhesive to form a coating of the bacteria culture on the seed surface before sowing. This helps in quick nodulation on the roots, which fix atmospheric nitrogen.

Sowing time. The sowing of crop is done January to February and August to September in plains, March to June in mid-hills and April to June in high-hills.

Sowing. Seeds are sown with a drill, or dibbled in rows 50 to 60 cm apart at 10 to 15 cm distance and 2 to 2.5 cm deep. 3-4 seeds are sown per hill and then thinned to two plants. Sufficient moisture in the soil is essential for optimum germination. Ridge and furrow sowing is also adopted. In hills, the seeds are sown in flat beds formed across the slope.

Spacing. Dwarf bush type-45 × 15 cm

Semi-pole types-75 × 15 cm

Pole types-90 × 15 cm between rows and plants.

Manure and fertilizer. If the land is under intensive cropping, apply 25 t FYM, complete fertilizer at the rate of 50 kg N, 40 kg each of P_2O_5 and K_2O/ha.

Irrigation. The crop should be irrigated as per requirement being shallow rooted the excess moisture will be harmful. It is essential to maintain optimum soil moisture during flowering, pod/fruit set and pod development.

Staking and training. In pole type varieties as the vines grows it requires staking and in bush types no staking is required. The pole types need training for weak and trailing vines in a nice way to expose to sun and proper aeration resulting high yield. Training of vines can be done either on bamboo or wooden sticks or angle iron 1.80-2.00 m tall. The trails system is installed properly and the vines are trained.

Hoeing and weeding. Hand hoeing is often necessary to control weeds. A pre-sowing application of Basalin @ 2 1/ha will check the weed growth. A shallow hoeing should be done 35 days after sowing and the plants be earthed-up.

Harvesting. The pods are harvested when they are tender and fleshy before the formation of fibre. Pods are normally ready for harvest 15-25 days after the first flowering. Delay in harvest will increase yield but the quality falls rapidly. Picking of pods is done by hand carefully without causing any injury to the tender plants. Now-a-days in advanced countries the mechanical harvesters are also used. Sometimes after the formation of seeds before they mature can be shelled and used. Pole beans pods over a longer period than bush beans.

Grading. On the basis of cultivars characteristics, the pods should be graded into A, B and C grades according to the ISI standards.

Marketing. The produce after proper grading and preparing for the market should be packed in suitable containers and immediately sent to the market so that it reaches to the consumers in fresh form.

Storage. The green pods can be stored for 4-5 days under ordinary room temperature and can be prolonged fore another 2-3 days by sprinkling water on the produce.

Yield. The yield of tender pods vary from 8-10 t/ha in bush type and 12-15 t/ha in pole type.

11.2. HYACINTH BEAN

This is otherwise variously known as Indian bean or Hyacinth bean or Sem or Bonavist or the Dolichos bean is a multiple purpose tropical vegetable. It is grown throughout the tropical regions of Asia. In India, the perennials with twining or creping habit are mostly cultivated as an annual. There are two kinds of beans *viz., Dolichos lablab* var. *lignosus* the common cultivated field bean and *Dolichos lablab* var. *typicus* as garden bean (annual type). The *lignosus* is a field crop in Tamil Nadu, Andhra Pradesh, Karnataka, Madhya Pradesh and Maharashtra. In North India, the field cultivars are rarely cultivated.

Uses. The crop is multiple purpose fully-matured grains used as pulse, the immature pods as vegetable (in 'typicus') and for forage. In fresh form, pods are a delicacy, cooked in a variety of ways and dishes are made, fried in oil and used as a savoury in south India. Seeds of field bean are roasted or baked and converted into flour, used for making soup and concentrate for livestock.

Nutritive value. Good source of protein content in the dry seeds varies from 15-25 per cent. The protein in field bean is more easily digestible and has a lower biological value.

Medicinal value. Seeds are considered febrifuge, stomachic, anti-spasmodic and aphrodisiac.

Origin. It has been originated from India.

Taxonomy. It belongs to the family *Leguminosae,* genus *Dolichos* and *species lablab.* There are two kinds of beans *viz., Dolichos lablab* var. *lignosus* is the common field bean cultivated as a field crop and *Dolichos lablab* var. *typicus* as garden bean (annual type) and are distinguished by the manner of attachment of the seed to the pod. In the garden bean the longer axis of the seed is parallel to the suture and in the field type it is right angle to suture.

Cultivars. Pole type-Co-1, Co-2, Co-3, Co-4, Co-5, Pusa Early Prolific, Rajni, Dasarawal, Deepallwal, JDL-79, jdl-53, KDB-403, KDB-405.

Bush type-Co-6, Co-7, Co-8, Co-9, Co-10, Co-11, Co-12, Arka Jay (Sel-1), Arka Vijay (Sel-2), Konkan Bushan (DPDL-1), Hebbal Avare-3, Wal Konkan-1, 125-36.

Climate. The garden crop prefers relatively cool season similar to that in cowpea as the fruiting starts in winter and sometimes indeterminately in spring. It is exclusively a dry land crop, grown mostly in low rainfall areas as a mixed crop with sorghum, castor and finger millets.

Soil. The lablab bean can be grown on a wide range of soils with average fertility.

Land preparation. The field is ploughed 4-5 times, well levelled and small plots are prepared.

Seed rate. 20-30 kg of seed is required for sowing one ha of land.

Sowing time. June-July is considered to be the best time for raising the pole type cultivars and bush types can be sown during *kharif, rabi* and summer season as most of them are photo-insensitive. In South India, the sowing is done in Dec-Jan. while in North India is done in March.

Sowing. Seed is drilled at a distance of 1 m in between fingermillet or sorghum crops. When the earheads are harvested, the stalks are left for giving support to the vines in winter. The vines when cut with sorghum straw give a mixed fodder of high nutritive value. In case of vegetable type the seeds are sown 2 m apart in circular pits, kitchen gardens. 2 or 3 seeds are sown in well manured pits of 0.5 m^3. It can also be planted along the borders of the gardens or border of the house compounds. Ridges and furrows are formed and on one side of these ridges the seeds are sown 15 cm apart.

Spacing. When grown alone a spacing of 1 × 0.75 m is recommended.

Manure and fertilizer. When raised as a mixed crop with fingermillet, it is fertilized with 20 kg Ammonium sulphate and 40 kg superphosphate per ha. after the first weeding. Before sowing 20 t/ha of well rotten FYM is applied and incorporated along with 18 kg of N, 72 kg each of P_2O_5 and K_2O either in pits or along the ridge or furrow. In pole types, top dress 18 kg/ha after 2 months and same quantity after 4 months after sowing as the duration extends upto 6-7 months. In bush types with short duration, the top dressing is done 30 days after sowing.

Irrigation. The first irrigation is given immediately after sowing followed by subsequent irrigation at a interval of 7-10 days depending on the soil moisture.

Hoeing and weeding. Inter-cultivation can be done to check weeds from growing in the field types but in garden types such a practice is not possible once the vines spread.

Stacking. In pole types, thin bamboo or wooden or angle iron poles have to be provided and the plants when starts putting forth tendrils have to be trained along with these poles.

Harvesting. Harvesting of tender pods commences 3-4 weeks after flowering. The pods are picked when tender, green and succulent prior to fibre development for the fleshy skin is valued as a vegetable. Pods when mature become fibrous and are unfit for consumption. On commercial scale, pods are harvested in the evening.

Grading. The pods are graded on the basis of uniformity in shape, size and colour. These are packed in wet gunny bags or bamboo baskets and well labelled with the sender's address and the destination.

Marketing. The produce is transported by trucks or trains from the warehouses to the important metropolitan cities in India. These are sold fresh during winter months in the principal markets of India.

Storage. Same as in case of French bean.

Yield. Pole type–80–120 q/ha. Bush type–40–60 q/ha.

11.3. LIMA BEAN

Lima bean is also called Butter bean or Double bean. Lima bean is not cross-compatible with French bean.

Uses. The tender pods as well as fully matured green beans which are cream in colour are edible after cooking. The green lima bean is grown for home use, fresh markets, and for canning and freezing.

Nutritive value. It is having high nutritive value.

Medicinal value. Trybin inhibitor present in raw beans helps in coagulation of human red blood cells.

Origin. The probable origin is Guatemala in Central America.

Taxonomy. It is a member of family *Leguminosae,* genus *Phaseolus* and species *lunatus.*

Cultivars. Two types —large and small seeded cultivars are grouped as pole types, semi-pole and bush or dwarf types.

Pole types. Florida butter, Challenge, Caroline Butter, Kodalkanal-1, Semi-pole type-Hopi, Wilbut.

Bush types. Burpee Bush, Fordhook-242, Henderson Bush, Baby Potato, Baby Fordhook.

Climate. Lima bean grows very well between a temperature range of 15-20°C. Temperature beyond 26°C hamper flowering, pod setting and formation result in reduced yield. It needs around 18°C temperature for seed germination. It cannot tolerate frost.

Soil. A well drained loamy soil rich in organic matter having a pH range of 6.0-6.5 is ideal for the growth of the crop.

Land preparation. The field is ploughed 3-4 times or given deep digging. Beds of convenient size are prepared.

Seed rate. A quantity of 20-35 kg in small seeded type or 45-60 kg in large seeded types would be required to sow one hectare.

Sowing time. In plains, it can be grown during winter while in hills it is cultivated during spring and rainy season.

Sowing. Same as in French bean.

Spacing. Pole and semi-pole types can be sown at a spacing of 60 × 40 cm, while the bush types can be sown at 35 × 25 cm.

Manure and fertilizer. About 20-35 t/ha of FYM is applied at the time of land preparation. Besides this 40 kg of N and 50 kg each of P_2O_5 and K_2O are to be applied per ha as a basal dressing. Excess N may increase the foliage growth and delay podding.

Irrigation. Light and frequent irrigation are needed. The soil should not be too wet.

Hoeing and weeding. Frequent shallow weedings will help the crop to come up rapidly.

Staking. Pole types should be trained on thin bamboo stakes for better growth and fruit set.

Harvesting. The tender pods become ready for harvest in 80-85 days. Lima bean should be harvested when the pods are filled and light green in colour (cream white for butter beans). Bush beans are harvested for about 3 weeks and pole types for about 4-5 weeks. Fully matured dried beans can also be used as an adjunct to vegetable.

Grading. Similar to French bean.

Marketing. Same as French bean.

Storage. Same as French bean.

Yield. Tender pod yield -5-10 t/ha. Fresh bean yield -0.8-1.1 t/ha.

11.4. CLUSTER BEAN

It is a very hardy crop and survive in the tropical plains in the country. Guar or cluster bean is raised in order to augment supply of vegetable to the market in lean months of May and June when vegetables are scarce in the market.

Uses. The tender pods are used as vegetable. In certain types the seeds are used for preparation of gum. These types are not suitable as vegetable. It is a suitable green manure crop because of legume and also fed to the cattle. The tender pods when salted and sun dried are a delicacy. Suitable for resistance for drought.

Nutritive value. Green pods are rich in food value as in French bean.

Medicinal value. It possess some medicinal value.

Origin. The probable origin is West Africa and India.

Taxonomy. It belongs to the family *Leguminosae,* genus *Cyamopsis* and species *tetragonaloba.* It is a bush type herbaceous annual and some cultivars have single stem bearing pods in clusters, whereas others produce branches needing more wider spacing for cultivation.

Cultivars. Pusa Sadabahar, Pusa Mausami, Pusa Naubahar, Vankadia, Agata Guar-III, Durgabahar, Rajasthan Guar-1, Bundel-1.

Climate. It is a very hardy crop and withstand very high temperature as well as severe drought conditions. It is a warm season crop adaptive to areas with very low rainfall. It cannot tolerate frost. *Kharif crop* makes better growth due to greater moisture availability of moisture during the monsoon season.

Soil. It is a shallow rooted, quick growing crop. It can be grown in all types of soils and it can tolerate alkaline soils with pH range of 7.5-8.0 in sandy loams it thrives best. It prefers well drained retentive soil.

Land preparation. The field is ploughed 3-4 times and rest is similar to other beans.

Seed rate. To sow one hectare, 30-40 kg of seeds would be required.

Sowing time. Northern plains–January-March.
Southern plains – December-January.
All over the plains–June-July.

Cluster bean grows almost around the year due to its wider adaptability to the different seasons.

Sowing. The seeds can be sown in flat beds or ridges and furrows. The seeds may be broadcasted or sown in lines by hand or kera method at a distance of 25-30 cm between rows.

Spacing. Row to row and plant to plant spacing should be 45 × 15 cm.

Manure and fertilizer. At the last ploughing, the FYM @ 20 t/ha is incorporated. 30 kg N, 65 kg each of P_2O_5 and K_2O/ha, half the dose of N, full P_2O_5, and K_2O are applied just before sowing. The rest half dose of N can be top dressed 30-40 days after sowing.

Irrigation. Irrigation is done immediately after sowing, on the third day and again once in a week or 10 days.

Hoeing and weeding. Shallow hoeing is given 2-3 times to check the weed growth. The plants can be earthed-up after top dressing and irrigation.

Harvesting. The tender pods should be harvested as frequently as possible before the pods become fibrous and unfit for marketing. The marketable pods are available from 45 days in early cultivars to 100 days in late cultivars and the crop duration varies from 80-90 days in the former and 135-145 days in the latter. Tender, green, long podded cultivars fetch premium price.

Grading. The harvested pods should graded and packed in suitable containers.

Marketing. The produce should be marketed immediately in fresh form like other vegetables.

Storage. Pods can be stored for 4-5 days under ordinary room conditions.

Yield. The yield of tender pods ranges from 5-8 t/ha.

11.5. BROAD BEAN

Broad bean also known as Faba bean or Pigeon bean or Horse bean or Bakla bean or Field bean or Ramfali, is a food legume sporadically cultivated as minor crop for dual purpose both for grain and as a vegetable. It is an important legume of bean group grown during winter season in sub-tropical parts of the country. It is worthwhile to mention that it is the fourth most important food legume crops of the world. Broad bean would help to improve the diet of people by growing it in kitchen gardens.

Uses. The immature green edible pods are mainly used as vegetable while the seeds of dried matured pods are very rarely used as pulse. It is an important food crop in some countries. It is an established excellent fodder for animals and birds. Besides, it fixes atmospheric nitrogen efficiently and thus increases soil fertility.

Nutritive value. The protein content in the green immature edible pods and dried seeds is 6-8% and 25-30%, respectively. Besides protein, it also contains significant amount of soluble vitamins, carbohydrates and minerals.

Medicinal value. It has got manifold medicinal properties.

Origin. It is believed to have originated in Europe and Asia.

Taxonomy. It belongs to the family *Leguminosae,* genus *Vicia* and species *faba.* Plants are erect, medium- tall and produce pods. Two types small and large podded.

Cultivars. Large Podded. Imperial, White Long pod, Master Piece, Green Long pod.

Small Podded. Palampur Local-2.

Others. Pusa Sumeet, BR-1 (Black seeded), BR-2 (Yellow seeded), Jawahar Vicia 73-81, Sutton White seeded (dwarf), Sel-2, Sel-3, Ramba Tall.

Climate. It is a hardy plant, only member of bean group grown during winter and can withstand temperatures as low as 4°C. It is mainly grown at higher elevations temperate and sub-temperate areas.

Soil. Broad bean can be grown in all types of soils. For better growth rich, well drained loamy soil with a pH range of 6.5-7.6 is preferable. In acidic soils, liming is essential for proper growth. It tolerate salinity to some extent.

Seed rate. Small seeded cultiva 70-80 kg/ha.

Large seeded cultivar —90–100 kg/ha.

Sowing time. In plains —October–November

Low-hills — October-November

Mid-hills — September-October

High-hills — March-April.

Sowing. The field is given deep ploughing and flat beds of convenient size are prepared and the seed is sown in shallow furrows of 15 cm wide at a spacing of 75 cm. In each furrow, two rows of seed are sown at a spacing of 25 cm in zig-zag manner along the furrow. It can also be sown in single row fashion with a spacing of 45 × 15 cm.

Spacing. Small seede – 45 × 10 cm between rows and plants.

Large seeded – 60 × 10 cm.

Manure and fertilizer. Apply 10 t of FYM, 50 kg N, 100 kg P_2O_5 and 50 kg K_2O/ha. Add full quantity of FYM, P_2O_5, K_2O and half N at the time of and preparation. Rest N is top dressed in two splits after one month and two months of sowing.

Irrigation. Immediately after sowing, the field should be lightly irrigated. It can be grown successfully as a rainfed crop. This should be followed by a life irrigation on third day after that irrigation may given once in 12-15 days.

Hoeing and weeding. Regular weeding and hoeing should be done.

Staking. Tall cultivars should be staked by using tree branches by tying the stems at 30-60 cm above the ground. Side shoots which arise from the base should be removed so as to have a straight growth.

Harvesting. The tender pods can be harvested 3-4 months after sowing when the pods are tender green shell stage. Picking of pods is done carefully without injury to the plant.

Grading. Similar to French bean.

Marketing. As in French bean.

Storage. The pods can be stored for 4-5 days at room temperature.

Yield. Small podded cultivar—8-10 t/ha.

Large podded cultivars—10-15 t/h.

11.6. WINGED BEAN

Winged bean is also known as four angled bean and Goa bean. It is an under exploited tropical legume of exceptionally high value. It can be cultivated from sea level upto 2000 m but prefers humid tropical climate.

Uses. It produces edible pods, seeds, tender leaves, flowers, tuberous roots and edible seed oil. The whole plant is a nutritious fodder to the cattle.

Nutritive value. In some cultivars, underground root tubers are formed which is also a rich source of carbohydrate and protein. The tender pods and fully mature seeds are rich source of protein.

Medicinal value. It has manifold medicinal properties.

Origin. It is a native of Papua New Guinea and South-east Asia.

Taxonomy. It belongs to the family *Leguminosae,* genus *Psophocarpus* and species *tetragonolobus. A* herbaceous climbing perennial and reach a height of 3-4 m if supported.

Cultivars. Local cultivars.

Climate. It is a tropical vine crop comes up well in areas of high temperature. It cannot tolerate frost. It is a very hardy crop and survives under severe drought conditions. The best growth, flowering and pod development takes place at temperature range of 25-35°C short days. It can serve as a very good cover crop to prevent soil erosion, as it forms a very rapid cover of foliage growth.

Soil. Similar to French bean.

Land preparation. The field is ploughed 2-3 times and after levelling, it is divided into small plots or ridges and furrows or channels.

Seed rate. 30-40 kg seed per hectare.

Sowing time. June-July.

Sowing/planting. The seeds are sown along the ridges or furrow or channels. The seeds are very hard and given water soaking for 24-48 hours before sowing. 4-5 seeds are sown per hill at depth of 2-3 cm. The seeds germinate in 7-10 days and then the plants are thinned to retain 2 plants/hill.

Spacing. 100 × 50 cm between rows and plants.

Manure and fertilizer. Ten tonnes of FYM is applied just before sowing along with the inorganic fertilizers at the rate of 40 kg N, 100 kg P_2O_5 and 25 kg K_2O/ha.

Irrigation. Immediately after sowing and on third day irrigation may be done and again once in 15 days.

Hoeing and weeding. One month after sowing the field is cleaned-off weeds carefully and repeated every month.

Staking. When the plants start throwing tendrills, long, thin bamboo poles or Subabool stem are fixed/planted at each hill and the two vines are trained along these bamboo poles.

Harvesting. The harvesting of tender pods should be done at very tender stage 20-35 days after flowering. The first harvest starts 70-75 days after sowing and can be continued once in 10-15 days.

Grading. Same as in other beans.

Marketing. Same as in other beans.

Storage. Same as in other beans.

Yield. A quantity of 7-8 t/ha green tender pods in a crop duration of 5-6 months. Tuber yield-0.6-1.2 t/ha and seed yield 1.5-2 t/ha.

11.7. COW PEA

Cow pea is grown throughout India for its tender thin pods and dry seeds rich in nutritive value. It is grown mostly as a rainfed crop during monsoon season in most parts of the country.

Uses. Cow pea is a dual purpose crop grown for tender pods as vegetable and mature seed as pulse. The plant as a whole is a nutritious fodder in green and dry form. It is a suitable inter-crop add atmospheric nitrogen to improve soil fertility with additional income.

Nutritive value. Green fresh pods contain protein, carbohydrates, vitamin A, B & C and minerals-calcium and iron.

Medicinal value. It is considered antibilious and prescribed in liver complaints with jaundice and diuretic. The seeds contain stigmasferol which can be used a substitute of soybean in the preparation of steriodal hormone.

Origin. Cowpea is a native of Central Africa.

Taxonomy. Cultivated cowpea consist of three main groups — the asparagus bean or yard long bean (*Vigna sinensis* var. *sesquipedalis*), the catjung (*V. sinensis* var. *cylindrica* or *V. unguiculata*) and the southern pea.

Cultivars. Pusa Barsati, Pusa Phalguni, Pusa Dofasali, Arka Garima, Pusa Komal.

Climate. Different cultivars respond differently to temperature and day length. The rainy season cultivar, if grown in summer, may give only vegetative growth. It is a warm season crop and cannot tolerate very low temperature. It can be grown both in summer and rainy season, do not withstand very heavy rains especially during flowering and pod set.

Soil. It is adaptable to a wide range of soils conditions ranging from coastal sand to clay loams, poorest type of soils. It is sensitive to ill-drained conditions. It grows well in open textured soils as it produces root nodules in conjuction with legume bacteria and improve soil fertility.

Seed rate. A quantity of 15 kg seed is required to sow one hectare.

Sowing time. South India —December-January
North India —February-March (Spring cultivars).
— June-July (rainy season cultivars).

Sowing. The field is ploughed 3 to 4 time. Then beds and channels of convenient size are formed and field is irrigated. The seeds are either broadcast or sown by kera method or drilled 2-3 cm depth.

Spacing. Row spacing is 45-60 cm is kept. After germination of the seeds, the seedlings are thinned to 10-15 cm in between plants.

Manure and fertilizer. 20-25 t/ha of FYM is applied at the last ploughing. A quantity of 20 kg N, 60 kg each of P_2O_5 and K_2O be applied just before sowing and mixed with soil.

Irrigation. Irrigation be given within 3 days of sowing and continue once in 7-10 days.

Hoeing and weeding. The weeds should be effectively controlled in first 25-30 days as the crop will cover the soil surface. Pre-emergence application of Prometryne @ 1 kg/ha or Alachlor @ 1.5 kg/ha is effective to control weeds.

Staking. Normally the crop is grown in between row of maize or arhar or any other tall growing crops which provides suitable staking to expose the plants to sun shine. However, staking is not necessary in non-spreading types of cultivars.

Harvesting. The tender pods can be harvested from 40-50 days after sowing and continued once in 5-7 days.

Grading. Similar to cluster bean.

Marketing. Similar to cluster bean.

Storage. Similar to cluster bean.

Yield. The tender green pod yield ranges from 2.5-8 t/ha.

11.8. SOYBEANS

It is also called edible soybean and vegetable soybean. In India, it occupies third place after groundnut and rape seed mustard in oil seed crops. It has capacity to provide residual effect of N in the range of 30-40 kg/ha.

Uses. Soybean is used as an important food and oil source in many countries. It is also used for the preparation of various nutritious products —soybean milk and oil and have industrial value.

Nutritive value. The green pods and seeds are rich in protein, fat, carbohydrates and minerals.

Medicinal value. It possess manifold medicinal properties.

Origin. Native of South-east Asia and has been cultivated in Japan, China and India.

Cultivars. PK-416, PS-564, PS-1024, Pant Soybean, Bragg.

Taxonomy. It belong to the family *Leguminosae,* genus *Glycine* and species *max.*

Climate. Soybeans are a warm season crop with an erect bush type growth.

Soil. It can grown in light textured soil to heavy soils and medium textured loam soil with natural pH, rich in organic carbon and having fairly good water holding capacity are the best soils.

Seed rate. 75-80 kg/ha.

Sowing time. May-June.

Sowing. Sowing of seed may be done by seed drill kera/pora method or broadcasting. Other practices are similar to French bean.

Spacing. 45 × 30 cm between rows and plants and seed depth should be 3-4 cm.

Manure and fertilizer. Apply 10 t of FYM, 20 kg N, 80 kg P_2O_5 and 40 kg K_2O/ha as a basal dose. If the soils are deficient in zink, foliar application of mixture of 5 kg Zink sulphate and 2.5 kg lime in 1000 litre of water is recommended.

Irrigation. Normlly it is grown with the onset of monsoon and no need of irrigation but a light irrigation at flowering to pod filling may be given in case of water stress condition.

Hoeing and weeding. Two hand weedings first at 25-30 days followed by 40-45 days after sowing should be done. Pre-emergence application of Lasso @ 2.0 kg/ha helps in controlling most of the weeds.

Harvesting. Soybeans are usually harvested as the immature seed. The pods are harvested when the seeds are fully grown but before the pods turn yellow. Pods are harvested over a 10 day interval. Soybean seeds are difficult to extract from the immature pods. The pods are usually placed in boiling water and cooked for 2 minutes and the seeds can be squeezed from the pods easily. These seeds are eaten similar to green shell beans. Mature dried beans may be used to produce sprouts similar to mung bean or lightly roasted to a sneck food.

Grading. Similar to other beans.

Marketing. Similar to other beans.

Storage. Similar to other beans.

Yield. 3-4 t/ha.

Crop protection (Bean vegetables)

Diseases/insects	*Symptoms*	*Control*
Diseases		
Anthracnose *(Colletotrichum lindemuthianum)*	Black sunken cankers with light coloured or grey centres are seen on the pods.	Use disease free seed. Follow crop rotation. Treat seed before sowing with Bavistin 50WP @ 2 g/kg seed. Spray the crop with Bavistin 50WP @ 0.05 % or Dithane M-45 @ 0.25% and repeat.
Angular leaf spot (*Isariopsis griseola*)	Reddish brown angular lesion appear on leaves.	Use health seed for sowing. Follow crop rotation. Spray the crop as in anthracnose.
Floury leaf spot (*Ramularia phaseolina*)	Appearance of floury patches on the underside of leaves followed by necrosis.	Use healthy seed. Follow three years crop rotation.
Fucous blight (*Xanthomonas campestris* pv. *phaseoli*)	Small translucent water soaked spots and yellowing of interveinal areas of leaves. Reddish streaks and cankers appear on stems.	Use disease free seed. Soak seeds in a mixture of streptocycline (1 g) and hexacarp (25 g) in 10 1 water for 4 hours before sowing.
Leaf blight		Spray Dithane M-45 @ 0.2%.
Common mosaic	Chlorosis, downward curling of leaves, vein banding, mosaic mottling, stunting of infested plants with less number of pods and seeds.	Grow resistant cultivars as Pusa Parvati, Contender and Kentucky Wonder. Vector (aphid), spray Malathian 50 EC @ 0.05%.
Powdery mildew	White or grey powder on the under side of leaves.	Dusting with sulphur compound.
Insect pests		
Blister beetle	Feed on vital parts of flowers resulting in poor pod set.	Spray Endosulphan 0.05% or any other insecticide.
Bean bug	Nymphs and adults suck sap from underside of leaves, turn yellow and fall.	Spray Methyldematon 0.025%.
Mites	Suck sap from tender foliage causing white speaks and patches leading to drying of plant.	Spray Malathina 0.05%.
Root Knot Nematode	Gall formation	Soil fumigaticn with nematicides-DD or Nemagon. Follow long crop rotations. Grow resistant varieties.
Aphids	Suck sap of leaves, stem, flowers and pods.	Spray Methyl dematon or Dimethoate @ 1.5 ml/l.
Pod borer	Feed and bore into the pods.	Spray with BHC 50WP 2 g/l.
Black fly	Suck sap of tender plant parts.	Spray Rogar or Metasystox 0.2 ml/l of water.

CHAPTER 12

CUCURBIT

Cucurbit forms the largest group of vegetables frost sensitive predominantly tendril bearing vines extensively grown through out the sub-tropical and tropical regions around the globe. These form a distinct group of species which are similar in botany, agronomy, ecological requirements and susceptibility to pests and diseases. Cucurbit grow well at day temperatures of 20-30°C, require comparatively dry, warm, long growing season, prone to frost and strong dry winds. Low temperature and short days stimulate development of female flowers. Nearly all are monoecious plants with unisexual flowers which are pollinated by insects. The various cucurbit grow very well in the plains.

12.1. CUCUMBER

Important member of cucurbit group commercially grown as a valuable off-season crop in the hills during summer and plains in rainy season. The fruits are available almost throughout year from different areas with mild climates *viz.,* hills, river beds, etc. Moreover, now several crops are raised in some areas in a year because of change in the cropping systems has occurred through change in cultivar maturity, wider adaptability, processing technology and consumers preference for the final product. The gherkin has emerged as a large export-oriented delicacy. Preserved in vinegar and acetic acid are its value-added products liked in the European countries fetching good amount of foreign exchange every year.

Uses. Tender fruits before maturity are used as salad, pickles as well as cooked vegetable. Cucumber fruit extracts are used in health and beauty products including perfumes, lotions, soaps and shampoo, Indigenous practitioners create medical concentrations from the roots, leaves, stems and seeds.

Nutritive value. Good source of carbohydrates, vitamin A & C and minerals.

Medicinal value. Pulp and seeds have cooling effect, tonic, diuretic and the former is beneficial in chronic or acute eczema. Cucumber seeds have a number of Ayurvedic uses. In the Unani system of medicine, the oil from its seed is good for brain and body.

Origin. Native of India.

Taxonomy. *Cucumis sativus* L. is monoecious annual trailing or climbing habit. The cucumber is distinct from *Cucumis anguina* in having triangular ovate leaves with shallow and acute sinuces unlike the deep roundish lobes of West Indian ghirkins *(Cucumis anguina* var. *anguria).*

Cultivars. Cucumber cultivars are pickling and slicing types. The former have light coloured skin with more pronounced waste at the immature stage. The later types are white skinned and mostly dark green exterior colour. The cultivars are Straight Eight, Japanese Long Green, Khira-75, Khira Local, Co-1, Khira-90, Dargeeling type, Poinset, Pua Sanyog, Temperate types — Kh-1, Hybrid Priya, Liberty, Himangi, Sel-75-1-10.

Gherkins-Ajax, Calypsoplus.

Climate. It requires relatively shorter growing season with a warm climate. It is more sensitive to fluctuations of light and temperature. When the Hght intensity, duration and temperature are high favour the production of male flowers and reduce that of female flowers. It is frost sensitive but can grow in cool weather conditions. It grows best at a temperature between 18-24°C.

Soil. It does well in a wide range of soil *i.e.,* clay to sandy loam. The soil pH should be between 5.5-6.7.

Seed rate. Depending on situation *i.e.,* location, cultivar and season, 2-3.5 kg/ha seed is required.

Sowing time. In South India — June-September.

— December-March.

North India — Summer crop — January-February.

Rainy season crop — June-July.

In hills — April-May.

Sowing/planting. The field is well prepared into a better tilth. The field is divided into beds of convenient size or furrows are prepared or long channels of 60 cm wide and 1.5 m apart. Either of these the pits of 45 cm are formed and filled with 10 kg FYM and 100 g of 6 : 12 : 12 mixture. Five seeds are sown in each pit or hill and followed by light irrigation or pot watering till they germinate. After germination the plants are thinned to three/pit. The seeds sown in poly-tubes and kept in green or poly-house or under protected conditions, shifted to the main field when they have 2 or 4 leaves formed and planted in the pits by giving a slit in the polythene tube. This operation should be done in the evening followed by immediate watering. The seed is also sown by dibbling method.

Thinning. The plants should be thinned when sown in hill/pits so that not more than three plants left standing in each hill and in furrows or side of the ridge allow one or two plants at each place.

Spacing. 150 × 50-60 cm.

Manure and fertilizer. Apply 25 t FYM, 100 kg N, 50 kg P_2O_2 and 50 kg K_2O kg/ha. Add total quantity of FYM, P_2O_5 K_2O and half N at the time of land preparation and rest N in two equal splits at a interval of one month of flowering.

Irrigation. The summer crop require enough soil moisture for its proper growth and development so irrigation should be given as and when needed and in rainy season crop, the irrigation is regulated accordingly.

Hoeing and weeding. Shallow interculture should be done during the early stages of growth. Hoeing and weeding are done twice or thrice at fortnightly intervals. Weedicides such as Glyphoset, Paraquat and Chlorambenl @ 2 kg/ha may be used to control weeds.

Sex. Ethral application (2.5 ml/10 lit) 4 times at weekly interval from 15th day of sowing can be done to increase female flower production.

Harvesting. Picking of tender immature fruits before the seeds become hard can be done from 45 day after sowing depending on cultivar and management. The full grown tender fruits should be picked once in 5-7 days on 8th-10th day of flowering. About 8-10 harvests can be made. Timely picking is most important in regard to the quality. Fruits are of highest quality when dark green, firm and crisp. Green-house types should be harvested after every day.

Grading. The fruits may be graded on the basis of shape, size, tenderness and colour according to the varietal characteristics.

Marketing. The marketing of cucumber fruits should be done immediately and are handled carefully in storage, packaging and transit causing no or minimum damage to the fruits and must reach to the consumers in fresh form.

Storage. The cucumbers should be stored not more than two days. For longer storage the temperature should be kept at 10°C.

Yield. 100-200 kg/ha.

12.2. MUSKMELON

It is an important dessert crop cultivated throughout India and is also called cantaloupe. It is commonly grown in river beds and occupies about 80% area under basin land of Indian rivers.

Uses. Its fruits are used for dessert and also eaten alone. Very rarely its immature fruits are cooked as a vegetable at green stage.

Nutritive value. It is very wholesome and nutritious and the nutritive value varies from cultivar to cultivar. Fruits contain protein, fat, carbohydrates, carotene, vitamin C and minerals like calcium, phosphorus and iron.

Medicinal value. It prevents constipation. Seeds are anthelmintic medicine and seed oil is used to counteract the poison of snakebite, to ward-off dandruff and a veriety of other ailments. Reduces diabetes mellitus by increasing carbohydrate utilization. Bitter melon also has been used to combat HIV infection.

Origin. It is a native of hot valley of Iran north-west India.

Taxonomy. It belongs to family *Cucurbitaceae* genus *Cucumis* and species *melo.* A large number of cultivars with different size, shape, very sweet with small seed cavity, thick flesh, good flavour, colours and resistance are cultivated in different parts of the country, the netted skin and musky types are common. The plants have separate male and female flowers on the same vine and are cross-pollinated by bees.

Cultivars. Durgapura Madhu, Punjab Sunehri, Pusa Madhuras, Pusa Sharbati, M-4, Arka Rajhans, Arka Jeet, Hara Madhu.

Local cultivars. Annamalai, Lucknow Safeda, Haridhari, Faizabadi, Kutana, Baghpat melon, Jaunpuri netted, Tonk melon, Maumelon, Hoshangabad, Goose, Jobner-96-2, Amritsari.

Hybrids-Punjab Hybrid-1, Hybrid-3, Hybird Swarna, MH4-3, MH-10.

Climate. It thrives best warm dry weather with good sunshine and low humidity and free from frost. The optimum temperature is 27-30°C. Sweetness and flesh flavour are hereditary and are influence by environment. Short day length promotes female flower production. For proper ripening and high sugar content, high temperature, low humidity and plenty of sunshine is essential. Cloudy weather will reduce fruit quality. Plants are sensitive to low temperature and frost. The seed does not germinate at temperature lower than 22°C.

Soil. Muskmelon can be grown in all types of soil but mainly grown in sandy and sandy loam soils at river beds. There should be sufficient organic matter in the soil. The optimum soil pH is 6.0-6.7.

Seed rate. Direct seeding — 3-7 kg/ha.

Transplanting technique — 1 kg/ha.

Sowing time. Plains — February-March.

North-eastern region — November-March.

Western region — September-October.

South India — October-November.

Hills — April-May.

Eastern India — November-December.

South India — December-January and rainy season crop-June.

Sowing/planting. The method of planting is the same as in watermelon. In muskmelon, transplanting of about a week old seedlings can also be done. Sowing may be done on ridges or furrows or pits/hills.

Spacing. 2.0-3.5 × 0.6-1.20 m between rows and plants.

Manure and fertilizer. The dose 25-45 t of FYM, 100 kg N, 50 kg each of P_2O_5 and K_2O/ha should be applied. Higher yield can be obtained by spraying boron at 50 and 75 ppm and maganese at 50 ppm.

Irrigation. Irrigation is given as and when it is necessary. Rainy season crop and crop grown in river bed do not require any irrigation except one irrigation is required for better establishment of plants.

Hoeing and weeding. 2-3 shallow intercultivation should be given to keep down weeds during the early stages of growth. Thinning of plants is also done. Mulching also supresses the weeds and increases the yield.

Harvesting. Muskmelon fruit is ready for picking in about 70-90 days after seed sowing depending upon cultivar, agro-climate, distance of market and method of transport. The fruits of muskmelon lakes about 28-30 days from fruit setting to reach maturity stage. The stage of maturity is generally judged by the change in internal flesh colour of the fruit, softening of the rind and development of abscission layer. The fruit when matures a crack develops around the penduncle at the base of fruit and slips out easily from the vine leaving a circular scar called 'full slip' stage. In netted muskmelon the green colour between the nets changes to yellow, yellow-green or brown and nets changes to dirty white. Harvesting be done when the fruits are fully ripe and at full slip stage for local market and harvest for distant market at half-slip stage. This is known with experience.

Grading. Fruits should be graded properly according to the specifications before marketing to earn better prices.

Marketing. Fruits are send to the market immediately after harvesting.

Storage. Normally muskmelons are not stored. However, these can be stored for 8 or more days at 0-1°C and 90 per cent RH.

Yield. 20-25 t/ha.

12.3. WATERMELON

Watermelon is a very common summer cucurbit grown from the lower Himalayan region to South India. It is also cultivated in riverbed and supplied to the markets before the hot summer starts throughout the country.

Uses. Fruits make a delicious and refreshing dessert, especially esteemed in hot weather. The pulp of the fully ripe fruit is juicy, sweet and delicious. In the desert areas, the juicy flesh serve as a substitute for drinking water. The rind may be pickled or candied.

Nutritive value. It is the richest source of iron among all the cucurbits.

Medicinal value. Seeds are anthelmintic medicine and seed oil is used to counteract the poison of snakebite, to ward-off dandruff and a veriety of other ailments. Reduces diabetes mellitus by increasing carbohydrate utilization.

Origin. Indigenous to tropical Africa, but according to Pangala, it is indigenous to India.

Taxonomy. Watermelon belongs to family *Cucurbitaceae,* genus *Citrullus* and species *lanatus.* Citron *(C. lanatus* var. *citroides)* is used differently *i.e.,* eaten cooked, pickled or candied.

Cultivars. New Hampshire Midget, Sugar Baby, Ashani Yamato, Charleston Gray, Improved Shipper, Durgapura Meetha, Durgapura Kesar, PKM-1, Arka Jyoti, Arka Manik, Pusa Bedana, Amrut, MHW-5, MHW-6, MHW-11, Nath-101, Nath-102, Suruchi.

Climate. Watermelon needs a long growing season with a relatively high temperature and low humidity. It cannot withstand frost and the seed do not germinate below 21°C. Dry weather during ripening with high temperature, enough sunshine and dry winds favours the development of flavour and high sugar content.

Soil. Deep sandy loamy soil is the best suited for this crop. It is generally grown on river beds. The optimum soil pH is 5.5-7.0.

Seed rate. 3-7 kg/ha. The germination percentage and storage life of seeds can be improved by treating freshly extracted seeds with *2%* HC1 or NaOH.

Sowing time. Plains — November-March.

Hills — February-March.

South India — January-February and June-July.

Sowing/planting. The land should be thoroughly prepared by giving 4-5 ploughings to bring into a better tilth. The seed is normally soaked overnight before sowing. The seed is sown by either of the following methods. **Shallow pit method** — pits of 60 × 60 × 45 cm size are dug at a distance of 1.5 to 2.5 m. Each pit is filled with a mixture of soil and 4-5 kg of FYM or compost, 30-40 g urea, 40-50 g single super phosphate and 80-100 g of muriate of potash. After filling the pits circular base are prepared and 5-6 seeds are sown per base at a depth of 2-3 cm and covered with fine soil, FYM or compost. **Deep pit method** — Pits of 60 × 75 cm diameter and 1.0-1.5 m depth are dug at a distance of 1.5- 2.5 m distance both ways. This method is mainly followed in riverbed cultivation. **Ridge method** — Seeds are sown on the side of raised bed. **Mound beds** — Seeds are sown on mounds and **Furrow method** — Furrows are prepared and seeds are sown on one side of the furrow.

Thinning. 2-3 plants may be kept/hill or pit by thinning at 4-6 leaf stage and retain only healthy plants.

Spacing. Normal spacing is 300 × 90 cm between rows and plants.

Induction of femaleness. Two sprays of TIBA @ 25-50 ppm or four sprays of ethrel 200 ppm at weekly interval starting from two true leaf stage (15 days after sowing) are given. This will help to increase the production of female flowers and thereby increase the fruit yield. Boron and molybdenum at 3 ppm and calcium at 20 ppm are also very effective.

Manure and fertilizer. Add 30 t FYM, 30 kg N, 65 kg P_2O_5 and 85 kg K_2O/ha. On 30th day of sowing, 30 kg of N should be top dressed and the plants irrigated followed by earthing-up.

Irrigation. The crop is irrigated by pitcher or walercane after sowing. The crop should be irrigated once every 7-10 days. The monsoon crop is grown as a rainfed crop. The seed is sown and left till the rains are received.

Hoeing and weeding. 2-3 hoeings should be done during the early stages of growth to keep down the weeds and conserve soil moisture till the vines covers the surface of the soil. Weedicides like Chloroxuron and Prometryne 3 and 2 kg/ha, respectively may be useful for controlling weeds.

Harvesting. The plant bear fruits in 4-5 months after sowing. The fruits should be harvested at the proper stage of maturity. The physiological maturity can be known by the following indications of ripening. **Withering of tendrils** —The tendrils that subtends the peduncle of the fruil ripens and it seldom ripe if the tendril is still green. But it may be unripe even if the tendril is dried in some cultivars. **Thumping.** — Ripe fruit, when thumped with the finger produces a muffled dull or dead sound, where as the immature fruits gives out a metallic and singing sound. **Colour of the ground spot** — It is white when fruits are green and they rest over it when the fruits are ripe they change to yellow. **Pressure on the fruit** — A ripe melon emits a crisp cracking noise on being pressed with the flat of the hand. Moreover the rind of the ripe melon, yields little under the presence of thumb. In some cultivars even slight pressure will crack the fruit. If the fruits are allowed to overripe, the pulp looses the sweetness and soon develops off-flavour and rot. It is therefore, very necessary that they should be harvested at the full ripe stage because they ripen very little on their way to the market.

Grading. Fruits are graded on the basis or variety, size, rind colour, sugar content and flavour, the chief attributes which do not increase after picking.

Marketing. Watermelons are transported in trucks without any individual packing and are liable to bruise and damage duing transit.

Storage. The harvested ripe fruits should be handled carefully storage and can keep well for 8-21 days at 2.2-4.4°C temperature and 80-85 per cent RH. These can be transported to long distances without refrigeration.

Yield. 20-25 t/ha in other cultivars and 40-60 t/ha in case of hybrids.

12.4. SARDAMELON

Normally it was introduced from Afghanistan, now cultivated in temperate areas of Himachal Pradesh like Kinnaur, Lahaul and Spiti districts. The Afghan melons are horticulturally very different from the ordinary melons cultivated in the plains of India. The fruits arc large in size, more sweet, very crisp and juicy with better shelf-life as compared to other melons. Moreover, Sardamelons are available in the market on the onset of winter in September-October when other melons are not available. Upto now its fruits are being imported from Afghanistan at a very high price by spending valuable foreign. At present, it is possible to grow sardamelon successfully in the temperate areas of India by the concerted efforts of the vegetable scientists of the Agricultural/Horticultural universities.

Uses. The sweet fruits are relished as raw before and as dessert after the meals.

Nutritive value. Good source of carbohydrates, sugar, vitamins and minerals.

Medicinal value. Seeds are anthelmintic medicine and seed oil is used to counteract the poison of snakebite, to ward-off dandruff and a veriety of other ailments. Reduces diabetes mellitus by increasing carbohydrate utilization.

Origin. Probable origin is tropical Africa.

Taxonomy. Sardamelon belongs to the family *Cucurbitaceae,* genus *Cucumis,* species *melo* and variety *raticulatus.*

Cultivars. Selection-1, Selcction-9.

Climate. It is a temperate crop and requires a long period of warm dry weather with plenty of sunshine and is not adapted to frost, snow and shade. Excessive humid weather is also not congenial for its growth and deveiopment. For good fruit quality and sweetness, dry weather during fruit development is necessary. Cool nights and warm days are ideal for accumulation of sugars in the fruits. This conditon is met in areas where temperate climatic conditions are available like Kinnaur, Lahaul and Spiti districts.

Site selection. Site should be open with plenty of sunshine and better drainage system.

Soil. It does well in sandy loam light, friable, rich in humus and well drained.

Seed rate. 3-4 kg/ha.

Sowing time. High-hills (1800-2200 m.a.s.l)-May.

Sowing/planting. This should be well prepared in advance of planting mixed with plenty of organic manure. Seed can be sown in polybages-a mixture of farm yard manure or leaf mould and soil in 1 : 1 ratio are filled and 2-3 seeds are sown in each polytube and keep in the poly-house till it attains 2-4 leaf stage. These are planted in the main field which are either prepared before snowfall or after when the soil becomes warm and weather is open. The poly-tubc plants are planted in the main field followed by irrigation. In case of direct sowing, furrows are made at a distance of 1.5 m and pits of about 30 cm depth are dug. These pits are filled with a mixture of FYM and NPK. Generally direct sowing has given good results and hill and raised bed system of seed sowing is followed and normally 2-3 seeds are sown per hill/spot. Finally one or two vines are allowed to trail per hill, flat on the ground. In areas where more rain are expected, raised bed system may be practised to facilitate easy drainage of water. Seeds are sown on both sides of the raised bed and depth of the seed should not be more than one centimetre.

Spacing. 1.5 × 1 m between rows and plants.

Manure and fertilizer. Well rotten 15-20 t of FYM, 100 kg N, 50 kg each of P_2O_5 and K_2O/ha should be applied. Full dose of FYM, P_2O_5, K_2O and half dose of N be added at the time of land preparation or pit digging and thoroughly mixed with the soil. Remaining dose of N is applied in two splits at months interval.

Irrigation. Generally hills or beds should be irrigated a day or two prior to planting of seeds and keep the soil in its optimum moisture condition by irrigating at an interval of 3-4 days till germination. Afler germination, irrigation at 4-5 days interval will be necessary to maintain good growth of vines. Application of water should be restricted to the base of the plant and over flooding of fields be avoided. Irrigation should be stopped at the time of fruit ripening *i.e.* after 100-120 days of sowing.

Pollination. The crop is andromonoecious and pollinated by insect pollinators during the month of July in District Kinnaur of Himachal Pradesh.

Isolation. The ideal minimum isolation to maintain the identity and genetic purity of a cultivar should be 1000 m between two cultivars or the vegetable crossable with it.

Hoeing and weeding. 2-3 hoeing and weedings are done to pulverize the soil and control the weeds.

Harvesting. Harvesting of fruits at the right maturity stage varies from cultivar to cultivar. Generally after 100-110 days of planting the fruits can be harvested when these turn yellow. The fruits are picked carefully without harming the vines. Fruits of Selection-1 and 9 normally do not slip easily at maturity from the vines. Fruits are harvested on the basis of external colour. Rind colour of Selection-1 turns yellow upto the middle of the fruit at full maturity, whereas Selection-9 emits slightly musky flavour and the rind colour turns greenish yellow, which indicates its fruit maturity.

Grading. The fruits are graded on the basis of size, shape and colour into various grades.

Marketing. The produce collected from the field should be taken to the collection centres and from where loaded in the trucks/vehicles and transported to the markets.

Storage. Harvested ripe fruits should be handled carefully before storage and can keep well for 5-6 days at 2.2-4.4°C temperature and 80-85 per cent RH. These can be transported to long distances under refrigeration.

Yield. 30-35 t/ha fruits can be expected depending upon climate and cultivar.

12.5. LONGMELON

Longmelon is an important cucurbit crop grown throughout India particularly kitchen gardens and riverbeds for its tender long fruits in tropical and sub-tropical areas. It is commonly grown in North India.

Uses. The tender fruits are consumed raw with salt and pepper. It is also consumed as vegetable.

Nutritive value. Similar to cucumber.

Medicinal value. Same as that of cucumber.

Origin. India.

Taxonomy. It belongs to the family *Cucurbitaceae,* genus *Cucumis,* species *melo* and variety *utilissimus.* The fruits are long (10-100 cm) dark green or pale green or yellowish green with or without stripes.

Cultivars. Long Green, Long White, Bariely Glory, Dark green, Faizabadi, Laila Ki Ungalian, Majanu Ki Pasalian, Arka Sheetal.

Climate. Similar to cucumber.

Soil. Same as in cucumber.

Seed rate. 3-4 kg/ha.

Sowing time. February-March.

Sowing/planting. The seeds are sown in well prepared field either in hills or spots, furrows or ridges or by kera method and also in polytubes.

Spacing. 2 × 1.5 m between rows and plants.

Manure and fertilizer. Same as in cucumber.

Irrigation. Same as in cucumber.

Hoeing and weeding. Same as in cucumber.

Harvesting. The fruits should be harvested carefully without damaging the vines and before the seeds become hard and the fruits are still tender.

Grading. Fruits of uniform size, shape, colour and having tenderness be put in a better grade to earn maximum returns.

Marketing. Since the fruits are very perishable and cannot stay more after picking and should be sent to the market immediately or packaging, transport and marketing must be well set prior to harvesting.

Storage. Similar to cucumber crop.

Yield. 30-35 t/ha.

12.6. PUMPKIN

Pumpkin is the most popular cucurbitaceous vegetable commercially grown and known by various names as *Kashiphal, Sitaphal* or *Lalkaddu.*

Uses. Pumpkin is normally used in green and mature stage as vegetable. The flesh is somewhat coarse and strongly flavoured with the result it is mil usually served as a baked vegetable. The young leaves, tender stems and flowers are also cooked. Besides a number of different preparations are made from the pumpkin fruits. It is also mixed with tomato in the preparation of sauce.

Nutritive value. The fruits contain protein, fat, carbohydrates and vitamin A.

Medicinal value. Pulp is used as a paultice and applied to burns, inflammation and boils. Seeds are anthalmentic, taenicide, diuretic and tonic.

Origin. Pumpkin was originated from tropical America.

Taxonomy. It belongs to family *Cucurbitaceae,* genus *Cucurbita* have four species *viz., pepo, maxima, moschata* and *mixta,* are annual herbaceous vines with numerous runners except a number of cultivars *pepo* and *maxima* that have short inter-nodes. Squash is employed to designate the forms of *C. pepo.*

Cultivars. Solan Badami, Large Red, Large Round, Red Flesh, Arka Suryamukhi, Arka Chandan, Local Cultivar, Co-1, Co-2, Pusa Vishwas, Ambli, Pusa Hybrid-1.

Sex expression in cucurbita. It is relatively stable and all the species are monoecious. This is because of the heavy and sticky pollen grains and need to be carried by some agent other than wind from the staminate flower to the receptive stigmas of the pistillate flower for fertilization to be accomplished by the domestic honey bees acts as the effective pollinator. The flowers are large showy with yellow or creamy corollas.

Climate. The crop requires long warm growing season with a comparatively low temperature and high humidity. Plants can be grown successfully between a temperature of 25-30°C and both very and low temperature conditions are deterimental. Short days low night temperature and high relative humidity are best for production of pumpkin.

Soil. Can be cultivated in all types of soil but loam, sandy loam and clay loam soils with pH 6.0-6.5 are considered best.

Seed rate. 6-8 kg/ha.

Sowing time. Plains of north India —January-March and June-July.

Rest of India — December-January. West Bengal and Hills — April-May.

Sowing/planting. Sowing is done on ridges or furrows or hills/pits and 2-3 seeds may be sown per hill. Sometimes dibbling method of sowing is also used.

Spacing. 2.5-3.0 × 1.0-1.5 m between rows and hills.

Manure and fertilizer. Apply 10 t of FYM, 90 kg N, 60 kg P_2O_5 and 55 kg K_2O/ha. Total quantity of FYM, P_2O_5, K_2O and half N at the time of sowing and remaining N is top dressed in two splits after one month of sowing and at the time of flowering.

Irrigation. No irrigation is required in rainy season crop and the summer crop should be irrigated at an interval of 5-7 days.

Hoeing and weeding. 1 or 2 weeding should be done during early stages of growth.

Harvesting. Pumpkin is harvested either in green stage or mature stage according to the demand in the market. In green stage, the fruit is separated from the vine carefully without any injury to the vine. The ripe fruits are collected after the vines get dry.

Grading. Grading of fruits is done on the basis of varietal characteristics as per the ISI standards.

Marketing. The fruits are packed in gunny bags or in trucks or boggies and transported to the various markets as per the demand and the price situation.

Storage. The fruits can be stored for 5-6 months in well ventilated rooms. The recommended storage temperatures are 15-20°C for the first 2-3 weeks and then 10-15°C as a holding temperature at 75% RH.

Yield. 25-30 t/ha.

12.7. SUMMER SQUASH

Squashes has a fine grained flesh with mild flavour. The plants are dwarf and bearing fruit at the axil of leaves.

Uses. Immature fruits are cooked by boiling and consumed.

Nutritive value. Suitable source of carbohydrate, protein, fat, vitamin and minerals.

Medicinal value. Seeds are anthelmintic medicine and seed oil is used to counteract the poison of snakebite, to ward-off dandruff and a veriety of other ailments.

Origin. Native of Mexico.

Cultivars. Pusa Alankar, Australian Green, Early Yellow Prolific, Platypan.

Climate. It can tolerate higher temperature.

Soil. It is grown in all types of soils but do well in loam, sandy loam and clay loams having pH value 6-6.5.

Seed rate. 3-4 kg/ha.

Sowing time. Plains — January-March;

June-July.

Hills — March-April.

Catch crop in potato or other — October-November.

Sowing/planting. For early sowing seeds are sown in poly-tubes, 2-3 seeds/poly-tube. These are kept in safe places or poly or green-house and allowed to grow to 2 or 4 leaf stage, then these are planted in the main field followed by irrigation.

Spacing. 90 × 60 cm between rows and hill/plant.

Manure and fertilizer. Apply 25 t FYM, 100 kg N, 50 kg each of P_2O_5 and K_2O/ha. Half N and all others are mixed in the soil at the time of land preparation and rest N in two splits at a month interval.

Irrigation. Irrigate the field as and when required. The summer crop should be irrigated after every 4th or 5th day and in rainy season crop no irrigation is needed.

Hoeing and weeding. As in pumpkin.

Harvesting. Fruits are ready to harvest after 50-60 days of sowing and should be harvested when they have attained proper shape, size, tender and are at mature green stage before the seed ripen. Harvesting may be done after every 4-5th day. The fruit is removed from the plant by a slight twist and with no portion of the stem attached.

Grading. Similar to other cucurbits.

Marketing. Similar to other cucurbits.

Storage. Fruits cannot be stored for a long period and does not stand long distance transport.

Yield. 25-30 t/ha.

12.8. BOTTLE GOURD

Bottle gourd is extensively grown through India under varied agro-climatic conditions.

Uses. The tender fruits are used in several ways as vegetable, preparation of some sweets, alongwith curd and cooked with pulse. The hard shell of the fruit is used for different purposes like domestic untensils —water jug, musical instruments, floats for fishing nets, decoration, novelty items, etc.

Nutritive value. Good source of carbohydrate, protein, vitamins and minerals.

Medicinal value. The pulp and the young stem and leaves have many medicinal values.

Seeds are anthelmintic medicine and seed oil is used to counteract the poison of snakebite, to ward-off dandruff and a veriety of other ailments.

Origin. Bottle gourd have originated from Africa and India and spread to other warm countries.

Taxonomy. Bottle gourd belongs to the family *Cucurbitaceae,* genus *Laginaria* and species *siceraria* (2n = 22), is also known as white flowered gourd is a monoecious annual vine. The fruits varies in shape and size because of cross-pollinated nature.

Cultivars : (*i*) ***Long varieties.*** Pusa Hybrid 3, Pusa Summer Prolific Long, Hot Long Green, Pocha's Long White, Samrat, Arka Bahar.

(ii) Round varieties. Pusa Summer Prolific Round, Pusa Alankar, Pusa Manjri, Punjab-Round, Ward MGH-1, Pusa Meghdoot, PBO 6-2 m CO-1.

Climate. It requires long periods of warm preferably dry weather with abundant sunshine and is a hardy crop can withstand drought but prone to frost. The seed germinate well when the day temperature is above 25°C. For normal growth, it needs optimum average monthly temperature of 25-30°C.

Soil. Bottle gourd can be grown in any type of soils, but sandy loam soils are best suited for its cultivation. The optimum pH is 6-7.

Seed rate. 3-6 kg/ha.

Sowing time. In plains — summer crop — January-February.

Rainy season crop — June-July.

In hills — April

Sowing/planting. The land should be prepared thoroughly by 3-5 ploughings into a better tilth. The seed is sown by dibbling method. Generally 3-4 seeds are sown per hill/pit at 2.5-3 cm depth.

Spacing. 2-3 m × 1-1.5 m between rows and hills/pits.

Manure and fertilizer. Apply 10 t of FYM, 100 kg N, 75 kg P_2O_5 and 50 kg K_2O/ha. Add FYM, P_2O_5, K_2O and half N at the time of land preparation and remaining N is top dressed in two split doses after one month of sowing and at flowering stage.

Irrigation. The summer crop requires frequent irrigation at an interval of 4-5 days while the rainy season crop should be irrigated when required.

Hoeing and weeding. 2-3 hoeing should be given to keep down the weeds during the early stages of growth. In case of summer crop, the vines are allowed to trail on the ground while the rainy season crop, the plants are staked often trained on tower made of tree branches or bamboo or angle iron, etc.

Harvesting. The fruits should be harvested when they are tender, green and attained the optimum maturity. Delay in harvesting causes the fruits to become unfit for marketing. Tenderness and edible maturity are judged by pressing the skin the little pubescence persisting or piercing the nail on the skin. Seeds should be soft, if examined in transverse section.

Grading. The grading should be done on the basis of varietal characteristics.

Marketing. The farmers sell their produce in the local/rural market or transport to distant markets without and individual packing or sometimes packed in jute bags.

Storage. It has short storage shelf-life for few weeks under 10°C and 60-70 per cent RH.

Yield. The average yield is 20-30 t/ha.

12.9. BITTER GOURD

Bitter gourd or Balsam pear is one of the popular cucurbitaceous vegetable grown extensively for its bitter fruits in different parts of India.

Uses. The fruits at tender stage are used as vegetable cooked in many ways preferably fried, boiled, stuffed and cooked also in curries.

Nutritive value. It is a highly valuable vegetable because of its nutritive value. Small cultivars are rich in iron and vitamin C.

Medicinal value. The fruit is wormicidal, good tonic, stomachic, carminative, have cooling effect, for rheumatism, gout, diseases of liver and spleen and most suited to the diabetic patients. The plant as a whole (leaves, stem and roots) is used as folk remedy.

Origin. Bitter gourd is believed to have originated in tropical Africa and Asia & widely distributed in China, Malaysia, tropical Africa and is growing wild in many parts of India.

Taxonomy. It belongs to the family *Cucurbitaceae,* genus *Momordica* and species *charantia.* The characteristic bitter taste in the fruits is due to a chemical constituent *'momorcidin'*. The related species of this genera are *M. cochinchinensis* Spreng and *M. dioica* Roxb. The former is commonly called sweet gourd of Kakrol, perennial, dioecious with tuberous roots. Fruits are ovate. 10-12 cm long, pointed and densely covered with conical spines. While latter species called Kakrol is also dioecious perennial, capable of yielding for 3-4 years. The fruits are very small 2.5-3.0 cm long covered with dense warts.

Sex form. The appearance of various intermediate sex forms like andromonoecious, gynoecious and trimonoecious, the colchine treated plants but remaining diploids is an interesting phenomenon.

Cultivars. There exist a good range of variability for shape, size and colour. The cultivars can be grouped into small fruited (7-10 cm long) grown in summer and long and large fruited (15-18 cm long) cultivated in rainy season. The cultivars are Solan-Hara, Solan-Safaid, Local-cultivar, Kalyanpur, Baramashi, Large White, Small Green, VK-1 Priya, Arka Harit, Pusa Do Mousmi, Pusa Hybrid-1, Pusa Vishesh, Coimbatore Long Green, Coimbatore Long White, Hirakani, Phule Green Gold, RHR BGH-1, CO-1, CO-2, MDU-1.

Climate. A warm season crop, grows well in hot and moist weather favouring its proper growth and development. Low temperature inhibit the seed germination. It grows best at temperatures between 20-30°C and the yields are high. The extremes of temperatures *i.e.,* below 18°C and above 36°C produces less female flowers resulting poor yield. Under moderate climate it can be grown throughout the year.

Soil. Bitter gourd can be grown in all types of soils but loam and silt loam is more suitable for its cultivation. It grows well on silty soils on river beds. The best soil pH is 6.5-7.0.

Seed rate. 4.5-6 kg/ha.

Sowing time. Plains—summer crop —January-March.

Rainy season crop —June-July.

Hills — March-June.

Sowing/planting. The plants can be propagated by tuberous roots. The tubers are collected separately from male and female plants and planted. The land should be well prepared. Seed is sown by dibbling method and 3-4 seeds are sown per hill/pit at 2-3 cm depth. Seeds are soaked in water overnight before sowing for better germination which can also be enhanced by soaking the seeds for 24 hours in a solution of 25 or 50 ppm boron. Seeds should be treated with Thiram @ 2 g/kg seed. In hills, the bitter gourd crop is raised on a trellis system of bamboo and the vines are allowed to trail at a height of 1-1.25 m and the person can move about for doing the intercultural operations like irrigation, weeding, etc. and also picking of the fruits easily.

Spacing. 1.5-2.5 × 0.6-120 m between rows and plants.

Manure and fertilizer. Application of 10 t FYM, 100 kg N, 50 kg P_2O_5 and 55 kg K_2O/ ha at the time of land preparation *i.e,* full dose of FYM, P_2O_5, K_2O and half N and rest N top dressed in two splits at months interval at the time of vining and flowering.

Female flowers. To increase the female flowers, ethrel 250 ppm (2.5 ml of ethrel mixed with 10 L of water) is sprayed when the plant is with two true leaves (15 days after sowing). This is repeated once in a week.

Irrigation. The soil should be kept in its optimum moisture condition. The summer crop be irrigated 5-7 days interval while in rainy season the interval will depend on rains.

Hoeing and weeding. 2-3 hoeing are done to keep the weeds under control. During early stages of growth. The rainy season crop is usually staked often trained on a trellis system or tower made-up of bamboo or wooden poles by using G.I wire.

Harvesting. Harvesting is done when the fruits are still young and tender at every alternate day. Picking should be done carefully so that the vines may not be damaged. The fruit should not be allowed to mature on the vine as seeds developed will afftect the quality of fruit and fruit bearing is reduced.

Grading. Grading of fruits should be done according to cultivar, fruit shape, size and colour or the recommended A, B and C grades.

Marketing. The fruits should be packed in bamboo baskets, crates, cartons, etc. if they are to be transported to distant markets and for local market onion bags can be used. While in transit the produce should be handled carefully.

Storage. Harvested fruits can be stored for 3-4 days in cool conditions or under shade.

Yield. 6-12 t/ha. Monsoon crop yields more than summer season crop.

12.10. SPONGE GOURD

Sponge gourd is also called smooth gourd or loofah, an annual is cultivated on a large scale in different parts of the country.

Uses. The fruit is edible when young and tender used as vegetable and herb. The dry inner fibre portion of the mature fruit is used for bathing purposes, cleaning utensils, in making shoe soles and also filters in factories.

Nutritive value. Some industrial oil is also extracted from its seeds.

Medicinal value. Plant extract in the form of clear liquid is useful in respiratory complaints. Tender fruits are considered diuretic and lactagogne, carminative, purgative, anthelmintic. Seeds have ematic and cathartic properties and seed oil substitute for olive oil which is useful for skin affections.

Origin. Sponge gourd is indigenous to tropical Asia probably India.

Taxonomy. A member of family *Cucurbitaceae,* genus *Luffa* and species *cylinderica* and the fruits are smooth skinned called 'Ghia tori'. The flowers are deep yellow in colour and blooming takes place in the morning hours.

Cultivars. Pusa Chikni, GFE SMG-108, Pusa Supriya.

Climate. These perform well under dry season in sunny, hot and humid climates. These are frost sensitive and somewhat drought tolerant. It is adapted to short day lengths.

Soil. Sponge gourd plants grow best on fertile, mildly acidic to neutral, well drained soils.

Seed rate. 4-5 kg/ha.

Sowing time. Plains —June-July.

Hills —March-May.

Sowing/planting. Under glass-house culture, plants require prolific feeding with nitrogen, temperature of 25-28°C and spraying for pest and mildew control. For field grown crops, seeds or transplanted seedlings should be planted in hills at the base of a sturdy trellis.

Spacing. 150 × 100 cm between rows and plants.

Manure and fertilizer. Apply 10 t FYM, 100 kg N, 75 kg P_2O_5 and 50 kg K_2O/ha. The total quantity of FYM, P_2O_5, K_2O and half N be applied at the time of pit/hill preparation and rest N in two equal spilts as top dressing after one month and at the time of flowering.

Irrigation. As in bottle gourd.

Hoeing and weeding. Similar to bottle gourd.

Harvesting. Immature fruits can be harvested 40-80 days after planting, harvesting of mature fruits begins about 3 months later.

Grading. The fruits should be uniformly graded according to the cultivar.

Marketing. The tender fruits after harvesting should be handled carefully while packing and in transit and immediately send to the market.

Storage. Fruits can be stored for few days under ordinary conditions.

Yield. 30-40 t/ha.

12.11. RIDGE GOURD

Ridge gourd commonly called luffa is cultivated both on commercial and in kitchen gardens throughout India.

Uses. Immature fruits are boiled, peeled or intact used in curries or cooked as vegetable and sometimes eaten as salad like cucumber. Leaves and immature buds are also edible used as green and mature seeds sometimes roasted.

Nutritive value. Good source of carbohydrates, proteins, fat, vitamins and minerals.

Medicinal value. Leaves are used as poultice in haemorrhaids, leprosy and splanstis, the juice of fresh leaves is useful in granular conjuctivitis in children. Decoction is useful for uraemia and amenorrhoea. Seeds possess ematic and puragative properties and seed oil is toxic.

Origin. Tropical Asia particularly India.

Taxonomy. A member of family *Cucurbitaceae,* genus L*uffa* and species *acutangula* and the fruits are having ridges called 'Kali tori'. The flowers are pale yellow in colour and blooming takes place in the evening hours. Crossing is therefore success only when artificially pollinated. In nature hardly any cross-pollination between the two species is observed.

Cultivars. Pusa Nasdhar, CO-1, CO-2, PKM-1, Satputia.

Climate. Luffa requires long and warm climate. Humid and warm climate is best preferably grows well during rainy season. Optimum temperature requirement is 24-27°C.

Soil. It can be grown on variety of soils but loamy soils with good amount of organic matter and optimum pH 5.5-6.7 are considered to be ideal.

Seed rate. 5-7 kg/ha.

Sowing time. Summer crop —February-March in plains.

January-March in eastern and western regions.

Rainy season crop—June-July through India.

April-May in hills of north India.

Sowing/planting. In north India, planting is done on raised beds or in channels while in south India its done in pits/hills.

Spacing. 1.5-2.5 × 0.6-1.2 m.

Manure and fertilizer. Application of 10 kg FYM and 100 g of 6 : 12 : 12 mixed fertilizer with top soil/hill or pit.

Irrigation. Summer crop should be irrigated soon after sowing and subsequently at an interval of 4-7 days. No irrigation is required in rainy season crop.

Hoeing and weeding. Weeds posses problem only in early stages and should be removed with in 20-25 days after sowing followed by another shallow hoeing as the next weed flush appears.

Staking. The plants being climber should be provided with suitable stake support.

Harvesting. The crop will be ready for harvest in about 60-90 days after sowing depending upon season and cultivar. The fruits attains marketable maturity in about 5-7 days after anthesis. Picking should be done at an interval of 3-4 days and only immature, tender fruits at green stage be picked before they turn yellow and fibrous or stringy.

Grading. Similar to smooth gourd.

Marketing. Similar to smooth gourd.

Storage. The fruits have poor shelf-life and dipping of fruits in BA 50 mg/L improves the shelf-life.

Yield. 12-20 t/ha.

12.12. ASH GOURD

It is an important vegetable in China, India, the Philippines and elsewhere in Asia. Ash gourd or wax gourd or white gourd or winter melon is commonly known as petha or petha kaddu is mainly grown in North India especially in U.P.

Uses. The immature, tender fruits are cooked as vegetable. Both mature and immature fruits of the bland-tasting but easily digested wax gourd are consumed. It is largely used in confectionery for the preparation of petha sweet, soups and pickle.

Nutritive value. Fruit contain high moisture content, low in calories and carbohydrates.

Medicinal value. Ash gourd is considered good for people suffering from nervousness and debility. Seeds are anthelmintic medicine and seed oil is used to counteract the poison of snakebite, to ward-off dandruff and a variety of other ailments.

Origin. It is supposed to have originated from south-eastern Asia, Japan and Java.

Taxonomy. A member of family *Cucurbitaceae,* genus *Benincasa* and species *hispida.* The fruits are round and oblong and size varies from 2-10 kg depending on cultivar.

Cultivars. Pusa Hybrid No.l, CO-1, CO-2, Local cultivars.

Climate. It needs a long, warm and humid climate but sensitive to frost and can be grown in mild weather. Optimum temperature range is 24-30°C is good and short days, low night temperature and humid climate are good for production of female flowers.

Soil. All types of soils are good for ash gourd but sandy loam soils with high organic matter and optimum soil pH 6-7 are considered best.

Seed rate. 5-7 kg/ha.

Sowing time. North India — summer crop — February-March.
Other parts of India — summer crop — December-January.
Rainy season crop — June-July.
Hilly areas — April-May.

Sowing/planting. It is sown on ridges or furrows or hills/pits and in river beds in trenches 2-3 seeds are sown on both sides of raised beds or each hill/pit.

Spacing. 1.5-2.5 × 6.0-1.20 m between rows and hill to hill.

Manure and fertilizer. 25 t FYM, 100 kg N, 50 kg each of P_2O_5 and K_2O/ha should be applied and N in 3 splits.

Irrigation. Frequent irrigation is required during vegetative phase of the crop. Summer crop may be irrigated at an interval of 7-8 days while the rainy season crop may not need any irrigation.

Hoeing and weeding. 2-4 hand weeding may be done to keep the field free of the weeds.

Harvesting. The fruits at full maturity have white waxy surface and should be harvested as immature fruits have a poor storage quality.

Grading. May be done on the basis of cultivar and size of fruit etc.

Marketing. The fruits can be transported to long distance markets in trucks and in local market in tractor trolleys.

Storage. The fruits have a good storage quality and can be stored for many days under normal conditions.

Yield. 10-15 t/ha.

12.13. SNAKE GOURD

The snake gourd is a very common vegetable in South India and is also grown in North India as a rainy season crop. It is cultivated in humid sub-tropical and tropical areas.

Uses. The fruits are cooked green as vegetable.

Nutritive value. It is a good source of carbohydrates, proteins, vitamins and minerals.

Medicinal value. Fruits taken helps to treat HIV.

Origin. The snake gourd is found growing wild in India and Indian Archipelago is thought to be its place of origin.

Taxonomy. It belong to the family *Cucurbitaceae,* genus *Trichosanthes* and two cultivated species *anguina* and *dioica.* The former is monoecious and the latter is dioecious in nature. The flowers are white and fringed. On the basis of colour, two types of cultivars are available *viz.,* light green with white stripes and dark green with yellowish or pale green stripes.

Cultivars. CO-1, CO-2, PKM-1, MDU-1, APAU Swetha.

Climate. It is a warm season crop and can be grown throughout the year in the south. The crop is generally grown during the rainy season but heavy rains during flowering and fruiting affect the yield. The optimum temperature for normal growth and yield is 25-35°C but cannot tolerate frost.

Soil. Snake gourd grows well in loam soils with pH 6-7. It can be grown in all other soils provided these are well drained. The seeds germinate in 7-10 days.

Seed rate. 5-6 kg/ha.

Sowing time. Summer crop — December-January.

Rainy season crop — June-July.

Sowing/planting. The land is thoroughly prepared by 3-4 ploughings. Seed is sown by dibbling method and 2-3 seeds are sown at each hill/pit and later one or two are left after thinning.

Spacing. Short fruited cultivars—1.5 × 1.5 m.

Long fruited cultivars. —2.5 × 1.5 m between rows and hill/pit.

Manure and fertilizer. Snake gourd respond well to manuring. Each hill/pit s applied with 10 kg of FYM, 100 g of 6 : 12 : 12 fertilizer mixture and mixed with the top soil.

Irrigation. Should be given as and when necessary. No irrigation is needed in rainy season crop.

Hoeing and weeding. Should be done to control the weeds and to make the soil loose and friable.

Staking. The crop is usually staked often trained on a tower made of bamboos or wooden poles or angle iron. Sometimes to have the fruits long and straight, a small weight is tied at the lower end of developing fruit. Staking is not needed for short fruited cultivars.

Harvesting. The full grown fruit should be harvested when they are still green. Delay in harvesting causes the fruits to become unfit for consumption. The crop is quick growing and the tender fruits are ready in 50-60 days depending on the cultivar. The period of harvest lasts for about 40-50 days.

Grading. The fruits should be graded according to the shape, size and colour.

Marketing. Harvested produce may be packed in gunny bags for marketing purpose.

Storage. Fruits can be stored of 7-10 days at 10°C and 60-70 RH.

Yield. Average yield is 10 t/ha.

12.14. POINTED GOURD

Pointed gourd or Parwal is commonly grown in north-eastern and southern states on commercial scale. It is also an important kitchen garden crop. The vines are perennial in nature and male and female flowers are borne on separate plants.

Uses. Immature fruits are boiled, pickled or used in curries and the young shoots and leaves are eaten.

Nutritive value. It is important for its high nutritive and wholesome value.

Medicinal value. Pointed gourd have manifold medicinal uses. It is easily digestible, diuretic and laxative, invigorates heart and brain and is useful in disorders of the circulatory system.

Origin. The West Bengal and Assam area is the primary centre of origin (India).

Taxonomy. It belongs to the family *Cucurbitaceae*, genus *Trichosanthes* and species *dioica.* It is a dioecious perennial vine bearing small fruits of 10-12 cm long.

Four different types. Small round fruits dark green with white stripes. Comparatively longer fruits dark green with white stripes. Long and thick fruits light green without stripes and Tapering fruits green in colour with stripes.

Cultivars. Sel.-1, Sel.-2.

Climate. Thrives best in warm and humid climate.

Soil. As in snake gourd.

Seed rate. Stem cuttings of 60 cm long/hill.

Sowing time. January-February and June-July.

Sowing/planting. It can be propagated by stem and root cuttings and these are prepared from one year fruiting vines of both male and female plants separately 60 cm long. These are planted in sand medium for rooting in October. These become ready in 3 months and are planted in the pits prepared in the main field. The vines die during winter and again sprout in the subsequent spring season for at least 3-4 years. After that the yield goes down and hence replanting has to be done.

Spacing. 2 × 2 m between rows and pit/hill.

Manure and fertilizer. Supplied with lot of organic manure as in snake gourd. 20-25 t FYM, 90 kg N, 60 kg each of P_2O_5 and K_2O/ha should be mixed in the soil in the furrow/pits/ hill prior to planting.

Irrigation. As in snake gourd.

Staking. The vines are trained over towers and exposed to sunlight.

Hoeing and weeding. Same as in snake gourd.

Harvesting. The fruits are harvested at tender stage when the seeds are most immature after about 80-90 days of planting. Picking should be done carefully without damaging the vines.

Grading. Should be done according to type and cultivar.

Marketing. Harvested produce is packed in gunny bags and send to the markets.

Storage. The fruits have poor shelf-life and spray of Malic hydrazide @ 1000 mg/L or Kintin @ 100 mg/L improve the keeping quality of fruit for a week. Fruits can be stored for a week at 10°C and 60-70 RH. Post-harvested dipping of fruits in 1% Salicyclic acid, 4% Citric acid and 10% waxol promote keeping quality of the fruits.

Yield. First year-2 t/ha, second to fourth year-9-10 t/ha.

12.15. ROUND GOURD

Indian gourd or Tinda is a summer crop extensively grown in North India and less important in South India.

Uses. Immature fruits are cooked as vegetable.

Nutritive value. The tender fruits has higher nutritive qualities than most of the other cucurbits.

Medicinal value. Fruits are considered good for cough and improvement of blood circulation.

Origin. It is believed to be Indian origin (Asian sub-tropics).

Taxonomy. It belongs to the family *Cucurbitaceae,* genus *Citrullus,* species *vulgaris* and sub-species *fistulosus.* There are mainly two types under cultivation *viz.,* light green colour and with dark green colour.

Cultivars. Arka Tinda, Punjab Tinda.

Climate. It can be grown under hot and mild climates but warm and dry climate is most suitable having optimum temperature of 27-30°C. Seed fail to germinate at low temperature (18°C).

Soil. It grows best on sandy loam soil which are well drained, rich in organic matter with pH 6-7. It produces a better crop in river beds.

Seed rate. 3.5-7 kg/ha.

Sowing time. North India :

Summer crop —February-March.

Rainy season crop —June-July.

Western India: Summer crop — December-January.

Rainy season crop — July-August.

South India —January-February, June-July.

Hills —May-June.

Sowing/planting. Sown in raised beds or ridged or furrows or hill/pit and 2-3 seeds are sown per spot or hill.

Spacing. 1.5-2.0 × 0.50-0.60 m between rows and hills.

Manure and fertillizer. 20-25 t of FYM.

Irrigation. First irrigation may be given when seeds have started germinating and later irrigation at an interval of 5-7 days in summer and practically no irrigation is required in rainy season crop.

Hoeing and weeding. Frequent weeding should be done in order to check the weeds timely. Nitrofen 21.25 L/ha and Alachlor @ 2,5 L/ha can control the weeds.

Harvesting. Fruits are ready for harvest after 60-90 days after sowing depending upon cultivar and season. The fruits takes about 6-8 days after fruit set to reach edible maturity. Picking should be done fruits are small in size and picking is done at an interval of 3-4 days.

Grading. On the basis of varietal characteristics, the fruits should be graded and marketed.

Marketing. Fruits can be sold in the local market or send to the distant intended markets after packing in baskets or crates or cartons or gunny bags.

Storage. Similar to other cucurbits.

Yield. 10-12 t/ha.

12.16. IVY GOURD

Coccinia or Kundru or tondli or ivy gourd is a typical dioecious species extensively grown in India. It is dioecious perennial vine.

Uses. The immature fruits are of good taste and are used for several preparations. The tender shoots of the plants are also eaten.

Nutritive value. The fruits are good source of protein (1.2%), vitamin A (250 IU/100 g) and vitamin C (28 mg/100 g).

Medicinal value. Its root, stem and leaves are easily digestible, used as medicine for the treatment of skin diseases, bronchitis, diabetes and diuretic. It is laxative, invigorates the heart and brain and is useful for disorders or the circulatory system.

Origin. Tropical Africa.

Taxonomy. A member of family *Cucurbitaceae,* genera *Coccinia* and species *grandis* or *indica, cordifolia.* On the basis of edible quality of tender immature fruits *Coccinia* can be classified into two distinct groups —bitter and sweet. The former are characterised by lobed or deeply dissected leaves and small or large oval or oblong fruits which are green in colour with white blotches. These are totally unfit for consumption cither raw or cooked. The latter generally have five lobed leaves with serrated margin and produce large oblong fruits which are light green in colour with white blotches. In parthenocarpic types, no male plants or flowers can be seen and the fruit set takes place by vegetative parthenocarpy.

Cultivars. Local cultivar 'Padappal'.

Climate. It is a warm season crop and does well in hot and humid climates. Low temperature inhibit the plant growth and in the north, the plant undergo dormancy. In south India because of mild winter, it can bear fruits throughout the year. The optimum temperature range is 20-30°C.

Soil. Coccinia can be grown in all types of soils but loam and silty loam soil rich in humus and well drained are the best.

Seed rate. 1.5-2.0 q cuttings/ha.

Sowing time. It is a semi-perennial crop and lasts for 4-5 years, producing fruits in summer (February planting) and rainy season (July planting).

Sowing/planting. Semi-hard stem cutting of 25-30 cm long, 1.5-2 cm thick are used for planting and the thicker cuttings sprout earlier. These cuttings are planted in a basin of 60 cm diameter hill/pits at a depth of 3 cm. About 10% male plants have to be planted to ensure good fruit set. Some can produce parthenocarpic fruits while some bitter fruits too.

Spacing. 2 × 0.60 m between rows and hills.

Staking. A systematic trellis/braces are erected at about 1.5 m in height to provide support to the weak vines and expose to sunlight.

Manure and fertilizer. 20-25 t FYM, 30-40 kg of N, 40 kg of each P_2O_5 and K_2O/ha should be applied as a basal dose and remaining 30-40 kg N be top dressed in two doses at monthly interval after planting. At least once a year the pits should be manure.

Irrigation. The soil should be kept in its optimum moisture condition by irrigating as and when required.

Hoeing and weeding. The weed should be kept under control by timely hoeing and weeding especially in early states.

Pruning and basin management. When fruiting is over, the vines are pruned. Normally under north Indian conditions the pruning is done twice a year — September and April. The shoots which are of finger thickness are pruned back to two buds. The soil in the basin is removed and left exposed for a week. Later on the basins are manured as per the schedule. In south India, the plants don't go into dormancy because of mild climate and fruiting is throughout the year. However, the peak harvest is only during April-November. During the lean period of harvest the basin is excavated and applied with manures and fertilizers.

Harvesting. Fruiting starts in 70-85 days after planting. In south India, fruiting is round the year while in north India fruiting terminates when the temperature comes down in November.

Grading. The fruits should be graded properly according to variety and market demand.

Marketing. The harvested produce after proper packing in suitable containers should be transported to the markets having great demand and bring premium prices.

Storage. The fruits have good keeping quality and can be stored for 10-15 days under ordinary room conditions.

Yield. A single vine bears 200-250 fruits weighing 3-4 kg and upto 8 kg which works to about 12-15 t/ha.

12.17. CHOW-CHOW

Chow-chow or chayote is also known as mirliton and vegetable pear, is one of the perennial vine crop.

Uses. The fruits before the maturity of seed in tender stage is commonly cooked and the roots which develop into tubers are also eaten. The tender sliced fruits are taken as salad either alone or mixed with other salad food, substitute for summer squash and also for various preparations. All parts of the plant make good fodder. Its plant extract is used for industrial uses like hat and buckets.

Nutritive value. It is probably the richest among the gourds in nutritive value particularly in carbohydrates (6.3%) and calorific value (29 calories/100 g).

Medicinal value. The leaves possessing cardiovascular modifying properties, have been used in herbal medicines for hypertension. Fruits and roots are considered diuretic and seeds are taken for intestinal problems.

Origin. Humid tropical America, Mexico, Guatemala and West Indies.

Taxonomy. It belongs to the family *Cucurbitaceae,* genus *Sechium* and species *edule.* Perennial plant, vine bearing large, pear shaped, light green edible fruit and tuberous roots, A perennial develop large succulent roots over several years. A large sized fruits white to dark-green pear shaped are produced often wrinkled and sometimes with a few spines.

Cultivars. Considerable variations are found to exist in the types under cultivation in size, spininess and fibre content of the fruits. Two distinct types are generally recognised *viz.,* the green fruited-Florida Green and white fruited-Florida White, Monticello White.

Climate. It is a warm season crop and hot and moist climate is favourable for its growth and development. Susceptible to frost and low temperature hindering the growth. Under moderate climates, it can be grown throughout the year and optimum temperature is 18-22°C.

Soil. Chow-chow can be grown in all types of soil but loam and slit loam soils with pH value 5.5-6.5, well drained with sufficient moisture are most suitable for its growing.

Seed rate. Propagation is by planting the whole fruit. The single seed is located near the broad end of the pear shaped fruit. The fruit germinate in 8-10 days.

Sowing time. April-May in hills, June-July in plains of north and south India and eastern states and Bangla Desh round the year preferably July planting is done in July-August.

Sowing/planting. The whole fruit is planted in a specially prepared pits in the field have better tilth in a sloping position broad end little exposed. Planting is done in the pit or basins of 45-60 cm diameter. Sometimes the seedlings raised in pits or poly-tubes are also planted.

Spacing. 1.8 × 2.4 m between rows and pit/basin.

Manure and fertilizer. The pits or basins are well manured with 10-15 kg of FYM and 100 g of N:P:K mixture basin/pit.

Irrigation. Irrigate the plants timely.

Hoeing and weeding. Should be done as and when necessary.

Trellis system. Pandal or trellis can be erected for the vines to trail over at a height of 2 m in homestead gardens, the vines are allowed to climb on small trees.

Harvesting. The vines start flowering in about 3-4 months and production is continuous. The fruits attaining the optimum size and tender are harvested carefully without injuring the vines.

Grading. The fruits are graded according to the ISI standards.

Marketing. The fruits are transported in baskets or gunny bags to the distant markets.

Storage. The fruit has good storage life and can be stored for 10-15 days or more at 0°C and 60-70% RH.

Yield. A well grown plant of about one year yields 500-600 fruits per year and the fruit weighs 200-450 g. The total yield is 25-35 t/ha.

Crop protection

Diseases/Insect pests	*Symptoms*	*Control*
Diseases		
Powdery Mildew (*Erysiphe cichoracearum, Spherotheca fuligines*)	Fungus forms white floury patches on leaves, stem and succulent parts. Fruits remain poor in quality and flavour.	Spray Karathane or Morestin 2 ml/L water 2-3 times at 10 days interval. Nimrod @ 0.05% or Saprol @ 0.1% or Benlate @ 0.05%.
Downy mildew (*Pseudoperono spora cubensis*)	Purplish spots appear on lower surface yellow on upper surface of leaves, fruits do not mature and attain right flavour.	Spray Dithane-Z-78 or Dithane M-45 or Blitox @ 0.2% once a week.
Anthracnose *(Collectotrichum orbiculare)*	Lesion on leaves and fruits, light and dark brown spots on plant parts.	Spray Dithane M-45 or Hexane @ 2.5 g/L at 15 days interval. Crop rotation with non-cucurbit.
Fusarium root rot (*F. solani & F. cucurbitae*)	Sudden wilt, stem base become dark brown, soften, fruit rot.	Seed treatment with hot water at 55°C for 15 minutes followed by Mercuric chloride (1 : 1000) treatment. Crop rotation.
Mosaic	Mottling of leaves with rough surface, green colour lacking, yellowing.	Grow resistant cultivar, Spray Metacid-50 EC or Metasystox-25 EC @ 1 ml/L of water to control the vector.
Insect-pests		
Red pumpkin beetle *(Aolacophora favecallis)*	Larvae and adult eat young leaves and flowers. Grubs bore into the root and fruits, lie on the ground and pupates in soil.	Spray Malathion 50 EC or Dichlorovos @ 2 ml/L of water and repeat.
Fruit fly *(Dacus cucurbitae)*	Female flies puncture soft and tender fruits, lay eggs below epidermis after hatching produce maggots, bore into the fruit and feed one the pulp result fruit rot and deformation.	Spray poison bait-50 g sugar/gur, 10 ml Malathion in 5 L of water. Bury the infested fruits deep in soil.
Mites	Suck sap from the tender foliage cause white specks and patches on leaves affect growth and vitality of plants.	Spray Malathion 50 EC 0,05% and repeat after 10 days.
Snake gourd Semilooper *(Plusia pepouis)*	Cut the leaf edge, make a nest, popate inside the nest.	Follow early sowing. Clean cultivation. Spray Carbaryl 0.2% or Endosulphan 0.05% and repeat.
Aphids *(Aphis* spp.)	Suck leaf sap and tender parts, leaves and vines turn yellow, plant loose vigour and yield.	Spray Malathion 50 EC 0.1% or Rogor 0.1-0.2% and repeat.
Scales and mealy bugs	Suck sap from the tender parts.	Spray Rogor @ 1 ml/L of water and repeat.
Nematodes *(Meliodogyne incognita acrita)*	Stunted plants and poor growth.	Green manuring with Tagetes or Xanthiuar leaf powder. Spray with Nemagon.

CHAPTER

13

SWEET POTATO

Sweet potato poor people's most important food through increased consumption by all sub-strata of the society, cheapest source of carbohydrates and colour, having the potentiality of wider adaptability under varying agro-climatic conditions. It is important crop of tropical and sub-tropical regions. About 124 million tonnes of sweet potatoes are produced annually in the world. In India, it is grown almost all over the country producing about 1.2 million tonnes with average yield of 8 tonnes per hectare.

Uses. Sweet potato is used as raw, cooked and for manufacturing of starch and alcohol. It is consumed after boiling. Tender leaves of sweet potato are used as vegetable. The plant parts (vines) is a suitable cattle feed.

Nutritive value. The tubers are rich source of carbohydrates and the starch content in tubers varies from 8-29 per cent. The tubers contain many vitamins in appreciable quantities. It is almost fat free and thus cholesterol free. It is fairly rich in dietary fibres which play a significant role in human health. It also contain protein, reducing sugars and carotene. The orange and yellow fleshed cultivars are rich in vitamin A.

Medicinal value. Vines and tubers contain fungicidal and bactericidal substances. Root is considered laxative. Tender shoots are used in poultices and leaves as a maturative cataplasm. A paste of root or leaves is used as an application to scorpian bites.

Origin. The sweet potato is believed to have originated in Central and South America.

Taxonomy. The sweet potato belongs to the family *Convolvulaceae* or *morning glory* family, genus *Ipomoea* and species *batatas.* It is a herbaceous trailing perennial. But cultivated as a annual. The adventitious roots developing from stem cuttings modify into tubers by the accumulation of starch.

Cultivars. R.S.-5, Cross-4, Kamlegh, V-35, S-30, Pusa Safed, Pusa Lal and Pusa Sundheri, Co-1, Co-2, Co-3, H-41, H-42, Sree Nandini, Sree Vardhini, Varsa, VL Sakarkand-

6, Rajendra Sakarkand-35, Samrat, Kiran, Gouri, Bhuban Sakarkand. Orange-fleshed-Sree Ratna.

Climate. It is a warm season crop widely grown in tropical, sub-tropical and warm temperate areas throughout the world from 40°N to 32°S but susceptible to frost. For optimum growth, a temperature of 34°C or more with abundant sunlight and warm nights as the cold nights and cloudy weather are not favourable for the growth. It need at least four months of warm growing season. Short days will promote root development.

Soil. It can be cultivated on a variety of soils, sandy or sandy loam with high organic matter content, friable and good drainage is ideal. Heavy clay, saline and alkaline soils are not suitable. The best pH range of the soil for its growth is 5.0 to 6.8.

Land preparation. The land is ploughed 2-3 times up to 15 cm depth as deep ploughing not required as the roots set at deeper level are long and slender. The field is divided into small beds or ridges and furrows are prepared. Ridge planting is advocated for rainy season crop while furrow method is suitable in water scarcity areas.

Seed rate. The seed material should be reasonably clean, healthy, firm and should conform to the characteristics of the variety. At least five quintals of tubers are required to produce sufficient vines for planting one hectare.

Sowing time. Season of planting varies according to the climate prevailing in the particular place. Under North Indian conditions, planting is done during February-March, June-July and August. In central India, planting is done in October-November. But in South India, planting is done during September-October, November-December and June-July. In Punjab sweet potato is raised by planting cuttings in April-July. Vines from the previous crop can be made into cuttings for planting during March-April. If the vines are raised from tubers, the planting is done in May-July during 15th October, the optimum time for planting.

Sowing/planting. The tubers are sown in the well prepared land and germinate after a month. Tubers with diameter of 3-5 cm are most suitable for planting. For raising planting material, vines from the summer crop are planted in the well drained uplands with the onset of monsoon. 1/15 to 1/20 ha of nursery will produce about 20-25 vines in about 80 days which will be sufficient for one hectare area/plantation. Terminal and middle portions of the vines are selected and basal portions are rejected for the preparation of cuttings. Planting of 40-50 cm long vines spaced at 30 × 30 cm apart increase tuber yields by more than 12%. Half of the vine length should be burried for better results. In some places, the middle portion of the cuttings is buried deep into the soil leaving both the ends exposed. Planting of vine cuttings taken from the top portion, yields more (up to 15%) than the middle or basal parts. In South India, 10 cm cutting is buried leaving the top exposed.

Sometimes the 'sprouts' or 'draws' from the tubers which have been buried 5-10 cm deep in the well prepared soil are also used for planting after clipping 40-45 days after the appearance and planted in the secondary nursery for further growth.

Spacing. Cuttings of 30-45 cm long with 5-7 nodes are generally planted on ridges 30-45 cm apart and the distance between the cuttings is also 30-45 cm. In south India a spacing of 60 × 20 cm is followed.

Manure and fertilizer. The crop should be fertilized with A basal dressing of 20 kg N, 80 kg P_2O_5 and 120 kg of K_2O/ha at the time of land preparation should be mixed with the soil. In the case of unsatisfactory growth of crop, it should be top dressed with 15-20 kg N/ha after about 40 days of planting.

Irrigation. The first irrigation is applied soon after planting and the subsequent irrigation after every 7-10 days in the early stages and every 12-15 days later on depending on the rains. In south India, the crop is raised as rainfed crop and the water requirement of the crop is 75 ha cm.

Hoeing and weeding. Before the vines spread and cover the field, all the weeds should be removed by proper hoeing and weeding after 20-30 days after planting.

Earthing-up. At least two earthing-up operations are necessary.

Harvesting. The tubers are harvested when the leaves turn pale and later slight yellow after 130-180 days depending on the cultivar in October-November (North India). When surface of the tuber is cut and exposed to the air and if it dries up soon, is an indication of maturity while the immature ones will remain moist and turn dark in colour. Hence, harvesting should be done at the correct stage of maturity. Tubers if harvested early may cause reduction in yield. However, considerable delay in harvest may also cause serious losses in yield. The tubers are dug out with a spade or plough taking care not to cut them. They are gathered and taken to the shade soon after harvest.

Curing. The curing process helps in the formation of the protective layer called callus on the injured portions. The curing is better at a temperature of 80°C and relative humidity of 30-40 per cent. Normally curing can be done under ordinary temperature or dried in the sun for about a week.

Grading. After harvesting, the tubers are cleaned, graded and should be properly cured.

Marketing. These are then stored in a safe place or send to the market.

Storage. The optimum temperature and humidity for tuber storage are 15°C and 85-90 per cent. Generally red skinned cultivars store better than white-skinned tubers. The best storage is possible in store houses provided with controlled temperature and humidity. The tubers can also be stored in pits covered with dry grass for 2-3 months but the damage due to insects, diseases, hardening, drying and sprouting is considerable.

Yield. The tuber yield varies from 20-30 t/ha and about 20/ha of vines are also obtained which can be used as a cattle feed.

Crop protection

Diseases/insect-pests	*Symptoms*	*Control*
Diseases		
Stem rot or wilt *(Fusarium oxysporium* or *F. batatas* or *F. hyperoxysporum)*	Leaves become dull in colour then yellow followed by wilting of vines. Stem get blackened inside and the roots develop a black ring.	Sow healthy cuttings. Follow suitable rotation Spray Bavistin 0.2%.
Black rot (C*eratastamella fimbriata*)	Dark brown and black spots develop on sweet potato and black cankers are formed on the underground parts of stem.	Same as for stem rot.
Insect-pests		
Sweet potato weevil *(Cylas formicarius elegantulus)*	Larvae of the weevil feed on the vine or the tuber.	Follow crop rotation. Remove alternate host. Spray with Fenthion (Labeycid) or Fenitrothion or Monocrotophos @ 0.05% and repeat. Dust the field with Dialdrin @ 2-25% at the base of the vine.
Stem borer caterpiller	The caterpillar bore into the stem.	Same as in sweet potato weevil.

CHAPTER

14

BHINDI

Bhindi or Okra or ladies finger is one of the most important warm season fruit vegetables grown in the tropical and sub-tropical areas. It is grown mainly for its tender non-fibrous edible pods extensively through India and is known as Ladyfinger. Okra is very popular among the farmers because of ease in growing and have wider adaptability range. In India, it occupies about 4.30 lakh hectares of land with an annual production of 40.31 lakh tonnes and productivity of 9.37 t/ha. Because of its high nutritive value and prolonged shelf-life as compared to others, okra has captured a prominent position among the export oriented vegetable crops and exported to middle-east countries, Western Europe and USA. It has a vast potential as one of the foreign exchange earner crops.

Uses. Its immature unripe fruits are popular, tasty, gelatinous, used in various ways like as cooked vegetable, boiled or fried, soups, *sambhar,* gravies stews in meat, frozen, canned and dehydrated forms. Sometimes leaves, buds and flowers may be consumed. It can be preserved in brine for future use. Fruits are sliced and sun dried for off-season use. Dried seeds provide oil, protein, vegetable curd and a coffee substitute after roasting and grinding. Roots and stems are used for clarification of sugarcane juice before it is converted into jaggery and brown sugar and also in the paper/textile industry.

Nutritive Value. Okra has a good nutritional value. The green tender fruits are rich in vitamins (A, B & C), proteins, calcium, iron, magnesium and other minerals. The extremely high calcium content is particularly valuable. It also contains iodine. The pods are rich in pectin and mucilage. Tender pods are richer in ascorbic acid than mature pods.

Medicinal value. The fruits also have medicinal values. Immature capsules are emollient, demulcent and diuretic. Useful against fevers, catarrhal attack, genitro-urinary disorders, spermatorrhoea, gonorrhoe and chronic dysentery. Mucilage is aphrodisiac in effect. Vapours from hot decoction are inhaled for inhibited throat, troublesome cough of phthisis. Root infusion is used in syphilis. Its mucilage in the form of soup is beneficial for the patients of chronic dysentery. Seeds are stimulant, cordial and antispasmodic.

Origin. Okra is known to be originated from Ethopia. Some recent reports cite it to be of African or Asiatic origin.

Taxonomy. Okra belonging to the family *Malvaceae,* genus *Abelmoschus* and species *esculentus.* The other two species grown commercially are *A. manihot* (L) Medikus and *A. moschatus* Medikus.

Cultivars. Pusa Sawani, Harbhajan, Perkins Long Green, S-l, A-4, MDU-1, CO-1, Punjab Padmini, Pusa Makhmali, Vaishali Vadhu, Belt's five, EMS-8, G-2 Selection-7, Selection-9, Selection-12, Lucknow Dwarf, Long Green, Velvet Green, Smooth Velvet, Long White, Red Wonder, Samalkota, Varsha Uphar, Gujarat Bhinda-1, MDU-1, Bhindi Gauray.

Hybrid. DVR-1, CO-2, CO-3 (Hybrid-8), GOH-2, GOH-3, Hybrid-6, Sheela-101, Lam Hybrid, KHR-OH-4.

Resistant cultivar. Parbhani Kranti, Arka Anamika (Selection-10), Arka Abhay (Selection-4), P-7, P-8, Hisar Unnat.

Climate. Okra requires a long and warm season and thrives well during warm humid season although it grows fairly well in the hottest summer. Okra is a tender plant susceptible to frost and continuous cold spell. It is a predominantly a tropical crop but it can be grown summer in the temperate zone, preferably where the average temperature ranges from 18-35°C. Seed germination is best at temperature between 25 and 30°C and fails below 20°C. When the day temperature exceeds 42°C, there is flower drop.

Soil. Okra can be grown on a wide range of soils *i.e.* sandy to clay soils which are well manured and supplemented with organic matter and impeded drainage. However, loose, friable and well manured soils are the best. It is slightly tolerant to acidity and the optimum soil pH range between 6-6.8.

Land preparation. The field should be well prepared with 2-3 ploughings and proper drainage system. The field is divided into beds of suitable size according to season and source of irrigation Ridges and furrow method is the most common. During rainy season they are sown on ridges and during summer in furrows.

Seed rate. Seed rate depends upon the season, method of sowing and the cultivar, etc. and there are about 14-15 seeds in a gram.

For summer crop — 8-10 kg/ha.

Rainy season crop — 14-16 kg/ha.

Sowing time. In south India (also parts of Maharashtra and Gujarat) okra is cultivated throughout the year. The main seasons are summer, rainy seasons and during October-February because of mild winter. In the northern plains usually two crops *i.e.* spring-summer (mid-February-early March, where there is danger of frost as in western U.P., Delhi, Punjab and Rajasthan, while in Assam, West Bengal, Orissa and Bihar, it is sown in late January or early February) and rainy season (May-July) crops are grown. In hills, sowing is done in April-July.

Spacing. In South India : summer crop — 60 × 30 cm

In Kerala : rainy season crop — 60 × 45 cm

In Tamil Nadu — 60 × 20 cm

Bangalore conditions — 50 × 15 cm

In North India — summer crop — 30 × 15 cm

Rainy season crop — 45-60 × 25-30 cm

In Himachal Pradesh — 45 × 15 cm between rows and plants.

Sowing method. Okra is a direct sown crop. Broadcasting, line sowing and dibbling methods are followed in various parts of the country. Seeds are sown in rows either in flat beds or on ridges or on furrows depending upon soil type, season and irrigation facilities available. Okra has hard seed coat, therefore, it is advisable to soak the seed for about 24 hours before sowing.

Manure and fertilizer. Depending on soil type and its fertility status, the quantity and method of application vary. In Himachal Pradesh, the recommended dose is 20 t FYM, 75 kg N, 50 kg each of P_2O_5 and K_2O. Whole quantity of FYM, P_2O_5, K_2O and half N should be applied at the time of field preparation and the remaining dose of N in two equal splits at one month interval after sowing. In South India, basal dressing of 50 kg N (110 kg of urea)/ha, 50 kg of P_2O_5 (300 kg of Super phosphate)/ha and 50 kg of K_2O (Muriate of potash)/ha is recommended. The fertilizer should be mixed and applied along one side of the ridges as band 10 cm away from the plants and mixed with soil.

Crop rotation. Okra is also sown inter-cropped with colocasia or around cotton, chillies, turmeric, ginger and banana fields.

Irrigation. The spring-summer crop needs irrigation after every 4-5 days but frequency of irrigation in the rainy-season crop depends upon the rains and field moisture in every 10-14 days.

Hoeing and weeding. The spring-summer crop should be given 2-3 hoeing and weeding but the rainy season crop may need frequent weeding. For commercial large-scale planting, pre-planting application of Basalin @ 2.5 L/ha a day after sowing or Lasso @ 5 L/ha a day after sowing have been recommended to check weeds. The weedicide-treated fields may, however, need one weeding 60 days after sowing.

Earthing-up. The plants are earthed-up at the time of fertilizer top-dressing. The second earthing-up is given 65 days after sowing.

Mulching. Under dry farming, mulching is beneficial for okra cultivation. Polythene is the best mulch followed by sawdust and straw. Mulching maintain optimum moisture, check weeds and increase pod production.

Harvesting. The crop is ready for harvest 45 days after sowing depending on cultivar, season and management practices. The best time of harvesting is 6-7 days after opening the flower. Usually the tender, young pods free from fibre should be harvested on every alternate days regularly. Pods increase its length rapidly in hot weather than in cold season, and during night. So it is better to harvest in the morning. A good crop gives 23 pickings, on an average of 15-16 pickings. The growth and bearing of the plant are adversely affected if the fruits are not harvested when tender young. The fruits are removed from the plants either by breaking or cutting from the stalk. Picking can be done as long as the fruit stalks break easily on banding the fruit. Pickers should bear gloves or wash their hands to remove the irritating or stinging effect while handling because of some bristles on the fruit.

Grading and packing. After harvesting, the fruits should be kept in shade and care should be taken to avoid bruises and injury. Damaged and insect bored fruits should be separated from the healthy ones. They should be handled so carefully that there may no rubbing or pressing which turns the bruised edges of the pods black. This will spoil them and lower their market value. Okra is graded according to size, maturity and general appearance. If they are to be sent to the distant markets, pack them in baskets or gunny bags. In case of export, fruits are packed in cartons after proper grading. If harvesting is done in the evening, water should be sprinkled on fruits during night to keep them cool and afresh for the next morning.

Marketing. The fresh fruits should be disposed-off as soon as possible after harvest. The produce need to be handled carefully in transit and while marketing so that it reaches afresh to the consumers. The small and tender fruits are sold at a premium.

Storage. Okra pods can be commercially stored at a temperature below 10°C at 85-95 per cent relative humidity for two weeks. Okra fruits deteriorate fast because of very high respiratory activity (120 mg CO_2/kg/hr). Polyethylene 400 gauze packaging provide modified atmosphere and consequently reduce decay, softening and loss of solids in okra and can be stored for several days in the refrigerator.

Yield. High yielding cultivars produce an yield of 100-200 q/ha. The spring-summer crop gives green fruits of 100-120 q/ha while the rainy season crop 150-200 q/ha.

Crop protection

Diseases/insect-pests	*Symptoms*	*Control*
Diseases		
Yellow vein mosaic virus	Veinal chlorosis and whole plant turns yellow including fruits.	Grow resistant varieties. Rogue out diseased plants. Remove collateral hosts. Control vector (white fly or jassid) by spraying 0.05% Thiodan or Endocil/Hildan/Malathion Don't use infested crop for seed production.
Powdery mildew	Blotches of greyish white powdery coating on the lower surface of the leaves, turn yellow and drop-off.	Dust fine sulphur or spray wettable sulphur @ 0.2% or Sulphex (0.2%) or Karathane (0.1%) and repeat.
Cercospora leaf spot	Shooty to dark olivaceous mould on the lower surface of leaves. Affected leaves roll, wilt and fall dwon.	Grow resistant cultivar. Spray Bordeaux Mixture (1%) or Dithane M-45 (0.2%).
Damping-off (*Pythium, Rhizoctonia & Fusarium)*	As in tomato.	Seed treatment with Capital or Thiram (0.2%).
Fruit rots (*Pythium aphanidermatum* &	Fruits rots occur when fruits are mishandled, bruised, packed tightly	Handle fruits properly in store and transit.

Phytophthora palmivora)	and transported or stored in humid and warm conditions.	
Fusarium wilt (*F. oxysporum*)	Yellowing and stunting of the plant followed by wilting and rolling.	Grow resistant cultivars. Suitable crop rotation. Removal of roots of diseased plants. Deep ploughing during summer. Seed treatment with Ziram (0.3%) at 45°C for half an hr.
Insect-pests		
Fruit and shoot borer	Caterpillars bore into the growing shoot where the buds appear and later enter into the fruit and damage them.	Spray Endosulphan (Thiodan) or Malathion 50 EC @ 0.05% or Carbaryl @ 0.1%.
Blister beetle	Beetles feed on the vital parts of flowers resulting in poor fruit set.	Spray Carbaryl 0.1% or Malathion 50 EC 0.05%.
Jassids (Leaf hopper)	They such sap from underside of the leaves, the leaves curl upward along the tips and margins, turn yellow and finally drp up.	Spray Malathion 50 EC or Cythion @ 0.05%.
Leaf roller	Conical leaf rools hanging on leaves, caterpillars feed on it and the entire lamina is cut.	Regular collection and destruction of leaf rolls. Spray Sevin @ 0.1% (contract insecticide).

CHAPTER
15

CORM VEGETABLES

15.1. ARVI (COLOCASIA)

Colocasia is grown in sub-tropical and tropical parts of the country under different names like taro, eddos, pokchoi, gabi, dasheen, Cocoyam, arvi, etc. and arvi might be considered as poor man's vegetable with cheaper price, low inputs requirements with high benefits. Arvi can be successfully grown by small and marginal farmers as a cash crop because of its wider adaptability to boost their income.

Uses. Its all parts *i.e.,* corm, young petioles and enlarged leaves are used in various ways as food because of its delicious taste, flavour and nutritive value. It is a subsidiary food after roasting, baking or boiling. The corms make good, slices, *achu,* chips, *esubaka, nia sese* and taro meal. Almost all the cultivars are free from acridity but some have and which is due to needle like crystals of calcium oxalate. The acridity is destroyed by cooking. In Hawai and other countries, a fermented product is prepared from taro and is very popular. Arvi is also fed to the animals.

Nutritive value. All plant parts contain a good amount of nutrients (corms are rich in) carbohydrates, protein, vitamin C, B-carotene and minerals-calcium, iron and phosphorus.

Medicinal value. Colocasia is recommended for gastric patients and taro flour is a good baby food. It has manifold medicinal and industrial properties. It is used as an effective abortijacient in Brazil, as stypton and poulices in Hawai for tuberculosis ulcers, as an anthelmintic and against jungal injection (thrush) in combination with coconut meal.

Origin. It has been originated in the tropics of the old world.

Taxonomy. Colocasia belongs to the family *Araceae,* genus *Colocasia* and species *esculenta.* A herbaceous plant of which the leaf blades are very large and petiole long. The underground stem consists of one or more large edible central corms and a large number of cormels.

Cultivars. Sar Kachu Bengali, Banda, Panchmukhi, Ashtamukhi, Sahasrmukhi, Kovvur, Sree Rashmi, Sree Pallavi, CO-1 (CE-16), Kaka Kachu, White Gaurya, Kimoor and Local cultivars.

Climate. It is warm season crop and is grown as a summer as well as rainy season crop. The annual rainfall required is 100-500 cm and the optimum temperature range is 21-25°C.

Soil. Colocasia can be grown in light to heavy soils having abundant supply of water, friable, rich in organic matter, better drainage with soil pH value of 5.5-7.0.

Seed rate. The seed rate is 7.5 to 10 q/ha depending upon corm size and other factors. The size of seed corm should be 4-6 × 2.5-3.5 cm and corresponding weight 20-40 g. The seed material should be reasonably clean, healthy, firm and should conform to the characteristics of the variety.

Sowing time. Plains : Summer crop —February-March.

Rainy season crop —June-July.

Low-hills — February-March and June.

Mid-hills — March-April.

High-hills — April-May.

Planting. Field is prepared thoroughly into a better tilth. For sowing ridges or furrows or beds are prepared. The cormels are planted by following optimum spacing and only selected ones are used for planting. Always use healthy, disease free, 2-3 buds/eyes in each cormel weighing each 20-25 g. Before sowing, treat the cormels with 0.25% Aresan or 0.5% Agallol for 10-15 minutes and dry in shade.

Spacing. Sprouted corms/cormels are sown in rows 45 cm apart and 30 cm with in the row and 10-15 cm deep in furrows.

Manure and fertilizer. Apply 25 t of FYM, 90 kg N, 60 kg P_2O_5 and 30 kg K_2O/ha. Apply FYM, P_2O_5, K_2O and half dose of N at time of field preparation and rest N should be applied in three equal splits *i.e.,* at the time of earthing-up and then 30 and 60 days after first application.

Mulching. Optimum moisture and mulching (as in case of ginger) condition will help in proper germination.

Irrigation. Colocasia needs adequate soil moisture at the time of planting for the cormel sprouting and development. During summer irrigation should be done at weekly intervals while in monsoon it may be done at fortnightly interval.

Hoeing and weeding. Weeding should be done periodically to promote growth and development of the corms and cormels.

Earthing-up. One or two earthing-up operation are done to provide adequate space in the soil for the formation of corms. If a large number of shoots comes out from each plant, pruning is practised, leaving one or two main shoots.

Harvesting. Plant leaves start yellowing and dry up indicate its corms maturity. The crop is ready after 4-5 months depending on variety and other factors. The corms are taken out by digging carefully without any injury with hoe or spade. The whole plant is pulled out and the corms are separated. These are kept under shade for proper curing for 10-15 days and then stored in trenches/pits or in stores. In some places, the crop is left as such in the field and covered with grass or plant leaves till it is harvested.

Grading. The corms should be trimmed, cleaned and graded on the basis of shape and size according to the cultivars into A, B, and C grades.

Marketing. Marketing will depend on the stage of harvest, normally immature corms are harvested when higher prices prevail in the market or there is a demand. Mature corms under proper grade should be marketed keeping in view the demand and supply and follow a suitable marketing channel.

Storage. The mature corms can be stored for 5-6 months in bags, baskets, heaps on the floor, spreading on the floor in a layer, storing in pits and sarkanda pyramid (kupi). The last two methods are safe and best for storing the corms.

Yield. The corm yield varies with the maturity stage and the average yield is 20-25 t/ha.

15.2. YAMS

Yams are under utilized tuber crops cultivated in the tropics. It is a tuber bearing climber and the underground stem (tubers) which bulk as the starch accumulation, normally single with variation in size and shape.

Uses. Yam tuber is consumed after roasting, boiling or with other vegetables. It is also used for the preparation of chips, flakes and flour.

Nutritive value. Tubers are rich source of starch.

Medicinal value. Betagenin obtained from yam is a promising material used in the treatment of rheumatiod, arthritis and rheumatic fever. Corms are aprient, carminative and expectorant and in fresh form acrid stimulant, increase appetite and taste, as an irritant to treat acute rheumatism, dysentery, piles and haemorrhoids, roots are useful to cure ophthalmiam, boils and an irritant.

Origin. Probable origin of yam is south-east Asia.

Taxonomy. Member of family *Dioscoreaceae,* genus *Dioscorea* and species *esculenta, alata, rotundata, opposita* and *japonica.* Deciduous perennial plant.

Cultivars. *Dioscorea alata* — Sree Keerthi, Sree Roopa, CO-1,

Dioscorea esculenta — Sree Latha,

D. rotundata — Sree Subhra, Sree Priya.

Climate. Widely grown throughout the tropics under both rainfed forest and sarvanna conditions where there is combination of adequate moisture and good drainage. The optimum temperature is 30-35°C and susceptible to frost. *D. opposita* and *D. japonica* can be cultivated even in a warm temperate climate.

Soil. A deep, rich, fertile well drained loam with a pH range of 6-6.5 is ideal for the development of tubers. In heavy soils the tubers are liable to rot and in poor soils low yields.

Seed rate. Mainly propagated vegetatively and tuber pieces or small whole tubers @ 20-35 q/ha are used. Tuber weighing 200-250 g is ideal for optimum production.

Sowing time. March-May.

Planting. The field is ploughed deeply 3-4 times and pits of 45 cubic cm are prepared. The pits are filled with FYM and mixed with the top soil and then mounds/hills or ridges are formed. The tubers are cut into pieces of 200 g, dipped in cowdung slurry + 0.2% Dithane M-45 and dried in shade. In case of lesser yam the whole tuber can be sown. The pieces or tuber should be planted in the centre of the mounds at a depth of 15-20 cm.

Spacing. Greater yam — 90 × 90 cm and Lesser yam — 75 × 75 cm between rows and plants.

Manure and fertilizer. Apply 15-20 t FYM, 60 kg each of N, P_2O_5 and K_2O as a basal dose before planting and mixed thoroughly. Top dressing should be done on 40th day of planting with 60 kg of N/ha.

Irrigation. Irrigate the mounds soon after planting through channels and subsequent irrigation are done once a week or 10 days depending on the soil moisture and rains.

Mulching. Immediately after planting is beneficial for increasing the tuber yield. Mulching provides protection from excessive temperature, conserve soil moisture, ensure quick and uniform sprouting of tubers and suppression of weeds. Yam take about one month for sprouting and another two months to develop sufficient cover.

Hoeing and weeding. Two intercultural operations would be enough to check the weed growth. The first weeding should be done one week after 50% sprouting and second one after a month.

Staking. The vine have to be staked on strong bamboo or wood or iron poles of 2 m height so that the leaves are exposed to the sunlight. Tuber yield from staked plants are generally higher than those of non-staked plants.

Harvesting. Greater yam is ready to harvest in 8-9 months and lesser yam in 7-9 months after planting. The maturity of the tubers is indicated by yellowing and drying of leaves. The tubers are dug out without causing injury.

Grading. Similar to colocasia.

Marketing. Similar to colocasia.

Storage. Similar to colocasia.

Yield. Greater yam — 20-40 t/ha.

Lesser yam — 20-25 t/ha.

White yam — 30-40 t/ha.

15.3. TAPIOCA

The cultivation of cassava or manioc or yucca is important because of its role in the tropical farming system, high carbohydrate yields per unit land and labour, adaptation to poor soils and water stress, compatibility with a variety of crops in association, an intermediate harvestability and tolerance to pests and diseases.

Uses. The tubers are consumed normally boiled or baked, the former are eaten with fish curry or side dish with rice. Tubers are taken after frying and fed to cattle. Leaves are also used as a base in making sauce and soups. It also serves as base for starch industry. The starch extracted from tubers is used to prepare glucose, vermicilli and other products.

Nutritive value. Tapioca is a rich source of carbohydrates.

Medicinal value. Some species have medicinal properties and their extracts are used for treatment of arthritis.

Origin. It is originated from tropical America.

Taxonomy. It belongs to the family *Euphorbiceae,* genus *Manihot* species *esculenta.* Cassava is a perennial woody shrub growing to a height of 3-4 m erect but grown as annual with branched stem having palmately leaves. There are two types bitter and sweet, the former produces higher yield and more commonly cultivated. The tuber colour varies from white to reddish white or brown. Most cultivars contain a poisonous glucoside, which is eliminated by boiling.

Cultivars. The important are M-4, Kalikalan, H-97, H-165, H-226, Sree Visakham (H-1687), Sree Sahya (H-2304), Sree Prakash (S- 856), CO-1 (ME-7), CO-2 (ME-167), CO-3 (ME-120-1), MVD-1 (S-2371).

There are many cultivars from Indonesia, Thailand, Philippines, China, Colombia and Nigeria considered for cultivation.

Climate. It can be grown from sea level upto an altitude of 200 m and humid regions to semi-arid regions having optimum temperature range of 25-29°C. It is the most drought tolerant species.

Soil. It can be grown on a wide range of soils in the tropic and sub-tropics. It is well adapted to low fertility and acidic soils but cannot tolerate water logging, high salt concentration and alkalinity. Optimum pH range is 5.5-7.0.

Seed rate. Propagated from the true seed or vegetatively from stem cuttings called stakes or setts. Each stem cutting should be 15-20 cm long and 10000 stakes or setts are sufficient per hectare.

Planting material. At the time of cassava harvest, mature, healthy and vigorous stems are selected and stored under shade as next season's planting material. Stems kept in vertical position with leaves intact sprout better.

Sowing time. Rainfed crop — May-June and September-October.

Irrigated crop — August or any part of the year.

April-May in the south India.

Planting. Field is ploughed 3-4 times into a better tilth. The setts should be prepared from the middle portion of the stem of fully matured plants free from cassava mosaic virus leaving the basal top portions. Each sett should have 5-6 buds. The basal ends of the setts can be dipped in a solution of azospirillum culture (prepared by mixing 30 g of culture per L of water) for 20 minutes and then planted with correct polarity.

Spacing. Between rows and plants 90 × 90 cm for branching type and 75 × 75 cm for non-branching type cultivars are followed.

Manure and fertilizer. 10-15 t of FYM and NPK mixture of 100 : 50 : 100 kg/ha should be applied.

Inter-cropping. It being a duration crop should always be cultivated with a companion cropping like multiplier onion, or any other short duration crop, which gives an additional income to the farmers.

Thinning. Twenty days after planting more number of spouts come up and they should be thinned to leave only two shoots. This helps to facilitate the regulation of top growth and encourage tuber bulking.

Irrigation. Normally grown as rainfed crop but in South India it is raised as a irrigated crop and the irrigation is scheduled depends upon the distribution of rainfall. Normally once in 10-15 days.

Hoeing and weeding. Interculture in the initial stage of crop growth suppress the weeds and light raking of soil followed by earthing-up about 70-80 days of planting records significant beneficial effect on the tuber yield.

Harvesting. Time of harvesting depends on the cultivar and the end use. Maturity of the tubers is indicated by the cracks formed in the soil, yellowing and falling of leaves. Most of the cultivars are ready for harvest at 8-10 months after planting for tuber consumption and starch production. The plants are cut leaving 30-60 cm of the basal end of the stem and the tubers are harvested by pulling the stem up. Then the tubers are separated using a bill hook giving last damage to the surface of the tuber. The soil adhering is cleaned and then the tubers are sent to the market or factory.

Grading. Grading and curing is done as in case of colocasia.

Marketing. The tubers are very tender and brittle and therefore enough care should be taken at the time of handling in transit, store and while marketing.

Storage. The best storage temperature is 14-15°C and can be stored for several weeks.

Yield. Average yield is 25-30 t/ha under good management practices.

15.4. ELEPHANT FOOT

Elephant foot popularly known as elephant foot or yam grown throughout the tropics and sub-tropics as a vegetable tuber crop for its edible corm.

Uses. Yam is grown for its corms which are used as vegetable as well as for preparations like chips, pickles etc.

Nutritive value. The corms are rich source of carbohydrates, vitamin A & B and minerals like calcium and phosphorus.

Medicinal value. The plant is employed in certain ayurvedic preparations. It is stomachic and tonic used in piles and restorative to dyspepsia and debility, etc. Root and corm is used in boils, opthalmia and in emmaenague.

Origin. The elephant foot is originated in Africa and Asia (India).

Taxonomy. Yam belong to the *family Araceae,* genus *Amorphophallus* and species *campanulatus.* Two types one with smooth corms and propagaged by small pieces of corms. This causes acridity and irrigation to the mouth and throat but gives a higher yield, but the acridity can be diluted or eliminated by boiling. The other type can be propagated by cormels or daughter corms and superior in quality and free from acridity. Fresh colour ranges from white to light pink.

Cultivars. Gajendra, Santragachi, Local cultivars.

Climate. It grows very well in tropical humid climate. A well distributed rainfall with warm humid weather during vegetable phase and comparatively low temperature during the development of corms will help to get high yields.

Soil. It does best in rich, sandy loam, well drained soil with a pH of 5-7 and rich in organic matter is preferred for its cultivation.

Seed rate. The sprouted corms can be cut into pieces in such a way that each corm piece weighing 500-700 g containing one sprout can be used for planting in the main field.

Sowing time. February-March.

Planting. The major constraint in elephant foot growing is the prevalence of corm dormancy. Propagation is done by means of corm cuttings of 500-700 g size or offsets (daughter corms) or corms. Corms exhibit long period of dormancy for about 3-4 months after harvest. As a result of this corm dormancy planting and harvesting are done at a particular time of the year, resulting in realisation of lower price of the produce due to glut in the market. If the dormancy could be broken by appropriate technique, early sprouting of the corms facilitates early planting and harvest during off-season resulting in better market price for the produce. Treating/incubating the corms at a temperature of 40°C for 6 hours/day for 6 weeks induced 100% sprouting of corms early by 45 days and this facilitate early harvest. The farmer can prepare a railing over the kitchen and keep the corms arranged which get warmed-up with the smoke and heat emerging from the kitchen during operation and the corms will sprout with in 30 days. Pits of size 50 × 50 × 30 cm are dug at recommended spacing and filled with a mixture of manure and fertilizer with top soil. The cut pieces or daughter or mother corms are dipped in cowdung slurry, dried in shade and then planted in these pits at a depth of 20 cm. Channels can be formed adjacent to one side of these pits. Planting is also done in wide ridge in south India.

Spacing. 75 × 75 cm between rows and plants.

Manure and fertilizer. Each pit is applied with 10 kg of FYM with top soil. 20 t FYM, 40 kg N, 60 kg P_2O_5 and 100 kg K_2O/ha is sufficient for better yield. 40 kg N/ha may be top dressed after 2-3 months of planting.

Rotation. Yam is often grown mixed with ginger and banana. Some crops like guar, groundnut, radish and methi etc. are sometimes grown as cover crops in the fields of Yam.

Irrigation. It needs a well distributed rainfall or irrigation. As a rainfed crop it requires a well distributed rainfall of 1000-1500 mm spread over a period of 6-8 months.

Hoeing and weeding. Two-three weeding should be done in the first few months to suppress the weed growth and later the spread of the leaves, the weed growth is suppressed.

Mulching. Immediately after planting, the pits are mulched with dry leaves which will induce better sprouting by conservation of moisture.

Earthing-up. The plants should be earthed-up properly to make the plants stable produce more yield.

Harvesting. The corms can be harvested 7-10 months after planting. The maturity of the corms is indicated by yellowing and drooping of leaves. The frequency of irrigation is reduced as the plants approach maturity Harvesting is done by digging the corms individually by a spade. The buds of the fourth year corms are removed and retained for planting the new crop.

Grading. The corms are cleaned, cured and graded before they are packed.

Marketing. The produce is transported to the local and distant markets depending on the demand and prevailing prices.

Storage. The corms of Elephant's foot yam can be stored under ordinary conditions in well ventialated rooms even for several months without damage.

Yield. 30-40 t/ha. Under better management the yield obtained are 75-100 t/ha.

Crop protection

Diseases/Insect-pests	*Symptoms*	*Control*
Disease		
Cassava mosaic virus	Affected plants show mosaic pattern in the leaves. Spread by white fly.	Use of disease free setts. Control of vector white fly by spray of Rogor or Metasystox 1 ml + 2 ml neem oil/ L of water.
Brown leaf spot *(Cercospora henningsli)*		Spray 0.1% Benlate or Bavistin.
Collar root rot *(Seclerotinia rolfsli & Rhizoctonia solani)*	Appear after 2-3 months and collar region is attacked.	Soil drenching with 0.2% Captan or 0.1% Brassicol twice at monthly interval. Proper drainage of soil.
Insect-pests		
Aphids, thrips and mealy bugs	Such sap of the tender parts leading to drying of plants.	Spray 0.05% Monocrotophos and repeat.
Root knot nematode		Deep ploughing during summer-Adoption of crop rotation. Burning of root residues.
Flea beetle leaf eating caterpillar and taro leaf hopper.	Feed on the crop colocasia.	Spray with 0.05% Endosulphan or 0.2% Carbaryl and repeat.

CHAPTER 16

SUMMER LEAFY VEGETABLES

16.1. AMARANTHUS

Amaranthus is tropical vegetable grown throughout India as a non-commercial crop essentially for home consumption. It is one of the cheapest leaf vegetable in Indian markets often described as a poor man's spinach. It is a very fast growing crop yielding 30 t/ha of fresh matter in 4 weeks under favourable conditions. It is, easy to cultivate and highly appropriate for nutrition and market gardens. Vegetable amaranthus are very common in India due to easiness in culture, nutritive value, fast growth rate, adaptability to varying agro-ciimates, high yield potential, relatively less susceptible to soil borne diseases and serious pests.

Uses. The leaves and succulent stems are cooked as vegetable and some grain species are good source of protein. The grains are used to prepare popped grain, gruel, cakes and other preparations like amaranth malt.

Nutritive value. The nutritive value of this cheap crop is excellent, because of highly nutritious contain carbohydrates content of dry matter (12.8 t/ha/year), protein, carotene Vitamin A and C, thiamin, riboflavin, minerals iron, calcium, phosphorus and potassium.

Medicinal value. Plant is beneficial in piles, as blood purifier diuretic and antisorbutic, leaves relieve chest congestion and serofulous sores. Roots boiled in honey is good laxative for infants.

Origin. Native of India or Southern China region.

Taxonomy. Amaranth belongs to family *Amaranthaceae,* genus *Amaranthus* and speries *tricolor and dubious.* There are about 65 genera and 850 species found in the world. They include species cultivated for leaf (greens), grains and some wild species. The most common species are : *A. blitum* and *A. tricolor* are known as choti and badi chauli, respectively. *A.*

caudatus is grown for seed and *A. mangostanus, A lividus* and *A. dubius* for green leaves in south India. It is an annual broad leaved dicotyledonous plant cultivated for vegetable, grain and both.

Cultivars. ***Vegetable type*** — Arka Suguna, Japanes Yellow, Pusa Kiran, Pusa Kirit, A-6, A-76, A-159, A-153, CO-1, CO-2, CO-3, CO- 4, Pusa Choti Chauli, Pusa Badi Chauli, Sirukeeral, Kannara Local.

Grain type — K-343, EC-321552, Annapurna.

Climate. Most of the amaranthus species are adapted to tropical climates. A temperature range of 20-30°C is preferred for better.

Soil. It can be grown under wide range of soil but sandy loam with slightly acidic nature is the best suited. Heavy clay and sand are not preferred.

Seed rate. A quantity of 2 kg seed is sufficient per ha.

Sowing time. Summer crop — March-April.

Rainy season crop — June-July.

Hills — May-July.

Sowing/transplanting. The field is prepared into better tilth by giving 2-3 ploughings and beds of convenient size and channels are formed. The crop is raised by both direct seeding and transplanting but the former method is common though the seed size is very small. The seed is mixed with 20 kg of fine sand and 5 kg of BHC 10% dust and the same is broadcasted on the beds. The seed is covered with a thin layer of sand or soil. The seed germinates in 5-7 days. In case of transplanting, the seedlings are raised and transplanted in lines as per recommendation.

Spacing. Between rows and plants in Choti chauli — 25 × 20 cm.

Badi chauli — 35 × 30 cm.

Transplanted crop — 45 × 30 cm.

Manure and fertilizer. At first planting add 10t of FYM and a combination of 50 : 50 : 20 kg of NPK/ha is applied as basal dose. But for clipping type a higher fertilizer dose of 60 : 50 : 25 kg/ha is recommended. N should be applied into two split doses one as a basal dose and another after 2 months or 5th clipping.

Irrigation. The irrigation should be done slowly as rapid water flow may wash-off the seeds to one end of the bed or field resulting in uneven stand of the crop. Subsequent irrigation's are given once in a week.

Hoeing and weeding. The crop should be kept clean in the early stages of growth by timely hoeing and weeding.

Thinning. If the seedlings are transplanted no thinning is required but in case of direct seeding, the thinning to optimum spacing is very important for initial growth of the plants.

Harvesting. In green types, the plants are pulled out after a months time. In clipping types, the first clipping can be done on 20-25th day of sowing and further clippings are repeated once in a week upto 90 days. In grain type, the plants are allowed to mature and the grains are separated by threshing, Choti chauli gives 6-7 cuttings while Badi chauli gives 9-10 cuttings.

Grading. The larger leaves or some part of petiole with leaves in choti chauli are bundled on the basis of cultivars characteristics of uniform weight preferably of one kg.

Marketing. The bundles prepared ease in handling in packaging, transit, marketing and in retail shops. These being highly perishable should be disposed-off immediately after harvesting.

Storage. The harvested produce cannot be stored for long under ordinary conditions.

Yield. 7-8 t/ha of green leaves.

16.2. INDIAN SPINACH

It is also called Basella or Malabar Nightshade and Poa in Hindi. Indian spinach is a common leafy vegetable grown in north-east and south India. The plant is a climbing vine with thick fleshy stem and leaves.

Uses. The succulent leaves or fleshy compound rosette of leaves with petioles and tender stems are cooked and eaten as vegetable.

Nutritive value. The plant is reputed for its high vitamin content and this quality has earned for it the name multivitamin green. It is a rich source of vitamin A, protein and fair source of iron.

Medicinal value. It has manifold medicinal values.

Origin. It is native to Asia.

Taxonomy. It belongs to the family *Basellaceae,* genus *Basella* and species *rubra.* There are different botanical forms of species *viz, B. abla, B. rubra, B. cannifolia, B. nigra, B. saponical.* Cultivars have smooth, or thick, dark green, savoyed leaves.

Cultivars. Cultivars having green leaves, petiole and stem and with reddish petiole and stem are grown. Red cultivar, Green cultivar.

Climate. Basella grows very well in warm moist climate. But it cannot tolerate extremes of temperature. It can be grown successfully under partial shade.

Soil. It can be grown under a wide range of soil right from sandy soil to clayey soil, sandy loam but grows well on any fertile with sufficient organic matter, well drained soil is the best suited. It is a shallow rooted crop.

Seed rate. About 12-15 kg of seeds would be required to sow one hectare.

Sowing time. June-July.

Sowing/planting. Basella is propagated by seeds as well as by stem cuttings. Both direct seeding and transplanting after raising the seedlings can be adopted. Rooted cuttings can also be used for planting.

Spacing. For trailing on the ground a spacing of 60 × 60 cm and if it is trained on trellises, a spacing of 60 × 30 cm or 60 × 20 cm can be adopted between rows and plants.

Manure and fertilizer. A basal dressing of 20-30 t FYM and 60 : 60 : 40 kg of NPK/ha has to be applied before transplanting/sowing.

Irrigation. Since the succulent leaves are to be harvested, frequent irrigation are necessary. During the rainy seasons, the frequency can be restricted. Water stagnation should be avoided.

Staking. Because of weak stem it is either staked on bamboo machan or trained on trellis system.

Hoeing and weeding. When the plants starts trailing, they should be trained on the support. Shallow hoeing in between the plants is done as and when necessary.

Harvesting. The first cutting starts from 45-60 days after planting and continues till the crops is over. The harvesting should be done carefully without injuring the vines. The entire spinach plant can be cut-off just at ground level when plants have 5-8 leaves. An alternate method is to harvest the outer leaves when they are 10-12 cm long, leaving the remaining leaves for later harvest. The entire plant should be harvested when a seed stalk begins to form.

Grading. Same as in spinach.

Marketing. Similar to amaranthus.

Storage. Similar to amaranthus.

Yield. A quantity of 15-20 tonnes of green matter can be harvested from a hectare in a crop duration of 120-150 days.

16.3. PORTULACA

Portulaca grows wild in summer season and in some places it is also cultivated. The important types normally have broad leaves. It has ornamental value and grown in kitchen garden. The succulent leaves and stems are cooked as vegetable.

It belongs to family *Portulacacae,* genus *Portulaca* and species *oleracea.* The fruit is a capsule and the seeds are collected after breaking them open. Portulaca is sown in early spring. The shoots grow erect when grown thickly.

The succulent branches are cut when they attain 15-20 cm length. The crop become ready for the first cutting in about 30 days after sowing.

Crop protection

Diseases/Insect-pests	*Symptoms*	*Control*
Diseases		
Damping-off	Seedling are killed both at pre and post-emergence stages. Infested seedlings topple down on the ground.	Treat nursery bed with formalin (1 part formalin and 10 part water). Drench beds with a mixture of Dithane M-45 (25 g) and Bavistin 50 WP (5 g)/10 L of Water.
Mosaic virus	Affected plants show mosaic pattern in the leaves. Spread by	Grow resistant cultivars. Control of vector white fly by spray of Rogor

	white fly.	or Metasystox 1 ml + 2 ml neem oil/L or water.
Leaf spot	Leaf spots appearance.	Spray 0.1% Benlate or Bavistin.
Root rot	Appear after 2-3 months and collar region is attacked.	Soil drenching with 0.2% Captan or 0.1% Brassicol twice at monthly interval. Proper drainage of soil.
Insect-pests		
Aphids, thrips and mealy bugs	Suck sap of the tender parts leading to drying of plants.	Spray 0.05% Monocrotophos and repeat.
Root knot nematode		Deep ploughing during summer Adoption or crop rotation. Burning of root residues.
Flea beetle, leaf eating caterpillar and leaf hopper.	Feed on the crop colocasia.	Spray with 0.05% Endosulphan or 0.2% Carbaryl and repeat.

The seeds can be treated before sowing and soil can be sterilised before sowing. To the extent possible it is advisable to avoid the use of any chemicals on the crop, since the leaves are the edible part.

CHAPTER 17

TUBER VEGETABLES

17.1. POTATO

Potato is a nutritious food rich in carbohydrates and protein. Mainly it is grown in tropical and sub-tropical parts of India. Being short duration, better fit in the cropping system, grown throughout the year, responds well to inputs and produces high returns per unit area and time, has high employment generation potential and also have a great potential to meet the increasing food requirements of the increasing population of the country. To meet such a huge demand in quality seed (seed tubers and TPS) has a great significance in potato trade.

Potato is cultivated in 11.09 lakh ha with a production of 118.43 lakh t, average productivity 15.99 t/ha and accounts for 0.67 per cent of total cropped area in India. Growth in potato has highly impressive with respect of production and productivity compared to other vegetables which increased from 1.5 million tonnes in 1950 to 25.07 million tonnes in 1996-97. Himachal Pradesh was the first state to organise a potato seed production programme on massive scale and still continuing besides seed plot technique and use of TPS techniques. Though many of the agro-techniques developed by the state are not relevant in recent day context when the varietal pattern has changed. Some new areas for production of this crop have also been identified.

Because of vast area under potato in our country, we used to import large quantity of tubers from other countries. Hence, there is still great need to boost production programme of potato in India.

Uses. Potatoes have great potential to meet the increasing food requirement. Better fit in intensive cropping system, have wider adaptability, high yielding per unit area and high employment generation potential both as crop and in post-harvest handling and processing.

Nutritive value. Potato is a nutritious food. It provides carbohydrates, proteins, minerals, vitamin C and number of vitamins of B group (like niacin, thiamine and riboflavin) and minerals like iron and magnesium. It also provides good quality fibre.

Medicinal value. It has manifold medicinal properties.

Origin. Potato is a native of high Andian region of South America.

Taxonomy. Potato belongs to family *Solanaceae,* genus *Solanum* and species *tuberosum.* There are a large number of related species both tuberous and non-tuberous. There are many cultivars either introduced or bred in the country which suits to each zone/region/state as per the requirements. Some are old and some new including hybrids. The former are still holding good in some areas.

Cultivars : *Old cultivars*. Satha, Up-To-Date, Phulwa, Dargeeling Red Round, Kufri Red, Kufri Kuber, Kufri Kisan, Kufri Kundan, Craig's Difiance, Kufri Safed, Kuferi Kumar, Great Scot, President, Kufri Neela, Kufri Sindhuri, Kufri Alankar, Kufri Sheetman, Kufri Khasi-Garo, Kufri Neelmani, Kufri Chamatkar, Kufri Moti, Kufri Lauvkar, Kufri Babar, Kufri Himalini, Kufri Sherpa, Kufri Lalima.

New cultivars. Kufri Swarna, Kufri Naveen, Kufri Sherpa, Kufri Megha, Kufri Khasigara, Kufri Chandermukhi, Kufri Jyoti, Kufri Navtal, Kufri Badshah, Kufri Bahar, Kufri Muthu, Kufri Jeevan, Kufri Dews, Kufri Ashoka, Kufri Jawahar, Kufri Sutlej, Kufri Giri Raj (SM/85-45), Kufri Pukhraj (JE X JC-166), Kufri Thenmalai (Hybrid D/79-56).

Suitable for chips. Kufri Chipsona-1, Kufri Chipsona-2, Kufri Anand.

Climate. It can be best grown in areas having both long-day and short day conditions *i.e.* long days for the growth phase and short days during the tuberization stage. Cultivars differ considerably in their response to varying photoperiodism. Potato is essentially a temperate crop but widely adapted in all climates and moderately tolerant to frost. The maximum tuberization takes place at a temperature of 20°C and beyond this temperature the tuberization retards and at 29°C it is inhibited. The yields at temperate regions are higher than in the tropics.

Soil. The shape, appearance and yield of the tubers-depends to a great extent, upon the texture and physical nature of the soil. Potato can be grown on almost all types of soils, but it does best on light and well drained soils which are rich in humus having a pH range of 5.2-6.4. Alkaline soils create favourable conditions for scab disease. Thus free and uniform development of tubers takes place in loose and friable soils as these are borne underground at the stolon ends. Excellent potato crops are grown under the river bed system of cultivation.

Seed. Potato is propagated from tubers which is called seed potato and these are planted either whole or cut into pieces (each piece should have 2-3 growing (eyes) buds). Always prefer certified. The usual size of seed piece should be 40-50 g with 40-50 mm diameter. The seed rate varies with the size of tuber.

Seed rate. The optimum seed rate is 10-15 q/ha.

Sowing time. Plains-autumn or main crop — end September-mid-January.

Spring crop — January-May.

South India — September (*Rabi*)-January *(Kharif).*

Hills — March-April.

Nilgiri Hills — April, August and January (three crops).

Planting of potatoes in optimum period is essential to secure high yield and the best time for planting would be when minimum and maximum temperature remains from 18-20°C.

Sowing/planting. The field is prepared by giving thorough ploughing into a better tilth. In hills, flat beds of convenient size across slope along the contour are prepared, which prevents soil erosion as well as conserve soil moisture as it is mainly grown as rainfed crop there. The different planting methods may be followed depending on the situation and these are ridge, furrow, flat, and double furrow method. The seed tubers are sprouted before planting so as to encourage initial growth. The seed tubers taken from the cold storage and are spread in shade for 8-12 days with one or two turning daily. This will encourage sprouting. The seed tubers from hills will be difficult to sprout and should be treated with 1 ppm gibberellic acid for one hour and dried in shade, these treated tubers are filled in gunny bags and kept in vertical position in dark place for 10 days enabling to encourage sprouting. Besides GA, chemicals like thiourea, potassium thiocynate carbondisulphide can also be used. The sprouted tubers can be treated with 0.2 per cent solution of Bavistin or Benlate for 20 minutes to avoid soil borne diseases.

Spacing. 45-60 × 20-25 cm between rows and plants according to the cultivar and size of seed tuber.

Manure and fertilizer. Potato is a shallow rooted and heavy feeder and require sufficient organic matter and nutrients for proper growth and development. A basal application of 20 t of FYM, 75 kg N, 50 kg P_2O_5 and 100 kg K_2O/ha. The manure and fertilizers should be mixed well in the soil. Where there is micro-nutrient deficiency, the micro-nutrient mixture should be applied and consisting of $ZnSO_4$ — 20 kg, $MnSO_4$ — 420 kg, $FeSO_4$ — 10 kg, $CuSO_4$ — 10 kg, Ammonium Molybdate — 1 kg and Sodium Borate — 1 kg/ha.

Irrigation. The potato crop requires 150-165 ha cm of water during the entire growing period. One irrigation should be applied 3-4 days after planting to provide optimum moisture for better and early germination. Light and regular irrigation are most effective. Frequent irrigation should be applied during the optimum period of growth and tuberization. Watering may be reduced gradually when the crop is heading towards maturity and later stopped a fortnight before harvesting.

Hoeing and weeding. The weeds should be removed as soon as they appear by hoeing and keep the soil loose and destroy weeds. Use of Nitrofen (Toke-E-25 25%) @ 1.0 kg a.i. or Alachlor (Lasso 50%) @ 2.0 kg a.i. or Zimazine (Tafazine 50%) @ 0.5 kg a.i./ha as pre-emergence spray just after planting and soon after the field is irrigated.

Earthing-up. Timely earthing-up is necessary to produce healthy tubers. After 30-35 days of planting the tuberization starts, this is the stage when the plants should be earthed-up. In case the planting is done on ridges, this operation can be delayed. In some areas, second earthing-up is done after 30 days from the first. This prevents frost damage and greening effect of sunrays on exposed tubers which actually affects the market quality of the tubers.

Harvesting. The harvesting of the crop is guided by the maturity and the sale price. The leaves start turning yellow and dry up, the crop is considered to have entered the maturity phase. It can be harvested at any time, depending upon the demand in the market and cultivar. In case of early harvest, the yield obtained is low and sale price is high whereas the produce from the late-harvest fetches low price but the yield is higher. Actually the time of harvesting is a judicious adjustment between the yield and the market price. It is better to harvest the mature tubers which are less prone to skinning and bruising and can be stored safely for longer periods. Delay in harvesting produce may result in the rotting of the tubers in the field. Every care should be taken to avoid cutting of tubers so that their commercial value is not reduced. The tubers are dug out along with haulms, cleaned and packed in gunny bags for ready market.

Grading. Grading and standardization of the produce is very essential as it brings higher income to the farmers and ensure a right grade of potato to the purchaser according to the requirements. For table purpose, the tubers of comparatively big size are preferred and cut or injured and green tubers are not accepted by the consumers. For seed, the basic qualities of the tubers are that it should be true to type and free from degenerative diseases. These will depend upon the reputation and reliability of the source where it has been produced. The size may vary from 2.5-3.75 cm in diameter. The healthy tubers are sorted out as over sized-used for chips, medium sized-fetches maximum price, small sized (pod) and miniature (natchupodi).

Marketing. Potato is a perishable and bulky commodity with high water content and thus require large storage and transport capacity. In cooler regions, storage is not a problem and the produce can be gradually released and transported to the local or distant markets within the country and elsewhere. Marketing in warmer areas, like plains of India, involves handling and movement of potato under unfavourable environmental conditions.

Storage. Potato being a semi-perishable commodity and needs proper storage facilities. Earlier the potato tubers were stored in sand pits, diffused light storage rooms, thatched mud wall rooms, passive evaporative cool stores, etc. These structures are suitable to hold potatoes up to the month of June-July. Now the present cold storage industry has given a big boost to store tubers for a desired period under controlled conditions. The stored produce is taken out as when it is needed in the market at premium prices. The tubers can be stored at 1-2.7°C and 90-95% RH.

Processing. Potato has been put to diversified use like a staple fresh food and processed products for human consumption, starch and alcohol production and live stock feeding in other countries of the world, in developing countries like India it is used as a vegetable for human consumption.

Yield. The average yield is 400-450 q/ha.

17.2. SEED PLOT TECHNIQUE

It is a easy and suitable method used for commercial potato seed production followed now-a-days in the plains of India. The following steps should be followed while adopting this method in potato crop.

— In the plots selected for potato seed tuber production, crops like tomato, brinjal, chilli, potato etc., should not be grown in the previous year.

— The soil should be free from soil-borne diseases like common scab, nematodes and bacterial wilt.

— The area should be free from aphids at least for 75 days and the minimum and maximum temperatures should be between 10-28°C.
— Seed tubers free from seed-borne disease and pest attack.
— Tubers should be planted at a distance of 45-50 cm (between the rows) and 20 cm (within the rows) for getting higher yields.
— Planting should be done when the aphid population is less, preferably in the first week of October (Jalandhar area) and third week of October (Patna and Babugarh area).
— Apply systemic granular insecticides (Thimet) to the soil at the rate of 15 kg/ha during planting against aphids and leaf-hoppers which act as viral and MLO vector.
— Full herbicides (Stomp, 2-4-D, etc.) to control weeds and avoid earthing-up in standing crop.
— Examine the seed plot two times to remove types. First inspection should be done soon after the emergence (20-25 days after planting) and second inspection should be done after 45-50 days of planting.
— Maintain an isolation distance of 30 metres between two varieties.
— In the first week of December, do spray with Dimethoate (1 ml/l) or Metasystox (1.25 ml/1) to prevent the attack of aphids.
— With hold the irrigation in the fourth week of December (7 to 10 days earlier to dehaulming).
— Kill the haulm (by cutting or by using herbicides) at the end of December or beginning of January.
— Harvest the crop after 10-15 days of dehaulming when the tuber's skin has matured. After harvesting, tubers are to be stored in a cool place.
— Grading should be done according to size (large, medium and small) and small and medium sized tubers should be used for sowing.
— Seed tubers should be treated with Organo Mercuric compound like Agallol at the rate of 0.3% for 30 minutes.
— Store the produce in old storage in seed bags.

17.3. TRUE POTATO SEED (TPS)

At present the farmers may not afford fresh healthy seed every year due to its high cost. True potato seed (TPS) or the botanical seed is free from most of the degenerative diseases and can serve as an alternative source of seed for raising a commercial crop. The potato seed resemble the tomato or brinjal seed. However, traditionally potato crop is raised from the seed tubers and the TPS technology has many advantages over it as : (*i*) low disease transmission, (*ii*) high resistance to many diseases, (*iii*) low incidence of virus, (*iv*) less amount of seed (150 g/ha) is required, (*v*) transport and storage cost are low, (*vi*) TPS can be produced in all potato growing regions and (*vii*) it gives tuber yield equal to or more than the seed tubers.

TPS cultivars. TPS-C (CPRI), HPS 1/13 (CIP).

Production methods. TPS can be used in two ways for commercial potato production, (*i*) crop raised through transplanted seedlings and (*ii*) crop raised from seedlings tubers produced in nursery beds. Both methods are economical and suitable for large scale production of potato. The former method is quite suitable in areas where temperature is mild (15-25°C) during crop season and crop duration is long more than 120 days. In areas (Indo-gangetic plains) where winters are severe and crop duration is short, healthy seed tubers can be produced through seed plot techniques, the use of seedlings tubers is a practical proposition. In these areas seedling transplants are not much successful because of low temperature after transplanting in field.

Transplanted Seedling Method

Nursery production. Nursery bed are prepared as in case of tomato and sow the seed in about 60 m^2 area enough for a hectare. Other management practices are similar to tomato.

Seed rate. 150 g/ha.

Sowing time. North-west plains — early October.

Eastern plains — late October.

Transplanting. The fields are prepared into better tilth. Divide the field into plots of convenient size linked with water channel. Or ridges and furrows may also be prepared.

Spacing. 50 × 10 cm between rows and plants.

Manure and fertilizer. Apply 15-20 t FYM, 120 kg N, 30 kg P_2O_5 and 100 kg K_2O/ha after soil test.

Irrigation. Light irrigation should be given in the furrows/plots before transplanting and rooted seedlings are transplanted on north side of the ridges near water level and after 3-4 days irrigation should be given. Gap filling may be done after 7-8 days. Irrigate the field regularly.

Seedling Tuber Method

The seedling tubers are produced by transplanting seedlings in nursery beds at 10 × 15 cm spacing or direct seeding of TPS (2 seeds/hole) at the same distance. About 40 g TPS and 300 m^3 nursery bed area is required to produce enough tubers for planting one hectare. Generally, the tuber yields in nursery beds ranges from 4.5-6.5 kg/m^2 and number of tubers 400-1000/m^2. Tuberlets can also be produced by transplanting the seedlings in field in suitable area as done above. Tuberlets of above 5 g weight can be used as seed for raising the commercial crop next year.

Spacing. The suitable spacing found are 50 × 20 cm for 20-40 g, 50 × 15 cm for 10-12 g and 50 × 10 g weight of tuberlets.

Seed rate. The approximate seed rate required is 30-33, 20-22 and 15-17 g/ha in each weight category, respectively. Tuber smaller than 5 g may be planted again in nursery bed at 10 × 10 cm spacing for tuberlet production. The other requirements are similar to above method.

Aftercare. Spray the plants with Durasban/Dermate after 6-7 days of transplanting to save the crop from cut worms followed by earthing-up and top dressing of half N when seedlings attain a height of 20-30 cm or after one month of transplanting. Earthing-up should be done in such a way that the seedlings come in the centre of the ridge. If needed another earthing-up can be done after about 2 months of transplanting.

The regular sprays of 0.25% Dithane M-45 and 0.15% Metasystox should be done after 50, 65 and 80 days of transplanting to control the diseases and insects. Dehaulm the crop after 90 days of transplanting.

Harvesting. The crop should be harvested after 8-10 days of dehaulming. The produce is relatively of smaller in size. Small sized tubers may be used as seed tubers for raising a commercial crop in next year. The large size tubers may be used as ware potato.

Crop protection

Diseases/Insect-pests	*Symptoms*	*Control*
Diseases		
Early blight *(Alternaria solani)*	Brown spots having concentric rings scattered over the leaves especially at the tip and margin, leaves wither.	Spray Dithane Z-78 @ 2 g/1.
Late blight (*Phytophthora infenstans*)	Brown patches on leaves starting from margin. Whitish haze on the under surface.	Grow resistant cultivars like Kufri Kuber, Kufri Kisan, etc. Spray Dithane Z-78 @ 2g/l.
Mosaic virus	Mosaic mottling of leaves including necrosis and spotting.	Rogue out diseased plants. Use certified seed and grow resistant cultivar.
Leaf roll virus	Leaves roll up and are thicker and rough to touch.	Rouge out diseased plants.
Bacterial scab		Maintain the soil pH between 5.0-5.3.
Root knot nematode		Treat the soil with DD @ 400 1/ha. Follow crop rotation.
Insect-pests		
Aphids, Jassids	Suck sap from tender parts and leaves and devitalize the plants.	Spray Nuvacron or Rogor @ 1 ml/l or Metasystox @ 2 ml/l of water.
Cut worm	Cut the small plants at ground level.	Apply Chlordane 5% dust @ 50 kg/ha.
Caterpillar	Feed on the leaves and stems.	Spray Endosulphan @ 1.5 ml/l of water.

CHAPTER

18

COLE VEGETABLES

The important crops in this group grown in India are cabbage *(Brassica oleracea* var. *capitata),* cauliflower *(Brassica oleracea* var. *botrytis),* knol-khol *(Brassica oleracea* var. *caulorapa),* Sprouting broccoli *(Brassica oleracea* var. *italica),* Brussels sprouts *(Brassica oleracea* var. *gemmifera)* and Kale *(Brassica olearcea* var. *acephala).*

18.1. CAULIFLOWER

Amongst the winter vegetables, the cauliflower is most popular. In India, two separate groups of cauliflower are commonly grown, Indian or tropical types and the annual tropical known as Efurt or Snowball types. In India, it is grown in an area of 2.20 lakh ha with a production of 24.73 lakh t and productivity of 11.24 t/ha. Early autumn varieties of cauliflower set seeds freely in the plains but late varieties produce best quality seed only in semi-temperate conditions in the hills.

Uses. Cauliflower is mainly grown for its white or cream tender curds consumed as delicious vegetable and as processed products. It is used as vegetable in curries, soups and for pickles.

Nutritive value. Cauliflower is rich in proteins and vitamin C and A. It also contains carbohydrates and minerals like potassium, sodium, iron, phosphorus, calcium, magnesium, etc.

Medicinal value. It has manifold medicinal properties.

Origin. It is said to native of South Europe in the Mediterranean region.

Taxonomy. Member of family *Cruciferae,* genus *Brassica,* species *oleracea* and var. *botrytis.* Cauliflower plant is characterised by forming a peculiar inflorescence consisting of thick, fleshy, strongly ramified flower stalks, which make a compact, often nearly spherical, 'curd'. Most cauliflower cultivars are annuals, and in the temperate zone make a curd in the year of sowing. In addition, biennials occurs, whose transition to the generative phase is not accomplished until after a period of low temperature.

Cultivars. Select the correct cultivar according to season and location as the different cultivars are season bound. As per the temperature and photoperiodism requirements, the cauliflower cultivars have been divided into three main groups.

Early. Early Kunwari, Pusa Katki, Early Patna, Pusa Deepali, Poosi, Ooty-1.

Mid-season. Improved Japanese, Dania, Pant Subhra, Pusa Synthetic, Maghi, Aghani.

Late. Snowball-16, Pusa Snowball-1, Pusa Snowball-2, PSK-1, Pusa Synthetic, Pusa Subhra, Hira Moti and Pusa Him Jyoti, Dania Kalimpong, Pusa Sharad.

Hybrid. Pusa Hybrid-2, Himani, Sweti, Moon, Raja, Rani, Neeta, TR-19, Gurdian, Sweta.

Climate. Being a delicate and sensitive crop, it needs more care. It needs specific temperature and photo-period for better curd development because it has a wide varietal variation. It produces best curds in a temperature range of 5°C to 20-30°C and moist climate. Comparatively higher temperatures and long day lengths are needed for early and mid-season varieties whereas late varieties respond better to low temperature and short days. The curds become ricey, leafy, loose and yellow resulting in poor quality at higher temperature. Snowfall at curd stage leads to soft rot. The tropical types are resistant to water-logging and heat.

Soil. Cauliflower can be grown in almost all types of soils with good fertility. Soil and site selected should be sunny, well drained, rich in organic matter, pH-range 6.5-7.5, free from soil borne diseases and insect-pests, etc. Early cultivars prefers rich sandy loam and late cultivars needs loam and clay loam. Don't grow cauliflower crop in the same field year after year and follow 3-4 years crop rotation, avoiding crucifers. Ensure good tilth.

Seed rate. Seed requirement for early cultivars is 500-800 g/ha and for mid and late cultivars 300-400 g/ha.

Sowing time. Early — May-June.
Mid-season — July-August.
Late — September-October.

Transplanting. The seed sown in beds (detail given in Nursery management chapter) and the healthy (3-4 weeks old) seedlings are pulled out carefully from the moistened nursery beds without damaging the roots and transplanted in the main field. Gap filling may be done in case of some damage to the seedlings with in a week or so. Before transplanting, the field is thoroughly prepared to have a fine tilth. The field should be divided into beds of convenient size or furrows or ridges and deep channel are formed to avoid water-logging. The seedling are transplanted when 4-6 weeks old depending on the season in a well prepared field.

Spacing. Transplanting distance depends on soil fertility, season, cultivar and market demand. It should be at a spacing of 30 × 30 or 45 × 30 cm in early cultivars, 45 × 45 cm mid-season and 60 × 45 cm in late cultivars.

Manure and fertilizer. Quantity of manure and fertilizer vary depending upon the cultivars. A quantum of 20-25 t FYM, 120 kg N, 80 kg P_2O_5 and 80 kg K_2O per hectare. Incorporate entire quantities of FYM, P_2O_5, K_2O and half N as basal dose. The rest half dose of nitrogen should be top dressed after 30-35 days transplanting.

Cauliflower shows boron and molybdenum deficiency symptoms when either grown in alkaline or highly acidic soils in such cases 10-15 kg/ha of borax may be applied in the soil or two sprays with 0.3% borax on the seedlings overcome boron deficiency. Molybdenum deficiency occurs in highly acidic soils and can be corrected by liming or application of about 1-1.5 kg/ha of Sodium molybdate.

Irrigation. Just before or after transplanting, a light irrigation should be given. For early and mid-season crop, light and frequent irrigation should be given without stagnation of water. Adequate watering is needed particularly during growth and curding phase. Keep the soil moist and irrigate at an interval of 8 to 12 days. Never allow the curd crop to suffer from excess or shortage of irrigation water.

Hoeing and weeding. Remove the harmful weeds to keep the field clean periodically without disturbing the plants as cauliflower is a shallow rooted crop. Weedicides like Diquat and Paraquat at 0.56 kg/ha will give better control the weeds. Basalin @ 2 kg a.i./ha also restricts the weeds emergence before transplanting along with one or two hand weedings.

Mulching. Polythene mulch will increase the yield and straw mulch cause adverse effect. Paddy husk can also be used as mulch to increase the growth and yield in cauliflower.

Blanching. It is an important operation done in cauliflower to get good quality curds. Curd are covered with inner leaves by tying them with thread or rubber band to protect the developing curds from direct sun scorching and yellowing so that they may not loose the white colour, flavour and attractiveness. The duration of blanching should not exceed 3-5 days in hot weather and 8-10 days in cool season. If it exceeds the limit, rotting and discolouration of leaves, curds begin to bolt and become ricey or begin to branch even during cool season. Late maturing cultivars have normally the character of self-blanching by incurbing of the inner leaves.

Harvesting. Harvesting should be done periodically without any delay as the curds reach prime maturity and attain proper size. Overmature curds will bolt and become loose, leafy, ricey or fuzzy unfit for marketing. The harvesting should be done either in the morning or evening so that the curds do not loose their colour and attractive. The curds are cut-off from the stalk with a large sharp knife after harvesting.

Grading. The harvested curds are separated into three grades, depending on size, colour, quality and cultivar.

Marketing. The normal method of packing and transport of curds is in big nets, bags, tractor trolleys and trucks. Tight packing is essential to prevent shifting and bruising. At present, curds are transported in plastic crates and wire bound containers/boxes. Also cellophane and transparent films are used after hydro-cooling to remove field and product heat for safe marketing.

Storage. Cauliflower curds with leaves can be stored for 30 days at 0°C with 85-90 per cent RH.

Yield. The yield may vary with the cultivar and the season of planting. Average yield of curds ranges between 20-35 t/ha. The highest may be upto 50 t/ha in late cultivars under better management.

18.2. CABBAGE

Cabbage is one of the most popular hardy winter vegetables in India. It is grown in kitchen gardens, truck gardens and off-season in the hills, available for consumption throughout the year. It is a very important off-season vegetable and the heads are available almost throughout the year. In India, it is cultivated in an area of 2.18 lakh ha with a production of 38.61 lakh t and productivity of 17.71 t/ha.

Uses. Cabbage is used as salad, boiled vegetable, cooked in curries and pickled as well as dehydrated vegetable.

Nutritive value. Cabbage is rich in digestible fat, minerals, vitamins A, B_1, B_2 and C. It streamline the digestive system.

Medicinal value. Glucoside sinigrinis the flavour principle present in cabbage.

Origin. It is probably native of Western Europe and the Northern shore of the mediterranean region.

Taxonomy. Member of family *Cruciferae,* genus *Brassica,* species *oleracea* and var. *capitata.* In cabbage, the thickening of main bud is called 'head'. They range in colour from green to purple, in leaf character from smooth to savoy leaves, in head shape from flat-topped to long-oval or pointed and in maturity from early (55 days after transplanting) to late (120 days or more after transplanting). The heads should be compact and round. The green rounded types are most common. Cabbage is biennial that requires a cold treatment to flower.

Cultivars : Early. Golden Acre, Pusa Mukta (Sel-9), Sel-8, Chaubatia Early, Sri Ganesh Gol, Express, Early Drum Head.

Mid. Pride of India, Pusa Drum Head, Aru Glory, Green Express, Copenhagen Market, Hari Rani, Meenakshi, Green Boy.

Late. Large Late Drum Head, September, Pusa Drum Head, Green Challanger, BSS-50 (Bajrang), BSS-32 (Suvarna), BSS-44, BSS-115 (Sudha).

Hybrid. Ganesh Gol, Hybrid-47, Green Challenger, Ravi, Vishwas, Bahar.

Red cabbage. (Early) Red Acre, Hako, Zeinth, Erfurt, (Late) Mohrenkopf, Kissendrup, Langedijk Autumn Red.

Climate. It thrives well in a relatively cool moist weather. It is mainly grown during winter in north India and in south India it is grown under moderate winter conditions. The optimum temperature required for proper growth and heading ranges from 15-20°C and never beyond 25°C. In hills, it is cultivated during summer and in some pockets 2 or 3 crops are raised because of mild climate.

Soil. Cabbage cultivars can be grown in almost all types of soils. Sandy loam soil is considered the best for early cultivars but to obtain higher yields, clay loam or silt loams are preferred. The optimum pH for cabbage is between 5.5 and 6.5 as it do not grow well under highly acidic soils.

Seed rate. 500 to 600 g of seed is sufficient for raising nursery for one hectare.

Sowing time. Early crop — August-September, mid-season — September and late crop — September-October in north India, while in south India the right sowing time is July-August. In hills, sowing is done in March-April for heads and July-August for seed production.

Transplanting. The field is prepared to better tilth. The method of transplanting is similar to cauliflower. Hardening of seedlings and use of starter solution at the time of transplanting give better results.

Spacing. Line to line and plant to plant spacing 45 × 45 cm and 60 × 45 cm is required for early and late varieties, respectively.

Manure and fertilizer. For cabbage head production 15-20 t FYM, 60-80 kg N, 40-60 kg P_2O_5 and 40-50 kg K_2O is required per ha where as for seed crop it should be 120 kg N, 60-80 kg each of P_2O_5 and K_2O/ha. Full dose of FYM, P and K and half dose of N should be applied before replanting of heads and rest N in two equal split doses at bolting and pre-flowering stage.

Crop rotation. Cabbage crop should be rotated with other crops/vegetables particularly in soils with low pH to control black rot, club root, etc.

Irrigation. The seedlings should be irrigated immediately after transplanting. Irrigation depends upon the frequency and intensity of rains and moisture level in the soil. Light soils needs frequent irrigation. In summer months field be irrigated at 10 days interval.

Hoeing and weeding. 2-3 hoeing and weedings should be done to remove the weeds and loosen the soil for aeration. Deep hoeing should always be avoided. Weeds can also be controlled by a pre-planting application of Trifluralin (0.5 1/ha) or Basalin (0.5 1/ha) or a pre-emergence application of Desmetroyne (0.25 1/ha).

Earthing-up. To produce healthy heads, the plants should be earthed-on 5-6 weeks after transplanting.

Mulching. The weed growth can be checked and the moisture is conserved by mulching the crop with black polythene sheet or crop residues.

Harvesting. Harvesting is done when the heads attain the suitable size, firm and tender. The head is cut or detached from the stump frequently accompanied by some wrapper leaves, which give them some degree of protection. Savoys and spring greens are sometimes harvested with a large proportion of the wrapper leaves, which are in part also consumed. The harvested heads should be kept in shade till marketed. The harvesting should not be unduly delayed, as the heads get cracked or eventually rot.

Grading. The grading of heads should be done according to the size and quality as per standards prescribed by the Indian Standards Institution. The uniform product is obtained by grading.

Marketing. The heads with wrapper leaves are packed in gunny bags used for onion or nets or crates or boxes or sometimes in trucks and transported to the markets. The marketing may be done by the farmer himself or the middlemen or the contractors.

Storage. The best storage temperature is 0°C at 90-95 per cent RH. A good air circulation will avoid condensation if a uniform 0°C storage temperature is maintained.

Yield. The average yield varies from 30-35 t/ha for the early cultivars and 35-45 t/ha for late cultivars.

18.3. KNOL-KHOL

It is an important member of the Cole group grown for its above ground enlarged stem fleshy edible part which is very nutritious. It is particularly popular in Jammu and Kashmir, West Bengal, and Karnataka. Knol-khol is grown in kitchen gardens by every house-hold.

Uses. Both bulb (knob) and leaves at tender stage are consumed raw or cooked.

Nutritive value. It is high in minerals like calcium, magnesium, potassium, phosphorus, sodium and sulphur. It also contains vitamin A and C.

Medicinal value. It has manifold medicinal properties.

Origin. It is originated in the coastal countries of Northern Europe.

Taxonomy. It belongs to the family *Cruciferae,* genus *Brassica,* species *caularapa.* The knob/tuber is characteristically formed by the thickening of the stem tissue above the cotyledons above ground level and the leaves grow out from this stem.

Cultivars. White Vienna, Early White Vienna, Purple Vienna, Large Green, King of North, King of Market and DPKK-1.

Climate. It is a cool season crop and the ideal temperature for growth and yield is 10-20°C. Continuous hot weather will hinder the development of knobs.

Soil. Similar to cabbage.

Seed rate. 1-1.5 kg/ha for transplanted crop and 2.5-3.5 kg/ha for direct sown crop.

Sowing time. Planting is done from August to November and in low and mid-hills, it is July-October and in high-hills March-July.

Sowing/planting. As in case of cabbage or cauliflower.

Spacing. Adopting a spacing of 30 × 20 cm between rows and plants.

Manure and fertilizer. Add 10 t of FYM, 100 kg N, 80 kg P_2O_5 and 85 kg K_2O/ha. Apply full quantity of FYM, P_2O_5 and K_2O at the time of sowing. N is applied in two equal split doses at the time of sowing and the other a month after transplanting.

Irrigation. The optimum soil moisture should be maintained at the time of transplanting and later irrigate at a interval of 10-15 days.

Hoeing and weeding. The field should be kept weed free and pulverize the soil by shallow hoeing.

Harvesting. The tender and developing knobs should be harvested before they are fully grown as per the requirement. For getting better knobs, harvest before they become tough, woody and stringy. The whole plant is pulled out and then the root portion along with stem is cut. Sometimes the foliage is removed in harvesting, but often it is left on the plant and then the knobs can be tied by it into bunches, as is often is done for market.

Grading. The knol-khol bulbs should be graded on the basis of bulb size, shape and colour considering the varietal characteristics.

Marketing. The produce should be marketed immediately after proper grading and packaging to the markets where it is in great demand.

Storage. Under ordinary conditions it can be stored for 2-3 days but under cold storage conditions it can be kept for a relatively long period.

Yield. 12-25 t/ha.

18.4. SPROUTING BROCCOLI

Sprouting broccoli is- a new potential rare Cole vegetable grown in some areas/pockets where the agro-climatic conditions are congenial for its growth and development. There is a great demand of sprouting broccoli in the five star luxury hotels and tourist resorts for its delicacy as it is relished by the tourists. The broccoli producing farmers of the hilly areas are regularly supplying their produce to the big metropolitan cities and earning lucrative returns every year. The area under the crop is constantly increasing and to meet the quality requirement, there is need to encourage its production.

Uses. A main head is produced terminally on a fleshy, branching, elongated attached stem are the edible part which may be green or purple depending on the variety. Besides, the terminal head, longer, more slender and smaller heads with a portion of fleshy flower-stalks appear in the axil of leaves are harvested and consumed as human food.

Nutritive value. Among the three types *viz.,* green, white and purple the green types are more nutritive and popular. The heading types resembling to cauliflower are highly nutritive and contains 3.3 per cent protein and is rich in vitamins A, B_1, B_2 and C.

Medicinal value. It has got better medicinal properties than cauliflower.

Origin. It has been originated in Southern Europe.

Taxonomy. It belongs to the family *Cruciferae,* genus *Brassica,* species *oleracea* and var. *italica.* Broccoli is an Italian word from the Latin Brachium means an arm or branch. A main head is produced terminally on a fleshy, branching elongated stem. The plant resemble to cauliflower and forms a kind of head, consisting of green buds and thick, fleshy flower stalks. The main heads, which can attain a diameter of 15 cm and more, are much looser than those of cauliflower and generally green coloured, while the flower-stalks are longer. The sprouts in the axils of leaves develop strongly, particularly after the central heads have been harvested, and also form bud-clusters.

Cultivars. Green : Pusa Broccoli KTS-1, Italian Green (Calabrese), Green Head, DPBG.

Purple : DPPB-1 (Palampur Samridhi), Bronzino.

Early : De Cicco, Green Bod and Spartan Early.

Late : Green Mountain, Coastal and Atlantic.

Hybrids : Premium Crop, Clipper, Cruiser, Stiff and Green Surf.

Climate. Broccoli is more adapted to warmer and less humid conditions. It must be grown during the cool months of the year. It is a cool season crop and some cultivars can withstand frost. Average day temperature of 20-25°C at vegetative stage and 15-20°C at heading are optimum. At higher temperatures its heads become loose.

Soil. The soil should have a high organic matter and friable. Broccoli can tolerate acid soils having pH of 5.5-6.5. It requires moist soil for proper growth while under dry conditions the shoots become fibrous.

Seed rate. Quality seed of 400-500 g/ha for transplanted crop and 1-2.5 kg/ha for direct sowing.

Sowing time. The seed is sown in the nursery bed in September-October and transplanted in the field in October or November.

Transplanting. Similar to other Cole crops.

Spacing. 45 × 60-75 cm depending on the cultivar.

Manure and fertilizer. A quantity of 20-25 t of farm yard manure, 100 kg N, 60-80 kg P_2O_5 and 40-60 kg K_2O_5 per hectare should be applied N is to be given in two split doses first as a basal dose and the next after the first harvest.

Irrigation. Generally the crop requires more moisture than other Cole crops. For getting higher yield, frequent light irrigation should be given at regular intervals.

Hoeing and weeding. Intercultural operations should be done like other Cole crops except thinning and it is carried in direct sown crop.

Harvesting. The central head should be harvested at the correct stage and time to avoid opening of buds. Heads should be cut with a few leaves. After sometime the small heads are formed in the axil of leaves which should also be cut and marketed. The central heads mature first, and by removing the main sprouts the growth of the lateral sprouts is promoted. The lateral heads do not mature at a time and harvesting should be done twice a week. Depending on the cultivar and management the duration of harvest may lasts for two months.

Grading. Broccoli sprouts is prepared for market by tying in bunches of bud clusters and intended for fresh consumption are often sold in bunches weighing one kg.

Marketing. The quality of harvested sprouts soon declines and they should be marketed as soon as possible. Cooled transport is important and an attractive product is obtained by freezing the sprouts.

Storage. Similar to cauliflower.

Yield. The broccoli yield varies from 5-10 t/ha.

18.5. BRUSSEL'S SPROUTS

The crop was grown in Brussel in Belgium and hence its name. The edible small sprouts resemble to cabbage heads are borne in the axil of leaves along and around the main stem progressively from the bottom upwards. At present, it has become popular around big cities to meet the demand from big hotels for tourists.

Uses. The sprouts are normally cooked and pickled.

Nutritive value. The sprouts contain 4.4 per cent protein and are fairly rich in vitamin A and ascorbic acid and contain appreciable quantities of riboflavin, niacin, calcium and iron.

Medicinal value. Similar to cabbage.

Origin. It has been originated in Brussels, Belgium.

Taxonomy. It belongs to the family *Cruciferae,* genus *Brassica,* species *oleracea* and var. *gemmifera.* The stems make normal longitudinal growth and in some cultivars may reach a length of over one metre. The buds in the axils of the usually petiole leaves develops into a miniature heads a few cm in diameter and it is these buds, which are generally called 'sprouts' that are harvested.

Cultivars Dwarf. Ctskill, Early Dwarf, Dwarf Dem, Early Morn, Dwarf Improved, Kivk, Hilds Ideal and F_1 hybrid-Jad cross.

Intermediate. Long Island, Half Dwarf.

Tall. Amager Market, Danish Prize, Evesham, Bed Fordshire, Cambridge No. 1, 3 and 5.

Climate. The crop need cool climate and can tolerate frost.

Soil. Brussel's sprouts comes up well in fertile soils rich in humus with good moisture retention capacity. Soil pH should range from 6.0 to 6.8 for better growth and development. Early crops are usually grown on light soils while late cultivars are generally better adapted for growing on heavier soils.

Seed rate. 300-400 g/ha.

Sowing time. September-October.

Transplanting. Similar to cabbage except the seedlings of 6-8 weeks old are transplanted.

Spacing. 5 × 5 cm between rows and plants.

Manure and fertilizer. Soil should be incorporated with 25-30 t of farm yard manure, 200 kg N, 50 kg P_2O_5 and K_2O/ha. N should be applied in equal splits *viz.,* at the time transplanting, after one month, at first picking and at second picking.

Irrigation. Field should be kept always moist with frequent irrigation. However, a light irrigation may be given soon after transplanting.

Hoeing and weeding. As in cabbage.

Harvesting. Harvesting should be done 120 says after transplanting when the lower most sprouts attain proper size and firmness before they become loose or burst. Regular and frequent harvesting should be done to avoid opening and yellowing of sprouts for a month or more. The leaf below the sprouts is removed and the sprout is then cut or picked by hand.

Grading. The sprouts should be solid and have their top leaves folded closely. The outer leaves should be tightly clasping and not yellow in colour as is sometimes the case. Soft, dirty, loose, yellow leaflets, pieces of petiole and damaged sprouts should all be removed. Grading of sprouts should be done into-under 2 cm, 2-3 cm, 3-4 cm and over 4 cm. Large, loose sprouts are sometimes are marketed separately as 'blowers'.

Marketing. The picked sprouts are generally transported in crates, boxes, bags, or nets or occasionally prepacked in transparent bags. At the end of harvesting period the tops of the plants are sometimes sold as 'Brussels green'.

Storage. As in cabbage.

Yield. Large sprout cultivars yield about 10 t/ha while others give 3-5 t/ha.

18.6. KALE

It is mainly winter vegetable grown normally on a small scale and is supplied at a time when other vegetables are in scarce.

Uses. Most forms of kale bear a rosette of leaves at the top of stem, which are used for food, though sometimes the individual leaves are picked. For human consumption it is mainly the curly leaved-cultivars that are used, whereas smooth-leafed cultivars are chiefly used for feeding livestock.

Nutritive value. Kale is very rich in vitamins, notably vitamin C, pro-vitamin A and in calcium.

Medicinal value. Have some medicinal properties.

Origin. The Kale is believed to have originated in Europe.

Taxonomy. It belongs to the family *Cruciferae,* genus *Brassica,* species *oleracea* and var. *acephala.* Different Kale types like Russian Kale, Head Kale, Jersey Kale or Tree Kale.

Cultivars. Dwarf : Dwarf Green Curled Scotch, Dwarf Moss Curled, Lage Groene Fijngekrulde, Dwarf Blue Curled Scotch, Dwarf Kale Siberian.

Medium-Tall : Medium Green Curled Scotch, Half Dwarf Moss Curled, Hammer, Hamburger.

Tall : Tall Green Curled Scotch, Winschoten, Westerwolde.

Other cultivars : Dwarf Brown, Tall Brown, Silver Heart.

Climate. Kale is the hardiest crop among the Cole group and hardy cultivars can withstand temperatures of 10-15°C but the little-hardy cultivars are sensitive to frost. Kale can also withstand high summer temperatures fairly well. The flavour of kale is usually improved by frost.

Soil. Kale does best in on medium-heavy fertile soils with a good moisture supply, but it can also be grown satisfactorily on lighter soils. It withstands drought reasonably well, and well drained soils is of importance. Kale is more salt tolerant than cabbage.

Seed rate. 600-800 g/ha.

Sowing time. Plains — September-October.

Hills — March-April.

Transplanting. Kale is normally sown on a seed-bed, though occasionally they are sown direct in the field.

Spacing. 45 × 45 or 75 × 60 cm between rows and plants.

Manure and fertilizer. As in case of cabbage.

Irrigation. Irrigation should be given at an interval of 10-15 days to keep the field in its optimum soil moisture condition.

Hoeing and weeding. Weeds are usually controlled by hoeings, which should be shallow if the crop has already made some growth in order to guard against root injury. Once the crop has made growth, further weed-control can generally be omitted.

Harvesting. Leaves are harvested before they become old, tough and stringy. Harvesting is done either cutting-off the entire plant from the growing level after days of seeding or the lower leaves are periodically picked. The inner leaves and bud are left to produce new leaves for a continuous supply. The whole top rosette is frequently harvested for the fresh market. In case of tall cultivars, the lower leaves, if adequately curled should be harvested. For processing industry the leaves are picked individually and large ribs must be removed.

Grading. The harvested leaves are graded on the basis of leaf colour, shape, and size, etc. according to cultivar.

Marketing. The leaves are picked and tied into bundles of 0.5 to 1.0 kg or entire plant, having reached their normal size. Sometimes the entire plant is harvested and marketed in bundles.

Storage. Similar to cabbage.

Yield. 10-25 t/ha. Normally the autumn crops yield best.

18.7. CHINESE CABBAGE

Chinese cabbage is also known as celery cabbage, but it is more closely related to mustard than to cabbage or celery. It produces more leaf yield in a short time. The demand for its green leaves is constantly increasing and thus the area both in hills and plains.

Uses. The leaves and petioles are cooked as vegetable.

Nutritive value. The plant is rich in vitamins and minerals.

Medicinal value. It provides sufficient fibre, maintain and improve the digestive system.

Origin. The Chinese cabbage is believed to have originated in China.

Taxonomy. It belongs to the family *Cruciferae,* genus *Brassica,* species *rapa* and sub-species *chinensis* and *pekinensis.* It is an annual plant. Two types are available-leafy type *(Brassica rapa* var *chinensis)* have thin, long, dark green leaves resembling to Swiss chard in growth habit and heading type *(Brassica rapa* var. *pekinensis)* produces larger, more elongated and compact head resembling Cos lettuce.

Cultivars. *Leafy types.* Crispy Choy, Pae Choy, Solan Selection, Palampur Green.

Heading type. Burpee Hybrid, Early Hybrid G, Michihli, Wonghok.

Climate. Chinese cabbage is a hardy, cool weather crop grown during winter but in hills in summer because of mild climate.

Soil. It requires a rich in humus, well drained moist soil.

Seed rate. Through seedlings — 600-750 g/ha.
Direct seed sowing — 1.5-2.0 kg/ha.

Sowing time. Plains — September-October.
Hills — March-April.

Sowing/transplanting. Normally seedlings are raised and transplanted in the main field. Seeds are also sown 1-1.5 cm deep in the soil. Chinese cabbage is sown on a seed-bed, though occasionally they are sown direct in the field.

Spacing. 45-60 × 30 cm between rows and plants.

Manure and fertilizer. Apply 20 t of FYM, 100 kg N, 60 kg P_2O_5 and 40 kg K_2O/ha at the time of land preparation and top dressed like cabbage.

Irrigation. Same as in case of Cole vegetables.

Hoeing and weeding. Same as in case of Cole vegetables.

Harvesting. In case of leaf type cultivars, the leaves are ready for harvesting after four weeks of transplanting. The leaves should be cut regularly at an interval of 10-15 days. The outer leaves may be picked by hand without disturbing the growing plant. The heads are harvested by cutting the entire head off at the ground level at the appropriate time and stage. The leaves are crisp and the inner leaves are faintly or dark green depending on the cultivars.

Grading. The green leaves of uniform size selected and tied into bundles of standard weight preferably of half or one kg. These are packed in baskets or any other suitable containers.

Marketing. The harvested produce being perishable in nature should be immediately sent to the market in fresh form without any delay otherwise it will be damaged or get dry.

Storage. Similar to spinach or other leafy vegetable. Leaves can be stored at 0°C and RH of 95%.

Yield. 30-40 t/ha.

Crop protection

Diseases/Insect-pests	*Symptoms*	*Control*
Diseases		
Alternaria leaf spot	Leaf spots appear on the leaves.	Seed treatment @ 2% by any of organomericurials 3 sprays of Manozeb @ 2% at 10 days interval along with sticker.
Sclerotinia rot	Rotting of curds in field, store and transit.	4-5 sprays of carbendazim @ 0.1% at 10 days interval.
Damping-off	Collapsing of seedlings in early and mid-season cultivars.	Drenching nursery beds with formaldehyde. Seed treatment with mercurial fungicide.
Yellowing	Plant become yellow in 2-3 weeks after transplanting.	Grow resistant cultivars. Clean nursery beds.
Black rot	Yellowing of foliage followed by blackening of veins and no curd formation.	Seed treatment with hot water (50°C for 30 minutes) + Streptocyline 0.1%. Long crop rotation. Grow resistant cultivars.

Black leg	Splitting stem vertical, severe black discolouration of sap stream and whole root system decays from bottom upward.	Hot water treatment of seed. Spray seed plant with copper oxychloride @ 0.2%.
Curd rot complex		Five sprays of Ridomil @ 2.5% + Streptocyline 200 ppm at 7 days interval.
Insect-pests		
Diamond back moth		Spray cartap hydrochloride @ 500 g a.i./ha at 15 days interval.
Cabbage maggot	First attack the young rootlets then burrow main root causing wilting of the plant.	Dusting aldrin or dialdrin controls the insect.
Cabbage and turnip aphid	Suck sap on later stage of the crop.	Spray with Malathion or Metacid @ 1 ml/L and repeat.
Cutworm	Attack on colorzone of young seedlings and plant dies.	Apply Chloropyrephos or Thiodan @ 0.2%.
Green cabbage worms	Feed on foliage of cabbage.	Spray Thiodan @ 0.2%.

CHAPTER

19

ROOT VEGETABLES

The most commonly grown root crops in India are radish, turnip, carrot and garden beet. From seed production point of view these vegetables are classified into two distinct groups *i.e.* Asiatic or tropical and European or temperate. The former can be grown for seed in the plains but the latter produces seeds only under the temperate climate. Both the types are adapted to cool weather and are highly resistant to frost. Temperate types undergo dormancy or rest period which can only be broken when the roots are subjected to a low temperature *i.e.* less than 10°C for a period of 4 to 6 weeks at any time either in storage or under field conditions. Due to this reason the seeds of later can only be produced in places like Kashmir, Kullu, Katrain, Darjeeling and Nilgiri hills where winters are severe.

19.1. RADISH

Radish is a popular root vegetable grown through out the year on commercial scale and as a kitchen garden crop. It is suitable for growing both in tropical and temperate regions. It is easy to grow as an off-season crop and an ideal source of income to the poor farmers.

Uses. It is relished for its pungent flavour in various forms, leaves and roots are used as raw or as salad or cooked in various ways. The green pods of radish are also cooked as vegetable. It is an ideal crop to grow as inter-crop and catch-crop. The long pods of rat tail radish are cooked as vegetable.

Nutritive value. Radish greens is very rich in vitamin A, B and C with little of carbohydrate iron and protein.

Medicinal value. Radish is credited with refreshing and defusative properties. It helps in curing piles, liver trouble, enlarged spleen, gall bladder and jaundice. It has diuretic cooling effect and increases appetite. In homoeopathy, it is used for neuralgic headaches, sleeplessness, chronic diarrhoea, and gastrodynia. Root ash is used in stomach troubles. Juice of fresh leaves is good diuritic and laxative. Seeds are good peptic expectorant, diuritic and carminative.

Origin. Probably it is a native of Europe or Asia/India or Central arid Western China.

Taxonomy. It is a member of family *Cruciferae,* genus *Raphanus* and species *sativus.* The species caudatus is grown for its long pods. It is a perennial plant and the fleshy roots edible portion of the root develops from both from the primary root and the hypocotyl. Pink colour of roots is due to anthocyanin.

Cultivars : *Temperate.* White Icicle, French Breakfast, RRWT, Sel-9, Scarlet Globe.

Tropical. Japanese White, Chinese Pink, Pusa Red, Arka Nishant (IIHR-1-1), Co-1.

Semi-temperate (Asiatic). Pusa Himani, Pusa Chetaki, Pusa Reshmi. Pusa Desi, Ganesh Synthetic.

Local. Jaunpuri, Bombay Red, Chinese Rose, Contai.

Climate. Radish require cool and moderate climate but the Asiatic varieties can resist heat more than the European types. It attain best flavour, texture and size at 10-15.6°C. It is not affected by frost of extreme cold. A long day as well high temperature lead to bolting without root formation. During hot weather the roots become rough, mis-shapen and pungent before reaching the edible size.

Soil. It can be cultivated in all types of soils but for good crop, the soil should be light, friable and rich in humus. Heavy soils should be avoided. The optimum soil pH is 5.5-6.8.

Seed rate. The seed required is 8-10 kg in tropical types and 10-12 kg in temperate types per hectare.

Sowing time. It can be grown throughout the year. In plains sowing is done any time between September and January. In hills, seed is sown in March-April.

Sowing. The soil should be prepared into a better tilth and free from clods, stones, weed plants etc. Divide the field into plots of convenient size for smooth irrigation. In some places radish is sown on ridges. The seed is sown directly in the field and are drilled 1.25 cm deep.

Spacing. Depend on the cultivar and seed is sown 6-8 cm between the plants and 30-45 cm between rows. However, the temperate types 20 × 10 cm and tropical types 30 × 10 cm.

Manure and fertilizer. Application of 10-15 t well rotten FYM, 100 kg N, 50 kg each of P_2O_5 and K_2O/ha is sufficient depending on the soil test.

Irrigation. Some of the cultivars are short duration and fast growing, needs optimum soil moisture conditions. The seed germinates within 4-5 days therefore pre-sowing irrigation is essential. Frequent irrigation is important for the proper development of the roots.

Thinning. Thinning should be done for proper plant spacing and for better root development.

Hoeing and weeding. Weeds need to be effectively controlled by giving shallow hoeing.

Harvesting. Depending on the cultivar the roots should be harvested, when tender and of optimum size. These are pulled along with leaves after light pre-irrigation. The washed roots are prepared for the market.

Grading. The roots along with tops are graded according to the cultivar and one kg bundles are prepared.

Marketing. The produce is transported to the market in baskets or gunny bags or mostly loose in trucks need to be disposed-off as soon as possible.

Storage. Radish produce is perishable and can be stored for a day or two.

Yield. Temperate types —7-9 t/ha and Tropical types —20-25 t/ha.

19.2. TURNIP

Turnip is a widely cultivated in the country. Mainly turnip is grown for its root and young tender leaves (tops) which are rich in minerals and vitamins.

Uses. Roots are taken raw as salad and cooked form also used for pickle. The turnip leaves are seldom used as a green vegetable are often fed to cattle. The young tender leaves are cooked as vegetable in hills.

Nutritive value. The tender leaves are rich in mineral matter (iron, calcium) and vitamins A and C.

Medicinal value. Turnip possess stomachic properties. A poultice of leaves is applied to abrasions. Aqueous extract of the leaves and roots inhibits the growth of *E. coli* and *Neurospora cressa.* It has antibacterial, diuretic, aperient and haemorrhage properties. Seed oil is used in dengue fever, rubbed on chest in bronchitis. In sensitive people, turnip cause haemoglobinuria and photosensitization.

Origin. Central and Western China, or Middle Asia (Punjab and Kashmir) or the Mediterranean region.

Taxonomy. Turnip belongs to the family *Cruciferae,* genus *Brassica* and species *rapa* or *B. camprestris* var. *rapa.*

Cultivars : *Temperate.* Purple Top White Globe, Golden Ball, Snowball, Early Milan.

Tropical. Pusa Chandrima, Pusa Swarnima, Pusa Sweti, Pusa Kanchan.

Climate. It needs a cool climate and tolerates frost to some extent. The optimum temperature is 18-23°C and high temperature will affect the quality of roots. It needs open sunlight for better root development.

Soil. Turnip can be grown in a wide range of soils but performs well in moderately deep, friable, well drained soil with optimum pH 5.5-6.8 (acidic soils).

Seed rate. 4.0-4.5 kg/ha.

Sowing time. Plains—September-October.

Low and mid-hills —September-October.

High-hills — March-May.

Sowing. As in radish.

Spacing. The 30-40 × 10 cm between and rows and plants.

Manure and fertilizer. Application of 10 tonnes of FYM, 100 kg N, 50 kg P_2O_5 and 50 kg K_2O per ha were found to be optimum. Application of manure and fertilizers is similar as for cabbage crop.

Irrigation. The soil if not in optimum moisture condition, a light irrigation should be given and the subsequent irrigations after 10-12 days interval till the roots are harvested.

Hoeing and weeding. Hoeing and weeding should be done periodically to remove the weeds and pulverize the soil.

Thinning. Thinning is an important operation in turnip crop to maintain optimum plant population per unit area.

Earthing-up. This operation should be done to cover the developing roots soon after top-dressing.

Harvesting. Turnip should be harvested timely as and when the roots attain optimum diameter depending on the variety. Before harvesting a light irrigation will be helpful for easy pulling of roots without any injury. The entire plant should be uprooted and cleaned for market.

Grading. The fresh turnip roots should be graded according to the cultivar-size, shape and colour, packed in proper containers and send to the markets.

Marketing. The produce should be transported properly without any damage and should be sent to the markets as soon as possible.

Storage. Similar to radish.

Yield. 300-400 q/ha.

19.3. CARROT

Carrot is an important cool season root vegetable cultivated almost throughout for its carotene richness.

Uses. Carrot roots are relished raw as salad, cooked in curries, vegetable and sambhar and processed forms as sweet meals. Forage is fed to the horses. Black carrots are used for the preparation of type of beverage called kanji which is supposed to be a good appetizer.

Nutritive value. It is rich in minerals such as iron, vitamins like thiamine, riboflavin, vitamin-A, niacin and ascorbic acid. The orange coloured cultivars are rich in carotene a precursor of vitamin A. Green carrot leaves are highly nutritive, rich in protein, minerals and vitamins. The outer area contains more sugar and vitamins than the inner one.

Medicinal value. Carrot provides relief for flatulence, fever, rheumatism, menstrual, discomfort, halrtosis, provide expectorant and anti-spasmodic preparations, as well as acting as appetite stimulant, digestive aid and several other benefits. Infusion of carrot is used as folk remedy for thread worms. It also causes a marked reduction in blood sugar and indolent ulcers. Beta-carotene helpful for relief of certain skin conditions and reduce the risk of cataract formation and several types of cancer.

Origin. The carrot is believed to have originated in Central Asia in the hills of Punjab and Kashmir with a secondary centre of distribution in Asia, Europe and North Africa around the Mediterranean.

Taxonomy. Member of family *Umbelliferae*, genus *Daucus,* species *carota* and sub-species *sativus.* Carrot root is the enlarged fleshy tap root and produces rosette of leaves during its vegetative phase and flowering shoot in the subsequent season producing seeds.

Cultivars: *Temperate.* Nantes, Chantaney, Kashmir Beauty, Zeno, Danvera, American Beauty.

Semi-Temperate. Pusa Yamdagni, Danver Half long, A Plus Desi, Ooty-1.

Asiatic. Pusa Indian, Long Red, Pusa Kesar, Imperator, Hybrid No-1, HG-202, HC 203, Carrot No. 1.

Climate. Carrot is widely adapted to cool climates but some tropical types tolerate quite high temperatures. The optimum temperature for the crop is 15°C and good germination takes place at a temperature range of 7.2-23°C. The colour development and root growth is affected by temperature. At temperature between 15-20°C produces good colour but beyond this colour development will be poor.

Soil. The land selected for carrot production should be deep with good drainage, fertile, rich in organic matter and free from disease inoculum. Heavy soils should be avoided as the roots formed are deformed, rough and coarse. The ideal soil pH is 6.0-7.0.

Seed rate. Use 2.5 to 3.5 kg certified seed rate/ha.

Sowing time. Plains — Tropical types — Mid-August-Early-December.

Temperate types — September-October.

Hills — March-July.

In some areas close to markets in cities, gap sowings are done to maintain continuous supply of fresh carrots.

Sowing. Land should be prepared into better tilth. To improve the germination, the seeds should be rubbed to remove fine hairs before sowing. The seeds being small should be mixed with sand before sowing. The seed may be sown on flat beds, single row or double row ridges, furrows or on flat beds about 1.5 cm deep. Carrot seed takes about 7-8 days to germinate.

Spacing. 30-45 cm apart between rows followed by thinning to 5-10 cm apart with in plants.

Manure and fertilizer. Apply 15-20 t of FYM, 40-50 kg each of P_2O_5 and K_2O at the time of sowing and top dress 75 to 100 kg N/ha in two splits after weeding. The FYM, P_2O_5 and K_2O are applied at the time of field preparation where as N is applied in two splits after 30 days and 65 days after sowing.

Irrigation. The irrigation should be given immediately after sowing for rapid and uniform germination. Because of the deep root forming nature, the crop needs continuous moisture in the soil. Frequent irrigation should be given to obtain good root yield.

Hoeing and weeding. Weeds generally possess a serious problem in carrot crop and both manual and chemical weeding are practised. Herbicides like Diuron and Monuron @ one kg per hectare applied 40 days after sowing effectively control the weeds.

Thinning. Thinning is an important practice done in carrot to improve the root quality. The early crop should be thinned to 5 cm between two roots whereas main crop is thinned 10-15 cm apart when the plants are 5-6 cm in height.

Physiological disorder. Splitting of root is a physiological disorder which is usually seen when there is a sudden increase in the soil moisture after a prolonged drought. Forking is another phenomenon wherein the hard soil does not allow the straight growth of the tap root which result in the formation of forked roots. Forked and split roots fetch poor price in the market. Keeping the soil moisture in its optimum condition will help the soil loose thereby help to avoid splits and forked roots.

Harvesting. Harvesting should be done at correct maturity stage when the roots has attained the optimum size according to the cultivar. Light irrigation should be given before harvest and the roots are pulled out from the soil without any damage.

Grading. The harvested roots are trimmed, washed and graded according to the cultivar before sending to the market.

Marketing. The mode of transport followed will depend upon the quantum of produce, distance from the market and prevailing prices. The produce should be immediately disposed-off after harvest as the quality of roots will deteriorate soon.

Storage. The tops should be removed of the harvested roots and stored in a cool, moist place. These can be better left in the field and covered with heavy mulch in areas where mild winter occur until required.

Yield. Depending on the cultivar and season, the yield ranges between 20-30 t/ha.

19.4. GARDEN BEET

Garden beet is an important root vegetable cultivated in home gardens and on commercial scale.

Uses. It is eaten as salad, cooked with other vegetables and meat, etc.

It is also used for processing-pickling, canning, etc. The young tender leaves can be used as greens.

Nutritive value. Garden beet is rich in minerals and vitamin C.

Medicinal value. Fat soluble extract is administered orally to treat vascular and metabolic disorders in human. Root juice exhibit antibial activity, against *Salmonella typhi* and *Micrococcouspyogenes* var. *auraus* and tumour. The plant contains alkaloids of which betaine is a mild diuretic and emmenagogue Infusion and decoction of the root are administered in stomach and boul complaints.

Origin. The native place of garden beet is probably the Mediterranean region of Europe or around Western Asia and Africa.

Taxonomy. It belongs to the family *Chenopodaceae,* genus *Beta* and species *vulgaris.* Also sugar beet, Swiss chard, mangel, palak (spinach beet) all belongs to *Beta vulgaris.* Garden beet is a biennial vegetable. Beet roots are usually round but may be flat or elongated.

Their fleshy roots are usually red but golden cultivars are also available. The seed is actually dried fruit or called 'seed ball' containing several tiny true seeds.

Cultivars. Crimson Globe and Detroit Dark Red.

Climate. Garden beet can tolerate both cool and warm climate and withstand some freezing condition. The optimum temperature for better growth is 18-21°C and if it lower down below 10°C for some days, bolting occurs affecting root development.

Soil. It can be grown in any type of soil but deep, light sandy soils are highly suitable and heavy soils should be avoided. Suitable soil pH is 6-7 but it can be grown well in saline and alkaline soils also.

Seed rate. Normally, 4-5 kg seed for monogerm cultivars and 7-10 kg in case of multigerm cultivars is required for sowing a hectare of land.

Sowing time. Plains —September-October.

Hills — March-April.

Sowing. The soil should be ploughed thoroughly into a better tilth. The field should be divided into fine beds. Garden beet is directly sown by using 'seed balls' which contain one or many seeds. If the seed is milled before sowing will help to eliminate thinning operation. Seed should be soaked in tap water for 6-8 hours before sowing.

Spacing. Seed/seed ball must be sown in lines 45 cm apart and 8-10 cm between the plants.

Thinning. After one month of sowing, thinning should be done 8-10 cm apart to maintain a plant population of about 70,000 to 80,000/ha.

Manure and fertilizer. The manure and fertilizers required for raising a good crop of garden beet are 30 t FYM, 150 kg N, 100 kg P_2O_5 and 80 kg K_2O/ha. At the time of planting, 50 kg N and full quantities of P_2O_5 and K_2O are added as a basal dose and the remaining nitrogen is applied in two splits *i.e.* at 30 and 60 days after sowing.

Irrigation. The number of irrigation depends upon soil-type, nature of crop/variety and surface evaporation. However, frequent irrigation after 10-15 days interval should be applied.

Earthing-up. Earthing-up is necessary for root crop during later stages to cover the swollen roots.

Hoeing and weeding. Weeding should be done by hoeing the crop at early stages to keep weed-free.

Harvesting. Depending on the cultivar and management, the roots will attain harvestable maturity with highest quality in about 60-70 days. A light irrigation before harvesting will be helpful and the entire plant is pulled out, the tops are removed and after washing the roots are marketed.

Grading. The roots should be graded according to shape, size and flesh colour into A, B, and C grades before sending to the market.

Marketing. Marketing should be done immediately to the markets having demand.

Storage. The roots after removing the tops can be stored at 0°C and 95% RH.

Yield. 25-30 t/ha.

Crop protection (Radish, turnip, carrot and garden beet)

Diseases/Insect-pests	*Symptoms*	*Control*
Diseases		
Alternaria blight		Treat seed @ 2% by any of organomercurials. 3 sprays of Mancozeb @ 0.2% at 10 days interval.
White rust		Clean cultivation and follow rotations.
Watery soft rot	Common decay in storage.	Resistant cultivars.
Black rot		Sanitation and crop rotation helps to control the disease.
Insect-pests		
Carrot rust fly		2 or 3 sprays with 0.1% Dimethoate.
Lygus fly		Seed treatment with insecticides.
Aphids	Suck the sap from leaves and devitalize the plants.	Spray Nuvacron @ 1.25 ml/1 or Metasystox @ 2 ml/1 of water.
Sawfly	Larvae feed on leaves voraciously.	Spray Sevin 50 WP @ 4 g/1 of water.

CHAPTER

20

BULB VEGETABLES

20.1. ONION

Onion (*Allium cepa* L.) is one of the most important and popular vegetable grown successfully in an area of more than 3.95 lakh ha with a production of 56.68 lakh t, productivity of 10.32 t/ha and rank only next to China. Onion is an export-oriented vegetable, fetching a huge amount of foreign exchange every year. It needs concerted efforts to increase cultivated area as well as boost the bulb production/unit area keeping in view the importance of the crop in recent years. A sizeable of quantity of onion bulbs are exported to various countries.

Uses. Onion is most popularly used vegetable and spice which is utilized by every house-wife in the kitchen, cooked as vegetable in various ways in all curries, fried, boiled, baked and in soup making, as spice and in various tasty preparations *viz.,* widely used in salads, pickles, chutney, stew, flavouring, cooked vegetables or sauces, and preparation of certain other products and extracts like onion powder, onion salt etc. It is consumed by all classes of people through the year as a ripe bulb and also relished as a salad while in green stage.

Nutritive value. Small sized bulbs are more nutritive. It contains little vitamin 'B' and 'C' and trace of iron and calcium. The pungency in onion is due to a volatile oil-allyl propyl disulphide.

Medicinal value. It has got manifold medicinal values. Onion extract have potent antibacterial and fungal properties. Cure smallpox, plausible remedy for hysteria, helps in lowering blood pressure as anthelmintics, as intestinal antispasmadics and externally as rebefacents or irritant and also helps in the treatments of diabetics, cancer and asthma. Onion juice is used to treat ophthalmia and earache. Onion possess tonic, stomachic, diuretic and appetite improving properties. Useful in jaundice, bilousness, stimulant, expectorant and respiratory affections, tumours and diseases of spleen, flatulence, dysentery and cholera, restoring consciousness in fainting and hystric fits. Reduces the insulin requirement of diabetic patients. Onion oil and dipropyl sulphide produce significant hypoglycaemic effect and reduce blood glucose level.

Origin. Onion has been originated from the region comprising North-west India, Afghanistan, Tajik and Uzbek of USSR and Western Tien Shan, Western Asia and the area around the Mediterranean regions. The Welish onion is probably of Chinese origin.

Taxonomy. Onion belongs to the family *Amaryllidaceae,* genus *Allium* and species *cepa.* It is a biennial in nature but can perennate by underground bulbs but behave as an annual whether grown from seed or bulb. It is a foetid, scapigerous herb possessing a tunicated bulb may be single or divided forming a cluster; the leaves are sub-distichous, fistular and shorter than the inflated scape. The aerial leaves are cylindrical, long, linear and hollow, a characteristic feature in *Allium cepa.* The true stem in onion is reduced and the bulbous structure above soil is the pseudo-stem constituted by the accumulation of the tubular leaf sheaths. Onion plant flowers and set seeds.

Cultivars : *Rabi.* Patna Red, Pusa Red, Brown Spanish, Bellary Red, Early Grano, Pusa Ratnar, N-25, VL-3, Punjab Red Round, Arka Pitamber, Arka Bindu, Bobby. Pusa Madhavi, Punjab Selection, N-2-4-1, N-257-9-1, Baswant-780, Phule Suvarna, Arka Neketan, Arka Pragati, Kalyanpur Red Round, Udaipur 101.

Kharif. N-53, Agrifound Dark Red and Arka Kalyan.

Hybrids. Arka Kirthiman, Arka Lalima, Arka Kalyan, Almora Hybrid, Hybrid BL-67, IIHR-F_1 Hybrid.

Hills. Brown Spanish and Early Lakiyar.

White onion. Pusa White Round, Pusa White Flat, S-48, Phule Safaed.

Export purpose. Phule Suvarna.

Climate. Onions require cool weather during early development of bulb crop and early growth of seed stalk. Later a moderately high temperature and a dry atmosphere are needed for the maturation of the bulbs and seeds. Relatively higher temperature as well as long photoperiod is essential for bulb formation in most of the commercial cultivars cultivated in India. The optimum temperature is 13-24°C is favourable for vegetative growth (before bulbing) and 16-21°C during bulbing is conducive. Onion also responds to day length *i.e.* bulb formation takes place under different day lengths depending on variety and some under short days varieties are grown in north Indian plains where as long day under hills.

Soil. Onion can be cultivated in a wide range of soils, a sandy loam or silt loam is the best. Preferably the soil should be rich in humus, well drained and friable. The optimum pH is 5.8-6.5.

Seed rate. 8-10 kg/ha.

Seed treatment. The raised beds of convenient size are formed and these are inoculated with Vesicular/Arbuscular *Mycorrhizae* @ 1 kg/m^2. The seeds are then treated with *Azospirllium* @ 100 g/kg of seeds before sowing.

Sowing time. The onion crop is raised during both *rabi* and *kharif* season *viz.,* in former case, seed is sown in mid-October to mid-November. and seedling transplanting is done in end of December and bulb crop is ready in May or early June. In *kharif* crop, the seed is sown in end May-mid-June, transplanting is done in end of July to early August, bulbs are lifted in late October or early November. The bulbs are stored until December.

Sowing/transplanting. The field is ploughed 4-5 times to bring into a better tilth. The beds and channels of convenient sizes or ridges and furrows are formed. The seedlings are transplanted and irrigated immediately.

Spacing. 20 × 10 cm between rows/ridges and plants.

Manure and fertilizer. Application of 20 t of FYM, 100 kg N, 80 to 85 kg P_2O_5 and 60-65 kg K_2O/ha is sufficient to raise the bulb crop. Along with 30 kg of zink sulphate or Ferrous sulphate is also applied.

Irrigation. Irrigation is necessary at the time of transplanting and then once in a 7-8 days. The critical stage is bulb formation stage and there should not be any moisture stress during the period. Otherwise the yield will be drastically reduced. On an average it may need 18-20 irrigation from transplanting to harvest. A dry spell followed by irrigation may cause splitting of the outer scales. Irrigation is stopped when the tops mature and start falling.

Hoeing and weeding. Deep interculture may be avoided since it is a shallow rooted crop.

Pre-harvest treatment. 15-20 days before bulb harvesting, the plants are sprayed with 500 ppm (500 mg/L of water) Maleic Hydrazide. This will prevent the sprouting of the onion bulbs in storage and keep them healthy for about 6-7 months.

Harvesting. Green onions are best to harvest when they are of the diameter of a lead pencil and until a small bulb is formed. They are uprooted and washed, bundled and send to the market. The ripe bulbs are ready for harvesting in May. The maturity is indicated by the tops drooping just above the bulbs while the leaves are still green. The mature bulbs can be pulled out easily by hand in case the soil is not hard or compact. In some place, the crop is ploughed with desi plough and the bulbs are collected. Precaution may be taken to cause minimum damage to the bulbs.

Curing. Onion bulbs should be properly cured before stored in crates or store. The length of time required for curing depends on mainly on the weather conditions and thorough curing needs 20-30 days. It should be done by piling in a thin layer as the thick layer may lead to rotting and loss.

Grading. Onion bulbs should be cleaned and graded after proper curing. All open necks, bottle necks and injured bulbs should be rejected. The Indian Standards Institution has fixed three grades for onions in the country.

Marketing. Onion is transported to the assembling centres in open bullock cart or tractor trolleys to the local markets and to distant markets, it is carried in jute bags in trucks. While loading bags in trucks care should be taken in loading up to 5-6 bags height as over loading will damage the bulbs in lower bags by pressure. While loading in trucks, the braces may be provided to support each layer of the bags. There will be injury to the bulbs meaning thereby loss in quality and weight. Use of hooks should be avoided as it injure the bulbs and such bulbs when stored loose more weight and also rot easily. Onion bulbs after reaching to the assembly centres are generally sold to the local whole sellers of distributing/consuming markets. These transactions usually take place with the help of commission agents. Exporters either buy their requirements directly from assembly centres through local commission agents or from whole sellers in the important assembling/regulated markets. Onion is sold by open auction in regulated markets. In other markets, sale often takes place by mutual negotiations which may either be direct between the buyer and seller or through commission agents or brokers. In certain markets under cover system is also present.

Storage. Onion bulbs are easily stored for 5-6 months after harvest which favours long marketing season. The onion bulbs should be mature, cured, dried and free from injury and diseases, etc. before storing in well ventilated stores/ware houses having uniform and comparatively low temperature and low humidity. The best storage temperature is 0°C and 60-75 per cent RH.

Yield. Hybrids — 40-50 t/ha.

Rabi crop — 25-30 t/ha.

Kharif crop — 15-25 t/ha.

20.2. GARLIC

Garlic is one of the important commercial spice or a condiment crop, second among the *Allium* species grown throughout India. It is also important foreign exchange earner apart from meeting the domestic requirement of the country. India ranks second in area (86,000 ha) and third in production (3,50,000 tonnes). The productivity in India is 4.07 t/ha.

The world area under garlic is 9,83,000 ha and production is 1,03,81,000 tonnes. China, Korea, India, Spain, Egypt and USA are the major garlic growing countries. China ranks first in area and production (5,57,000 ha and 76,74,000 tonnes). India though ranks second in area (86,000 ha) its position is third in production (3,50,000 tonnes). In productivity Egypt *tops* the list (21.43 t/ha) followed by USA (18.51 t/ha), China (13.78 t/ha) and Korea Rep. (10.28 t/ha). The productivity in India is 4.07 t/ha. In India, area production and productivity of garlic have improved by about 48.28, 69.90 and 14.19, respectively (FAO, 1998). According to Director of Economics and Statistics, Ministry of Agriculture, Government of India, the annual area under garlic is 111,900 ha, production 475,300 tonnes with average productivity of 4.25 t/ha. Among different states of India M.P. is the leading state accounting to more than 35% of area and 38% of production with average yield of 4.58 t/ha. The other major garlic producing states are Gujarat, Rajasthan, Odisha, U.P. and Maharashtra. In India per ha yields are highest in Punjab (12.44 t/ha) followed by Haryana (12.00 t/ha and Maharashtra (6.76 t/ha).

Uses. It is consumed almost in every home kitchen garden for seasoning and flavouring the food as it has got manifold uses. Garlic is consumed almost all walks of life who takes onion in every meal.

Chemical composition. The uninjured bulb contains a colourless, odourless water soluble amino acid *allin.* On crushing garlic bulb the enzyme *allinase* breaks down and *allin* to produce *allicin* of which the principal ingredient is the odoriferous diallyl disulfide. Garlic contains about 0.1% volatile oil. The chief constituent of the oil are diallyl disulfide (60%), diallyl trisulfide (20%), allyl propyl disulfide (6%), a small quantity of diethyl disulfide and probably diallyl polysulfide. Diallyl disulfide is said to possess the true garlic odour.

Nutritive value. It has higher nutritive value than other *Allium* species. It is rich in proteins, phosphorus, potash, calcium, magnesium and carbohydrates. Ascorbic acid is very high in green garlic.

Medicinal value. On the basis of Unani and Ayurvedic system prevailing in the country, garlic is carminative, diuretic, diaphoratic, expectorant, rubefacient, tonic and is a gastric stimulant and thus helps in digestion and absorption of food. *Allicin* present in aqueous extract of garlic, reduces cholesterol concentration in human blood. The inhalation of garlic oil or garlic juice has been generally recommended by the physicians in case of pulmonary tuberculosis, rheumatism, arthritis, sterility, impotency cough and red eyes. Garlic possess insecticidal action. 1% extract gives protection against mosquitoes for 8 hours. Extract of garlic along with chilli and ginger has beneficial action against soil nematodes and many fungi. *Allicin* of garlic has also got bacterial properties so also diallyl disulfide, diallyl trisulfide and essential oil including many medicinal properties.

Origin. It is belived to have originated in Central Asia and Mediterranean region.

Taxonomy. Garlic belongs to the family *Alliaceae* genus *Allium* and species *sativum.* It is a herbaceous annual for the bulb production. The edible underground stem is the composite bulb made of numerous smaller bulbs or bulblets called cloves (5-30/bulb). Leaves have solid thin blades. Some cultivars produce flower but these flowers do not set seed whereas others produce vegetative bulbs on the top called bulbils which are also used for propagation in some cases.

Cultivars. GHC-1, Selection-1, T-56-4, T-54-4, Solan Phavari, Pusa Selection-10, ARU-52, Yamuna Safed (G-l), Agrifound White (G-41), Yamuna Safed-2 (G-50), G-282, Agrifound Parvati (G-313), G-323, Godavari (Selection-2), T-56-4, Sweta (Selection-10), Co-2. Other varieties I.C.42889, I.C. 42860, Madrasi, Tabiti, Creole, Eknalia, Jamnagar, HG-1, HG-6, Ooty-1.

Climate. Higher quality yields are obtained in a mild climate. Excessive hot and long day are not good for proper bulb formation. Therefore, the crop is usually planted in winter and harvested when the hot season sets in. Garlic is frost hardy plant requiring cool and moist period during growth and relatively dry period during maturity of bulbs. Bulbing takes place during longer days and at high temperature, exposure to low temperature subsequent to bulb formation favours the process.

Soil. Garlic can be grown on variety of soils but thrives better on fertile, well drained loamy soils. Under heavy clay soil conditions are deformed, mishappen and make harvesting difficult. The bulbs get discoloured in badly drained soils and the cutting and pulling of bulbs from hard soils causes splitted and bruised bulbs which do not keep well in storage. The sandy or loose soils also produce bulbs lighter in weight and large discoloured bulbs with poor storage quality. The pH of soil between 6-7 is suitable for good crop. However, highly alkaline and saline soils are not suitable for garlic growing.

Propagation. The garlic is propagated vegetatively by using cloves. Bulbils produced in some varieties are also used as planting material. Now-a-days, tissue culture technique has been developed to produce healthy garlic bulbs. It needs lot of labour for planting and other operations as being narrow spaced crop. Moreover, in most parts labour is not available at times because of industrialization and this input has become costly.

Seed rate. Well developed, uniform bulbs having appropriate shape, size and compactness as per the cultivar are selected and about 500 kg cloves of 8-10 cm diameter are required to plant a hectare.

Planting time. The time of planting differs from region to region. It is planted from August to October in M.P. and Maharashtra, Karnataka and Andhra Pradesh and from September to November in North India. In Gujarat, planting is done during October-November. Proper season for planting in hills is March-April.

Planting material. Bigger cloves of 8-10 mm diameter should be selected from the outer side of the bulbs and long slender cloves present in the centre should not be used for planting, as such cloves produce poorly developed bulbs. The planting material are cloves which are detached from the bulbs with hands.

Land preparation. Land should be prepared to fine tilth thoroughly by repeated ploughings and plankings. Field should be divided into small beds and channels for easy intercultural operations.

Planting Methods. Garlic can be planted by dibbling, furrow planting and broadcasting. The common method is since dibbling or furrow planting by hand. Mostly because labour constraint, broadcasting method of sowing in furrow is followed which produces low yields of poor quality. This method is commonly used in Gujarat. In temperate areas in hills, bulbils are first grown in nursery bed and after 30-40 days they are transplanted in the main field at proper spacing. In advanced countries, kidney bean planter is used for planting of garlic to reduce the cost of production, (*a*) **Dibbling** —Fields are divided into small plots convenient for irrigation. Cloves are dibbled 5-5.7 cm deep keeping their growing ends upwards. (*b*) **Furrow planting** — Furrows are prepared at appropriate spacing with hand hoe. In these furrows cloves are dropped by hand. These are then covered lightly with loose soil and followed by mulching and (*c*) **Broadcasting** —Cloves are scattered evenly in well levelled field/seed beds by hand. They are then covered by harrowing and the field is divided into small plots for irrigation.

Spacing. The spacing followed 10 × 7.5 cm. The plant spacing vary in different regions of India. In Punjab 15 × 8 cm have given best result and has been recommended to most of the pockets. Closer planting invite more disease infection especially purple blotch. Wider spacing of 15 × 10 cm produces larger sized bulbs with bigger cloves, however, very wide spacing should be discouraged as it produces thick neck of bulb which is a undesirable character.

Manure and fertilizer. Garlic responds very well to organic manure. For a normal soil, apply 50 tonnes of FYM, 100 kg N, 50 kg P_2O_5 and 50 kg K_2O/ha. However, these doses varies from region to region depending on agro-ecological situation, soil type and soil tests, etc. The total FYM, half N, complete dose of P_2O_5 and K_2O maybe applied at the time of land preparation, before planting. Another half dose of N in two splits be added after one and two months of planting, respectively. Excessive N results in thick neck, sprouting before harvest and poor storage. Micro-nutrient application helps in enhancing the yield. Application of 5 kg boron, zink and molybdenum along with fertilizer dose produced maximum amount of allyle-propyle-disulfide. Also application of borax up to 10 kg/ha increased bulb size and yield.

Mulching. The garlic crop should be provided with a thin (4-5 cm thick) layer of mulch @ 5-6 tonnes of dry leaves or crop residues or 10-12 tonnes of green/wet leaves or well rotten FYM or compost. Mulching increases soil temperature, ease germination, maintain optimum moisture condition, add organic matter, protect from direct sun, check weed growth, diseases. Pests and soil erosion, resulting in more production of better quality.

Irrigation. At the time of planting cloves, the soil should be in its optimum moisture condition, otherwise irrigation may be applied immediately after planting. In general, garlic needs irrigation at an interval of 8 days during vegetative growth and 10-15 days during maturation. First irrigation is given after sowing. There should not be scarcity of moisture at any stage of the crop, otherwise bulb development will be affected. Garlic being shallow rooted (5 cm depth) and the soil should be kept wet to this level. Excess irrigation results in sprouting of bulbs. Irrigation after a long spell of drought results in splitting of bulbs and irrigation at maturity reduces storability and decreases market value of the bulbs.

Hoeing and weeding. Garlic is a shallow rooted crop and 2-3 shallow weeding and hoeing are done. Weedicides like Goal @ 0.95 ml (a.i.)/ha or Stomp @ 3.5 litre and one hand weeding at 40-50 days after planting gave better yields.

Croping systems. Crop rotation followed in a particular crop have a significant impact to enhance productivity, quality yields and make best economic use of the resources and soil without depleting the soil fertility. The cropping systems planned and followed in a region or tract for this crop with other crops varies depending up on the prevailing situations. A suitable crop rotation will give better results like Garlic (October-May), Chillies/French bean (June-September), Garlic (October-May) — Maize (June-September) and Garlic (October-May) — Ginger/Capsicum (June-Sept.).

Harvesting. The crop is considered ready for harvesting when the tops turn yellowish or brownish colour and show signs of drying up and bend to the ground. The bulbs begin to mature in about 4-5 months after planting, depending upon cultivar and season/soil, etc. G-282 is early maturing cultivar. Harvesting at the stage when tops have fallen over gives good quality bulbs. Early harvesting results in poor storage quality bulbs whereas delayed harvesting results in splitting and sprouting of bulbs. In India, harvesting is done manually by hand digger or in some areas where soil is loose the plants are pulled out or pulling is done by loosening the soil with country plough. Bulbs are taken out along with the tops and store at a dry place.

Curing. Curing is additional process of drying to remove the excess moisture and to allow the bulbs to become compact and go into dormant stage. It is done for about a week in the field to dry the bulbs thoroughly. Bulbs are covered along with the tops of each other to avoid damage to the bulbs from sun. These also are cured for 7-10 days in shade either with tops or after cutting the tops by leaving 2.5 cm to avoid the sun injury, above the bulbs and removing the roots. Harvesting at 100% neck fall and curing by windrow method has been recommended under Karnal conditions resulting in lowest storage losses in garlic (G-l).

Sorting and grading. Garlic after curing are run over a grader or it may be done manually before they go into storage or for marketing. The thick necked splitted, injured, diseased bulbs with hollow cloves are sorted out. Size grading is done after sorting depending on the varietal characters.

Packaging. In India, for domestic use, garlic bulbs are packed in open mesh jute bags. Garlic is packed in 90 kg packings. The packages should be well labelled with complete information, *viz.* lot number, name and address of both dispatcher and destination.

Marketing. Garlic is consumed in every home and use in processing industry has a fairly constant market demand. Garlic is transported to the assembling centres in open bullock cart or tractor trolleys in open. It is also carried in jute bags in trucks. While loading bags in trucks care should be taken in loading up to 5-6 bags height as over loading will damage the garlic bulbs in lower bags by pressure. There will be splitting also meaning thereby that cloves will be detached. Use of hooks should be avoided as it injure the bulbs/cloves and such bulbs when stored loose more weight and also rot easily. Garlic bulbs after reaching to the assembly centres are generally sold to the local whole sellers of distributing/consuming markets. These transactions usually take place with the help of commission agents. Exporters either buy their requirements directly from assembly centres through local commission agents or from whole sellers in the important assembling/regulated markets. Garlic is sold by open auction in regulated markets. In other markets, sale often takes place by mutual negotiations which may either be direct between the buyer and seller or through commission agents or brokers. In certain markets under cover system is also present.

Export. India has been exporting garlic for many years to the major importing countries *viz.*, Qatar, Saudi Arabia, Zambia, UAE, Behrain, Mauritius, Kuwait, Bangladesh and Sri Lanka. The export has been ranging between 2-3% of the total domestic production. The quantum of export has been fluctuating due to frequent and sudden change in the policy of garlic importing countries. China, France, Spain and Egypt are however major garlic exporting countries. These countries being at higher latitudes produce bigger cloved garlic which are more in demand. In India, the production of bigger cloved garlic is though not on big scale, it is picking up in northern hills and Nilgiri hills in view of increasing demand in export market. It is hoped that in the near future increase in area under those varieties having bigger cloves and have demand in the international market will be produced to the extent by 10-15 times easily. The export is mainly arranged from the ports of Mumbai, Tuticorin, Cochin, Chennai and Kolkata.

Storage. Bulbs are easily stored for 5-6 months after harvest which favours long marketing season. Thoroughly cured garlic bulbs keep fairly well under ordinary ventilated rooms. Garlic with dried leaves can be stored by hanging in well ventilated rooms. This is, however, not possible on commercial scale because space requirement is more storage without tops in nylon netted bags gave better performance at Nasik and Karnal as such the same has been recommended for storage to minimize the post-harvest loss. The losses in 5 months period *i.e.,* May to September may be about 25% mainly due to driage. Storage of garlic in bundles with top helps to reduce storage losses.

Dehydration. Some portion of garlic produce (surplus) is subjected to processing especially dehydration *i.e.* drying under controlled conditions of temperature and humidity. The dehydration is important because of the concentrated form, low cost, convenience and easy transportability and dehydrated garlic in the form of powder etc. has become highly popular among the civilians, military and para-military forces, besides export. Garlic makes an excellent dehydrated product and its use in the dry form has a great scope particularly in foreign countries where there is scarcity.

Yield. The yield of bulbs varies between 100 to 200 q/ha depending upon the variety and the regions where they are grown.

20.3. LEEK

Leek (*A. porrum*) is a non-building biennial crop grown for blanched stem. Bulbs little or not at all developed, the elongated foliage leaf bases (false stem) eaten.

Uses. The green stem and leaves are consumed as salad or cooked with other vegetables or mild flavouring soups, steves and spice curries. It is a very good substitute for green onion during summer and winter.

Nutritive value. The long white stem, leaf base and green tops are edible and nutritious, good source of carbohydrates, protein, minerals-phosphorus, iron and vitamin C.

Medicinal value. Plant contain sufficient amount of non-toxic saponine which give it expectorant properties.

Origin. Leek is believed to have originated in Mediterranean region.

Taxonomy. It belongs to the family *Amarilidaceae,* genus *Allium* and species *porrum* with its tunicate, narrow bulb. It is propagated by seed.

Cultivars. London Flag, American Flag and Elephant, Varna, Titan, Otins, Furar, Tenor, King Richard, Pancho, Partons, Alaska.

Climate. It is a cool season crop. However, it can tolerate heat more than onion. It thrives best in a temperature range of 12-18°C.

Soil. It can be grown in all types of soils but medium soils which are rich in nutrient and organic matter with a pH range of 6-8 is the best suited.

Seed rate. 5-7 kg/ha.

Sowing time. Plains — August-October.
Hills — March-April.

Sowing/planting. Normally propagated by seed and the nursery is raised like that of onion. The 40-45 days old seedlings or 12-15 cm tall are planted in the well prepared beds or narrow trenches.

Spacing. 30 × 10 cm between rows/trenches and plants.

Manure and fertilizer. Apply 20 t FYM, 50 kg N, 65 kg P_2O_5 and 130 kg K_2O/ha as band and mixing the soil. The top dressing is done with another 50 kg N, 30 days after transplanting.

Irrigation. The crop should be irrigated regularly for proper growth and plant development at an interval of 7-10 days.

Hoeing and weeding. This operation is very important and should be done as and when necessary to keep down the weeds.

Blanching. Blanching is an important operation in the cultivation of leek. The trenches in the centre of which the seedlings are transplanted are fdled-up with top soil thereby the plant bases are earthed-up. This makes the base blanched. The earthing-up is continued as the plants grow.

Harvesting. Like that of green onion, leek is harvested and kept under shade in cool conditions. Leeks are harvested whenever they are large enough for a desirable taste, some are used as baby leeks for salad otherwise ready in 75-110 days. Harvesting is done by hand with the help of fork or spade.

Grading. The trimming of soiled and yellow leaves should be done and after thorough washing, bundles are prepared and keep in shade.

Marketing. The properly packed produce is send to the market immediately after harvesting, grading and packaging in the cities where it is in a great demand.

Storage. The green leek can be stored at 0°C with RH of 85-90 per cent for 30-60 days.

Yield. A quantity of 20-25 t/ha can be harvested in a crop duration of 70-90 days.

20.4. CHIVE

In India, it is grown as a herb in kitchen gardens and is very popular particular in hilly areas. It also has ornamental value. It do not or scarcely form bulbs at all, its food reserves are being stored in well developed rhizomes to this its name may have reflected tuberous (swollen or enlarged). It is both wild and cultivated plant. In the recent past, chive gained popularity among domesticated herbs. Now it is a popular plant in the home garden but not cultivated commercially in our country. However it is growing wild in the Himalayan range is collected by the tribals and is processed dried and sold to the near by markets. Also it is imported or carried by Tibetans (Lamas) and is made available even in far-off distances.

Uses. Chive add a delicate tint of garlicy and oniony flavour to many different foods. The green leaves are sold or used as dry cut leaves or in powdered form. It is also used for culinary purpose during winter months fresh as well as dried leaves. The chopped leaves are used as mild substitute for onion in salads and sauces. Seeds are used in picklingly. It also act as repellant against aphids, mites and rabbits. Having tufted habit, attractive green foliage, and purple flowers make them useful ornamental edging plant or for growth in clumps as a herb.

Nutritive value. Plant as a whole is nutritious, good source of carbohydrates, protein, minerals-phosphorus, iron and vitamin C.

Medicinal value. It is carminative, diuretic, diaphoratic, expectorant, rubefacient, tonic and is a gastric stimulant and thus helps in digestion and absorption of food.

Origin. Arctic to tropical latitudes in Euthopia and Celone.

Taxonomy. Member of *Amarilidaceae* family is a hardy bunching perennial herb. Two types of chives *A. schoenoprassum* having rush like leaves similar to onion and another Chinese chive *A. tuberosum* having garlic like leaves. In Himalayan range it is commonly called as zimmu and is found growing in thick tuft and produce leaves in spring and regularly upto the next cold season. The scape is solid and has two or more sharp angles running along the whole length. The flowers are white widely stare like borne in flat topped umbel of.

Cultivars. Fine leaves, Straight delicate leaf, Stars, Local cultivars.

Climate. It is a cool season plant growing wild in the high altitude temperate areas of the country.

Soil. It can be grown in all types of soils rich in humus but light loamy soils are best.

Seed rate. 8-10 kg/ha seed.

Sowing time. February-March.

Sowing/planting. It is first propagated by seeds which after maturity is easily divided and multiplied by its very small oval bulbs or rhizomes which is divided by the thick tuft of compact mass. In kitchen gardens, the plant tufts developed by seed, being perennial, grows for 2-3 or more years in a place and later on the clumps are replanted for another time span. But for commercial plantings the seed is sown in spring which develop into a scallion like plant in rows. The plants are also sold in pots or polythene bags (tubes) ready to plant even for harvest, if the care is taken up properly. The seed or seedlings are dibbled in furrows and later earthed-up from both sides.

Spacing. 70 × 30 cm between and within rows.

Manure and fertilizer. Similar to leeks.

Irrigation. Similar to leeks.

Hoeing and weeding. Same as in leeks.

Blanching. The blanching of plant or leaves is also done depending on the requirement.

Harvesting. Chives are at their culinary best when their tubular leaves are young, narrow and tender before the plant flowers. To harvest these leaves, cut them off in clumps about 2 cm from ground. Do not cut-off the just tips as the leftover leaves will turn brown and become useless. To rejuvenate a plant that has flowered and turned tough, cut it all off close to the ground, it will grow quickly. The cutting stimulates the fresh growth and several harvesting can be taken number of cutting. The harvesting tops are then carried, washed, cut into pieces, packaged and frozen immediately.

Grading. As in leeks.

Marketing. The green fresh leaves are packed in cartons or crates or baskets and marked.

Storage. Like that of leeks.

Yield. 10-15 q/ha when the season is favourable.

Crop protection

Disease/Insect-pests	*Symptoms*	*Control*
Diseases		
Purple blotch	Small whitish sunken lesions with purple centre on leaves, stem, bulbs and seed stalks. Leaves and seed stalks fall.	Grow resistant cultivars. 4-5 sprays of Dithane M-45 @ 0.25% along with sticker trition.
Stemphyllum blight		As above.
Smut	Elongated dark slightly thickened areas at the base of seedling leaves. Raised black lesions near the base of the scale at bulbing stage.	Treat the seed with Arasan @ 15 g/kg of seed.
Soft rot	Bulbs start rotting at the neck, gradually become soft and smell badly in storage.	Thorough and rapid drying at harvest. Remove damaged bulbs before storage.
White rot		Treat the cloves with Agrosan @ 6 g/kg of cloves.
Downy mildew	A violet furry growth on the surface of the leaf or stem which break down.	Spray with cuprous oxide, Grow resistant cultivars.
Insect-pests		
Thrips	Cause whitish blotches on the leaves and the tips turn brown and die.	Spray at 15 days interval 0.04% Quinophos or Endosulphan or 0.1% Carboryl.
Head borer		Spray Endosulphan 2-3 ml/1of water at 7 days interval.
Maggots	The larvae of small grey fly feed on the leaves or suck sap.	Spray the soil around the plant with 4 : 4 : 50 Bordeaux mixture.
Aphids	Suck sap on leaves and stem.	Spray Methyl dematon @ 1 ml/1 of water.
Physiological disorder		
Rubbering in garlic	Garlic become spongy and rubber like.	Judicial use of nitrogen.

CHAPTER

21

GARDEN PEAS

Garden pea is a popular vegetable and is grown in an area of 2.23 lakh ha with a production of 23.41 lakh t and productivity of 10.49 t/ha in India. Canned, frozen and dehydrated, garden peas are popular at the world over. In India, it is grown throughout the year and the pods are available all the year round from various regions particularly from hills where it is grown in off-season. The quality of pods in off-season produce is found to be much better. Therefore, it is exported to the middle-east countries for earning foreign exchange and beside domestic consumption. It is cool season crop and high temperature adversely affects the pod setting thus reducing the pod/seed yield. But the flowers and pods are badly affected if the severe frost occurs.

Uses. The tender fully developed seeds are the economic part consumed as vegetable except some edible podded varieties. The green fresh pods are used for fresh market or freezing, canning or dehydration. It is an excellent food for human consumption taken either as a vegetable or in soup, canned, frozen or dehydrated. Its straw is a nutritious fodder.

Nutritive value. Garden peas are highly nutritive and contain a high percentage of digestible protein, carbohydrates, vitamins and minerals.

Medicinal value. Fresh pods possess high degree of typotropic antisclerotic substances especially choline. The deficiency of choline leads to growth and development of malignant tumours. The garden pea containing upto 263 mg of choline has no harmful effect in daily consumption.

Origin. Euthopia is believed to be the probable origin of garden pea.

Taxonomy. Garden pea belongs to the family *Leguminoseae.* It is grouped as *Pisum sativum* sub-sp. *hortense* and the field pea as *P. sativum* sub-sp. *arvence.* The edible podded cultivars are found in both these sub-species. The garden pea plant is a herbaceous annual with a trailing, climbing or dwarf growth habit, there are three types *viz.,* bush type, medium tall and tall types. Based on seeds, the cultivar can be grouped into round/smooth seeded and wrinkle seeded. The flowers are born singly or in pairs on elongated peduncles arising in the axil of the leaves. The garden pea is a self-pollinated crop. Early opening of the anthers followed by self-fertilization before the flower bud open, avoid cross-pollination even if flower is visited by insects.

Cultivars : *Early cultivars.* Asauji, NP-29, Alderman, Alaska, Arkel, Matar Ageta, Early Badger, Pusa Vipasa, Palam-Priya, Pant Uphar, Little Marble, Sylvia, Newline Perfection and Punjab Ageta Azad pea-1, Azad pea-3, Pant matar-2, Pant sabji matar-3.

Mid-season cultivars. Bonnvillae, Lincoln, VL-3, VL-7, Shalimar Matar and Solan Nirog, T-19, T-17, Jawahar matar-1 to 4, Pant Uphar, Arka Ajit, JP-83.

Late cultivars. Kinnauri and Early Giant.

Edible podded. Sylvia.

Resistant /tolerant cultivars. Pusa Pragati, Palam-Priya.

Climate. It is a winter vegetable in plains and summer vegetable in hills. It cannot tolerate extreme temperatures as well as frost. The optimum temperature germination and initial growth is 18-20°C. But for further growth, flowering and pod set, a temperature of 12-15°C will ideal. In case of high temperature, there will be drastic reduction in yield. The wrinkled seeded cultivars are more sensitive to high temperature. The blossom and pods are susceptible to frost also.

Soil. A well drained silt loam soil is ideal for proper growth of garden pea. Soils with better retention capacity and continuous moisture supply are better suited as frequent irrigation leads to vegetative growth. The optimum pH is 6.0-7.5. In very acidic soils, liming is essential. It is highly sensitive to water-logging.

Seed rate. Early cultivars — 100-120 kg/ha.
Mid. and late cultivars — 80-90 kg/ha.

Sowing time. North plains — Mid-October to mid-November.
Hills — Mid-March-May or July-August.

Seed treatment. To check root rot in early sowings, the seed should be treated with Thiram or Arasan @ 2g/kg seed. It is advisable to treat the seeds with bacterial culture *(Rhizobium)* before sowing in areas where sowing is done for the first time. This help in quick nodulation and early fixation of atmospheric nitrogen.

Sowing. The land should be ploughed into a fine tilth and beds of convenient size be prepared. The seed is generally sown on flat land in lines. At the time of sowing, the soil should be in its optimum moisture condition for better germination.

Spacing. 30 × 10 cm, 22.5 cm row spacing as most appropriate for higher seed yield. Bold seed has always been considered ideal for getting the maximum crop yields.

Manure and fertilizer. Apply 15 t FYM, 15 kg N, 60 kg P_2O_5 and 40 kg K_2O/ha as a basal dose just before sowing. The basal dose of N is valuable for stimulating early growth of legumes. At flowering, apply 15 kg of N should be top dressed. Garden pea being a leguminous crop and can fix atmospheric nitrogen by itself with the help of *Rhizobium* available in the root nodules. As it has a specific feature in the response to nitrogen application and should be applied as per the requirement.

Irrigation. The soil moisture should be maintained optimum for plant growth as excessive irrigation help in more nitrogen uptake leading to more vegetative growth and less productivity. Frequent irrigation of pea crop have been found to encourage the incidence of pea leaf miner. Light irrigation should be applied at an interval of 10-15 days during the dry period.

Hoeing and weeding. Garden pea is a shallow feeder and a light hoeing should be given 25-30 days of sowing to keep the field weed free. A pre-sowing application of Basalin @ 2-3 L/ha or Stomp 3.5 1/ha controls most of the weeds.

Staking. In case of semi-tall and tall cultivars the vines should be supported by thin stakes of tree branches or bamboo. In some areas, the pea is inter-cropped in wheat or any other crop, the plants of which provides support to the vines. Staking is an expensive proposition and the commercial growers do not stake the crop.

Micro-nutrient. At flowering, foliar application of 0.1 per cent Ammonium molybdate is recommended to get increased quality grain yield.

Harvesting. The market maturity of the pods is indicated by the change of pod colour from dark green to light green within which the grains are well filled up. The quality of the pea is judged by its sugar content. The pods must be picked up at the proper stage of maturity, because they start loosing their quality rapidly after reaching the edible maturity. The deterioration is hastened if the temperature is high at the time of picking. Picking is done manually by giving a simple jerk to the pedicel and every care should be taken not to injure the vines while picking pods with a jerk. The picking is continued in 10 days interval. The number of pickings varies with cultivar and management. The picking should be done either early in the morning or late in the afternoon so that the quality may not lower down during the heat of noon. Uniformity is an important criterion for canning and dehydration. The quality of pods can also be measured with the help of tenderometer. In advanced countries on large scale, the harvesting of pods is done by machines. The shelling percentage ranges from 35-45.

Grading. The Indian Standards Institutions has fixed three grades of garden peas in pods *viz.* A, B and C.

Marketing. The produce being perishable in nature should be immediately sent to the market under proper grade, packed in bags used for onion transport, preferably picking for the purpose must be done in the evening to carry the same either during night or in the next early morning or in the morning to be transported by evening.

Storage. Fresh pods may be kept for 12-15 days at 0°C and 90-95 RH. Garden pea pods can also be stored in crushed ice for about 15-25 days and the pods will freeze at — 10°C.

Pod Yeild. Early cultivars — 2.5-4.0 t/ha.

Mid-season cultivars — 6.0-7.5 t/ha.

Late cultivars — 8-11 t/ha.

Crop protection

Diseases/Insect-pests	*Symptoms*	*Control*
Diseases		
Powdery mildew	White powdery patches on leaf surface, tendrils, pods and stems. Entire plant is covered.	Spray Sulfex or Elosal or Hexasual @ 3 kg/ha. Repeat after 15 days interval.
Downy mildew	Symptoms appear on lower side of lower leaves than on upper leaves.	Spray crop with Dithane M-45 @ 0.25%.
Fusarium wilt Rust	Wilting of plant occurs. Yellow spots having accia in round or elongated clusters and plant dies.	Seed treatment with Benelate or Dexan Spray crop with Dithane M-45 @ 0.25%.
Insect pests		
Pod borer	Bore into the pod and eat the grains inside.	Apply 5% BHC dust @ 18-25 kg/ha. Spray Thiodan or Sevin @ 2L/kg/ha.
Leaf miner	Larvae feed by making tunnels in the leaves.	Chlordane dust 5% or Dimecron 100 EC 25 ml/L or Metasystox 20 EC 1 ml/1.
Pea stem fly	Maggots damage internal stem tissues and entire plant dies.	Apply Furadan @ 30 kg/ha or Thimet granules @ 10 kg/ha and mix with soil.
Pea aphid	Suck sap of cells, owing to which leaves turn pale yellow.	Spray Dimecron 100 EC 25 ml/1 or Metasystox 20 EC 1 ml/1.

CHAPTER

22

WINTER LEAFY VEGETABLES

Leafy vegetables supply the roughage required in our daily diet and play an important role in the balanced diet of human beings. They are cheaper and very rich in minerals and vitamins A & C, possess the capability to combat malnutrition and undernutrition. The leafy vegetables comprise some 700 species of plants belonging to 125 plant families.

22.1. BEET LEAF

Indian spinach or beet leaf or desi palak or common palak or Spinach beet is commonly grown good leafy vegetable throughout tropical and sub-tropical regions of the country.

Uses. The tender leaves along with petioles are cooked as vegetable.

Nutritive value. Palak leaves are rich source of vitamin A & C, protein, carbohydrates B-carotene and minerals-calcium and iron.

Medicinal value. It acts as laxative by improving the digestive system and cure constipation.

Origin. Palak is a native of Indo-Chinese origin.

Taxonomy. Beet leaf belong to the family *Chenopodiaceae,* genus *Beta,* species *vulgaris* and sub-sp. *bengalensis.* It has leaves different to that of spinach with entire leaf margin and produces bisexual flowers. The spinach leaves have lobed leaf margin and the plants produces three types of flowers *viz.,* staminate, pistillate and hermaphrodite.

Cultivars. Based on the pigmentation of mid-ribs and leaf veins the cultivars are classified into :

(*i*) Reddish mid-rib and leaf veins.

(*ii*) Green mid-rib and leaf veins.

Some of the improved cultivars are, Pusa Bharati, Pusa Jyoti, Pusa Harit, Benerjee's Giant, Long Standing, All Green, Shalimar Green, HS-23, Pant Composite, Jobner Green.

Climate. It has a wider range of adaptability to climatic conditions. It can tolerate frost as well as high temperature and grows well in hot weather. Very high temperature of 35-40°C lead to early bolting rendering the leaves unpalatable. Therefore, under tropical conditions beet leaf can be grown during winter season.

Soil. Fertile soils with good drainage are ideal for growing palak. It can be grown in saline and alkaline soils also as it has been proved to be highly salt tolerant vegetable.

Seed rate. 25-30 kg/ha.

Sowing time. South India — November-December.
North Indian plains — September-October and June-July.
Hills — March-May.

In some areas where mild climate prevails it can be grown throughout the year.

Sowing. The field should be well prepared into a better tilth and levelled. Beds of convenient size should be prepared. Each seed ball contain 2-3 or more seeds and during sowing only one seed is sown in each hill. The depth of sowing seed should not be more than 3-4 cm. Commonly broadcast method is followed.

Spacing. 20 × 10 cm between rows and plants.

Manure and fertilizer. Leafy vegetables require lot of nitrogen and apply 15-20 t FYM, 25 kg each of N, P_2O_5 and K_2O/ha as a basal dose. 25 kg of N should be top dressed after each cutting followed by irrigation.

Irrigation. A light irrigation should be given immediately after sowing. Subsequent irrigation should be given at an interval of 7.10 days depending on the soil moisture.

Hoeing and weeding. To keep under control the weeds and pulverize the soil, hoeing and weeding should be done once in 15-20 days.

Harvesting. Well developed green succulent leaves are cut with petiole when they attain the 15-20 cm length. The main consideration should be the tenderness and succulence of the leaves. The first cutting is ready in 20-30 days after of seed sowing. The number of cuttings depends on cultivar and management and ranges 4-6 cuttings. During summer 3-4 cuttings are taken. The cultivars with large sized leaves produces about 40 per cent higher yield as compared to normal cultivars.

Grading. The uniform sized leaves are selected which are healthy, clean and complete with petiole must be tied into bundles of half or one kg weight which smoothen handling and marketing.

Marketing. The harvested produce should be send to the market immediately in fresh state to earn better price.

Storage. Similar to Chinese cabbage.

Yield. Total green yield — 8-10 t/ha.
Pusa Bharati — 40-50 t/ha both in winter and early-spring seasons.

22.2. SPINACH

Spinach or 'Vilayati Palak' is commonly grown all over the plains throughout the country preferably in southern states.

Uses. Leafy vegetable foliage of the plants are cooked and eaten.

Nutritive value. The leaves are rich sources of protein, vitamins like vitamin A, thiamine, riboflavin, vitamin C and minerals like iron, phosphorus and potassium.

Medicinal value. The lipids from the leaves possess antibacterial properties. The fruits are demulcent and diuretic and are employed for the treatment of fever and inflammation of the bowels.

Origin. It has its origin in South West Asia.

Taxonomy. Member of family *Chenopodaceae,* genus *Spinacia* and species *oleracea.* It is an annual plant with rosette of leaves and compact stem. When it produces in florescence the central stem elongates. The leaves of spinach have lobed leaf margin. Usually dioecious in nature but occasionally monoecious plants are also observed. There are four types of plants-extreme males produce seed stalks sooner than do the vegetative males, females and hermaphrodite or monoecious plants.

Cultivars. Based on the seed type, the cultivars are classified as prickly seeded and rounded seeded while on leaf type, smooth and savoy leaved cultivars are recognised. The improved cultivars are Pusa palak, Verginia Savoy, Early Smooth leaf, Shannihon (AG-41), All Green, Prickly Seeded, Bloomsdale, Long Standing and Pusa Bharati.

Climate. Spinach is mainly a cool season vegetable. It grows very well in a temperature range of 15.5-18.5°C and the seed germinates at a temperature of 10.15°C. At higher temperature and long days, the plants tend to bolt and flower and the quality of leaves is affected freezing temperature causes injury to young plants. At higher atmospheric humidity, the leaves will be more succulent and tender.

Soil. Spinach can be grown in different soil types like sandy loam upto clayey soils. A soil pH range of 6.0-7.0 is ideal for proper growth and at lower pH the growth is adversely affected.

Seed rate. 40-45 kg/ha as it needs higher seed rate because 50 per cent of the population will turn into male plants which produce poor vegetative growth.

Sowing time. Plains — September-October.

Hills — April-May and August.

Sowing. The well prepared field is divided into small beds or ridges. The seed should be sown either in beds or on ridges and furrows.

Spacing. 60 × 2.5 cm between rows and plants.

Manure and fertilizer. This crop being a leafy vegetable needs more nitrogen. Apply 20 t FYM, 150 kg N, 40 kg P_2O_5 and 60 kg K_2O/ha. The N may be applied in two split doses half at the time of sowing and the rest half at 30th day of sowing.

Irrigation. Immediately after sowing one light irrigation is given and the subsequent irrigation should be given once in 10-15 days.

Hoeing and weeding. Shallow hoeing should be given to control weeds so that root system of the crop is not much disturbed.

Harvesting. The plants should be harvested after they attain full size but before any of the leaves turn yellow, form seed stalk or die. Normally the crop is ready for harvest in 25-30 days of sowing. The harvesting is done manually and the subsequent cuttings are taken at an interval of 15-20 days. A total of 4-6 cuttings can be obtained.

Grading. After harvesting, damaged and yellow leaves should be removed and the soil, dirt, etc. adhering to the leaf stalks is washed-off and these are tied into bundles of one kg containing about 15-20 plants.

Marketing. The harvested produce should be immediately sent to the market.

Storage. Under ordinary conditions it is not possible to store for more than a few hours. The leaves can be stored at 0°C and 95 per cent RH for a short period of 10-15 days safely.

Yield. 6-10 t/ha green leaves and petioles.

22.3. FENUGREEK

Methi having wider adaptability to hot climate is cultivated throughout India and other parts of the world. In India, in the states of Rajasthan, Madhya Pradesh, Gujarat and Maharashtra.

Uses. The green leaves are used as vegetable while fully matured seeds as condiment. The leaves can also be dried and used for flavouring. The plants are used as fodder.

Nutritive value. The green leaves are rich source of minerals, protein and vitamin A and C. In industries, seeds are used as dye making and for extraction of alkaloids or steroids.

Medicinal value. The leaves and also the seeds in particular have medicinal value. It prevents constipation, remove indigestion, stimulates the spleen and the liver and is appetizing and diuretic. The seeds are used in the treatment of diarrhoea and many other ailments.

Origin. The methi is believed to have originated in South Eastern Europe.

Taxonomy. Methi belongs to the family *Leguminoseae,* genus *Trigonella* and species *foenum-graecum* (non-scented or common or desi methi) and *corniculata* (scented or kasuri or champa methi). These differ in their growth habit. The common methi is quick growing and produces upright shoots, 2-3 white flowers at the base of each leaf and has 6-7 straight long pods, and kasuri methi is slow growing initially and remains in a rosette condition during most of its vegetative growth period, produces bright orange yellow flowers on long stalk and has smaller sickle-shaped pods.

Cultivars. The cultivars may be non-scented and scented.

Common. IC-74, Pusa Early Bunching, Lam Selection-1, Co-1.

Kasuri. Pusa Kasuri Selection, Methi No. 14, No. 47, EC-491.

Climate. Methi being a cool season vegetable is widely adapted to hot climate too and can tolerate freezing temperature to a certain extent. Kasuri methi needs comparatively cooler climate.

Soil. It can be grown in all types of soils but clay loams are found to be the best for growing method. The optimum pH is 6-7.

Seed rate. Common methi — 25 kg/ha.
Kasuri methi — 20 kg/ha.

Sowing time. Plains — September-November.
Hills — March-April.

Sowing. Land is well prepared and divided into beds of convenient size. The seeds are sown by broadcasting and raking the bed surface. Line sowing will be better than broadcasting to facilitate intercultural operations in the initial stages. The seeds germinates in 7-10 days under rainfed condition and 4-5 days under irrigated condition.

Spacing. 25 × 10 cm between rows and plants.

Manure and fertilizer. Apply 15 t FYM, 25 kg N, 50 kg P_2O_5 and 40 Kg/K_2O/ha as a basal dose. Top dressing of 20 N should be done after first cutting in about 25-30 days after sowing.

Inoculation. Methi being leguminous crop, respond well to the inoculation of Rhizobium by fixing atmospheric nitrogen and produces a lot of vegetative growth.

Irrigation. A light irrigation should be given immediately after sowing and subsequent irrigation may be given 10-15 days interval. Water stagnation should be avoided as it leads to damping-off.

Hoeing and weeding. At the early stages of crop growth, weed may pose problem because initially methi plants grow slowly as compared to many weed species. Hence, shallow cultivation is essential after about 20-25 days after sowing. During cuttings, weeds *viz.*, motha, pyazi, jangli chauli, etc. should be uprooted separately.

Thinning. When methi is grown as greens no need of thinning, however, seed crop must be given proper plant spacing.

Harvesting. The first cutting is made in about 25-30 days after sowing and subsequent cuttings can be taken once in 12-15 days. The kasuri methi gives a number cuttings. In case of common methi, the shoots are nipped-off in about 25 days after sowing and later on, the whole plant is often pulled out. After 2-3 cuttings the plants can be allowed for seeding.

Grading. The harvested produce is bunched into bundles preferably of one kg after grading and packed in crates, baskets or gunny bags.

Marketing. The produce being perishable need to be send to the market where it is in great demand.

Storage. The leaves can be stored at 0°C and 95 per cent RH for a short period of 10-15 days safely.

Yield. Common methi — 7-8 t/ha.

Kasuri methi — 9-10 t/ha.

22.4. SWISS CHARD

It is a type of beet that was developed for the large crisp leaves.

Uses. The large green crinkly leaves and fleshy leaf stalks of Swiss chard are used.

Nutritive value. Similar to beet leaf.

Medicinal value. Similar to beet leaf.

Origin. It was originated in Mediterranean region and Canary Islands. It is a favourite crop of people of Switzerland.

Cultivars : ***White ribbed.*** Fordhood Giant, Large White Rib, Lucullus and Perpectual.

Red Ribbed. Burgundy, Rhubarb Chard and Ruby.

Taxonomy. It belongs to the family *Chenoopodaceae,* genus *Beta,* species *vulgaris* and sub-species *cicla.* The leafstalks and midribs are usually white but red cultivars are also available.

Climate. Chard does not produce seed stalks during hot weather. Climatic requirements are similar to beets.

Soil. Similar to spinach.

Seed rate. Same as in beet leaf.

Sowing time. September-November.

Sowing/planting. The seedball is sown in the well prepared soil. Plants emerge in 6-10 days. Each seedball contains 5-8 seeds and the plants need to be thinned to the optimum spacing.

Spacing. 45 × 5-10 × 3-4 cm between rows and plants and deep in the soil.

Manure and fertilizer. The basal dose of FYM and N, P, K is similar to beet leaf. For rapid and continuous growth, additional nitrogen fertilizer should be applied about a month after planting.

Irrigation. Keep the soil in its optimum moisture condition by frequent irrigation.

Hoeing and weeding. Timely removal of weeds and pulverizing the soil helps to increase the leafstalks yield.

Harvesting. The small chard plants can be harvested when the row is thinned and used as greens. Large leaves and stems are harvestable 50-60 days after planting. The outer leaves are cut-off about 2-3 cm above the ground with a sharp knife, while they are still young and tender. Care should be taken not to injure young leaves or the central bud. Leaves should be harvested continuously to stimulate the production of young new leaves from the central bud. During the final harvest; the entire plant may be dug up, placed in a soil and stored in a cool place. Plants are placed upright with roots still containing some soil. They should be watered lightly prevent wilting. The leaves can then be harvested during the winter months.

Grading. The leaves are washed and of uniform size should be bundled in one kg weight and send to the market.

Marketing. The produce should be carried to the market immediately after harvesting in suitable containers *viz.,* baskets, crates, bags etc. without causing any damage to the leaves and must reach to the consumers in fresh form.

Storage. The leaves can be stored at 0°C and 95 per cent RH for a short period of 10-15 days safely.

Yield. 7-8 t/ha of green leaves.

Crop protection

Diseases/Insect-Pests	*Symptoms*	*Control*
Diseases		
Damping-off	Dieing and collapsing of plants.	Brassicol or Bavistin seed treatment and drenching @ 0.3%.
Cercospora Leaf spot	Appearance of spots on the leaves.	Spray 0.2% Blitox or Coprox at 15 days interval.
Powdery mildew	Powdery substance on the leaves.	Spray Cosan, Thiovit, Karathane WP or Sulphur dust @ 2.5 kg a.i./ ha.
Insect-pests		
Aphids and leaf eating caterpillars	Suck sap and eat up the tender leaves and stem.	Spray Malathian 0.05% or Quinalphos 0.04%.

CHAPTER

23

SALAD VEGETABLES

23.1. LETTUCE

Lettuce is the most popular salad cropland it is gaining importance in the country.

Uses. In some cultivars, stems are thick which are peeled and eaten raw or as cooked vegetable.

Nutritive value. It is a nutritious leafy vegetable rich in vitamin A and C, thiamine and niacin, etc., carbohydrates, protein and mineral matter.

Medicinal value. Lactucarium from lettuce is used as hypnotic in bronchitis and asthama. It is used in poultices for burns and painful ulcers.

Origin. The Lettuce is believed to have originated in Mediterranean region.

Taxonomy. Lettuce belongs to the family *Compositae* or sunflower family, genus *Lactuca* and species *sativa.* It is an annual plant with milky juice. There are distinct types *viz.,* non-heading type *(crispa)* do not form head and open leaves called leaf lettuce, asparagus type *(asparagina),* Cos or Romain lettuce *(longifolia)* forms a loose upright head and heading type *(capitata)* form compact head. It is further have two types —butter heading and crisp heading.

Cultivars : ***Butter heading.*** Heads small, loose with broad oily crumpled and soft textured leaves. Big Boston, White Boston, May King, etc.

Crisp heading. Heads are round and large with brittle texture, tightly folded green leaves outside and yellowish leaves inside. Non-wrapper leaves will be wrinkled. New York 515, Imperial-44, Great Lake, etc.

Cos lettuce (Romainer). Cultivars with elongated leaves forming a loaf shaped loose in appearance but with good eating quality. Outer leaves are dark green and inner leaves are light green. Effel Tower, Paris Island, Paris White, etc.

Leaf Lettuce. The plants do not form any head but produce rosette of leaves.

Climate. Lettuce is a temperate crop and need very cool climate. However, in tropical and sub-tropical regions, it can be grown at higher altitudes. The climatic need of head lettuce are more critical than that of leaf lettuce or crisp/heading type which is commercially cultivated. The optimum temperature required for growth and head formation is 10-18.5°C while for germination it is 7.2-23°C. Higher temperature checks heading, cause bitter flavour and seeding. When the soil temperature exceeds 25°C, thermodormancy will be induced and there will be poor germination.

Soil. Almost all the soils are suitable for lettuce cultivation, fertile loamy soils rich in organic matter with a pH of 6.0-6.5 are the most ideal. In warm weather heavy soils would be desirable. Lettuce has a small root system so adequate moisture and good drainage are essential.

Seed rate. Direct seeding — 1-1.5 kg/ha.

Transplanting — 400-500 g/ha.

Sowing time. Direct seeding — September-October.

Transplanting — October-November.

Sowing/transplanting. Before sowing/transplanting, the land should be prepared into a better tilth. It can be grown either as direct sown or transplanted crop. In former case seeds are sown in the beds in rows either in dry soil followed by light irrigation or pre-irrigate the beds and then seeding is done when the soil is in optimum condition. The seed is sown thinly in lines. In the later case, seedlings are raised and transplanting is done accordingly.

Spacing. Direct seeding — 35-40 × 35 cm between rows and plants.

Transplanting — 45 × 30 cm between rows and plants.

Manure and fertilizer. Apply 10-15 t FYM, 30 kg N, 60 kg P_2O_5 and 60 kg K_2O/ha as a basal dose. At the time of heading/peak vegetative growth of non-heading type, top dress 55 kg N/ha followed by irrigation.

Irrigation. The first irrigation should be given at the time of sowing/transplanting and generally later irrigation can be applied once in 8 or 10 days. There should not be any soil moisture stress which leads the plants to bolt quickly.

Hoeing and weeding. Hoeing should be done after 25-30 days of sowing/transplanting to keep the weeds under control and repeated at same interval.

Harvesting. Leaf lettuce should be harvested whenever the leaves are large enough to use. Plants that have been thinned from the row are also eaten. The inner leaves of the leaf cultivars are of high quality and the entire plant should be harvested. Butterhead and Cos types are ready in 60-70 days. Crisp head types are harvested after the formation of solid, firm and full heads when it is intended for sending to the market whereas for home use, the heads are harvested before the head is well formed. Usually the harvesting is started about 80-85 days after sowing/transplanting depending on cultivar and continued upto 95-100 days.

Grading. Lettuce may be washed dripped dry and stored in an airtight containers in the refrigerator. The harvested heads/plants are graded and neatly packed in baskets or crates or cartons.

Marketing. The produce being perishable should be marketed as soon as possible otherwise the quality will get deteriorated.

Storage. Lettuce heads can be stored for 15-25 days under refrigerated conditions. After packing they can be stored at 0°C and 95 per cent RH.

Yield. The average yield is 10-14 t/ha.

23.2. CELERY

Celery ranks second in importance amongst the salad crops. It is mostly grown in kitchen or home gardens as a salad crop.

Uses. The fleshy stalks (petioles) are used as salad and cooked like a leafy onion. They are also used in soups, sauces, curries fried and spiced. In England, celery is canned. Principally used as a pre-dinner appetizer and as flavouring in soups and dressings. Excellent vegetable either stewed or creamed and its seed are used as condiment. A pale yellow volatile oil extracted from seed is much valued as fixative and an ingredient of several perfumes.

Nutritive value. Leaves are rich in protein, vitamin C, B-carotene, riboflavin and minerals-calcium and iron.

Medicinal value. Celery seeds are credited with stimulant and carminative properties and prescribed as nervine sedative and tonic. Its decoction is a household remedy for rheumatism, useful to some extent in liver and spleen troubles, theropeutic utility in various prychiatic and epilepsy disease. Fatty oil (17%) from seeds is used in many medicinal preparations as antispasmodic and nerve stimulant. The roots are credited with diuretic, anasaria and colic.

Origin. The celery is believed to have originated in Mediterranean region.

Taxonomy. It belongs to the family *Umbelliferae,* genus *Apium* and species *graveolens.* There are three types — var. dulce (Blanched celery), secalinus (Leafy type) and repaceus (Edible rooted type). It is a biennial herb with well developed leaves and expanded petioles. The flowers are small, white and borne in compound umbels among the leaves of the flower stalk.

Cultivars : *Self-blanched.* Florida Giant, Golden, Self-blanching, Golden Self-blanch.

Green leaved. Standard Bearer, Wright Grove Giant, Ford Hook Emperor, Giant Pascal, Emperor of Jeen, U-late 52-70.

Climate. It is a cool and humid season vegetable grown in hills behave as biennial but as annual in the plains. The ideal temperature for the growth is 15-20°C but at very high temperature bolting occurs and leaves become bitter.

Soil. A well drained sandy loam soil is suitable to grow celery. The optimum soil pH ranges 5.5-6.7.

Seed rate. Through seedling — 200-250 g/ha.
Direct seeding — 1.5-2.0 kg/ha.

Sowing time. Plains — July-September.
Hills — January-March.

Sowing/planting. Deep tillage is not very essential as it is a shallow rooted. The field should be prepared into a better tilth. The top soil should be pulverised and properly levelled by planking. It is a transplanted crop and 50 m^2 nursery area is sufficient to plant one hectare. The seeds should be soaked overnight and then broadcast on the beds or sown in lines and covered by a thin layer of soil.

Spacing. 45-60 × 15-20 cm between rows and plants.

Manure and fertilizer. Application of 20-25 t FYM, 100-120 kg N, 40-60 kg P_2O_5 and 30-40 kg K_2O/ha is done. One-third of N and entire P_2O_5, K_2O and FYM as basal dressing and rest dose in two splits is top dressed at earthing up. Foliar application of 50 ppm of N can also be given frequently to enhance the plant growth.

Irrigation. Celery is a very delicate crop as far as moisture stress is concerned. The soil must be kept in optimum moisture condition as drought and water stagnation are detrimental. Irrigate at an interval of 10-12 days. Irrigation should be done carefully so that the soil put around the plant for blanching is not washed. Moderate and well distributed rains are favourable.

Hoeing and weeding. Celery is a long duration crop so weed control is necessary to get good harvest. Frequent hoeing is advocated but they should not be too deep. A pre-planting application of Basalin @ 1.0 L/ha or Linuran @ 14.8 kg/ha is advised to keep-off the weeds.

Mulching. Mulching with alkathene or hay is useful to check weeds and maintain optimum moisture in the root zone.

Blanching. Blanching is an important inter-cultural operation in the cultivation of celery which make the crop crisp, reduce acrid flavour, improve good flavour, quality and tenderness so as to form a wholesome salad. When the plants are 30 cm high, the outer old leaves are removed and the remaining leaves are tied by holding with hand loosely into bundles. Then blanching is done by any one of the method. It is the process of shutting down the sunlight for the petiole by wrapping (*i*) dark coloured stout brown paper strip, (*ii*) old news paper board around the leaf stalk or (*iii*) even by earthing-up-in this case, it should be noted that the soil should not enter into plant bunches but it should loosely cover the entire leaf stalk. The only disadvantage of soil blanching is that the produce rot very easily but in frost prone/temperate areas, it prevents frost injury.

Harvesting. It can be harvested at different stages of plant growth. The crop is ready for harvest in 75-90 days after transplanting depending on cultivar and management. When the plants are 40 cm tall, side suckers are removed, the plants are cut just below the soil surface. If the cut is given too high then the outer leaves will shatter should be tied into bundles and sent to the market.

Grading. The produce should be graded on the basis of leaf colour, compact and shattered leaves.

Marketing. Properly blanched fresh produce is sent to market immediately after harvest. It should properly be packed in suitable packings. It can also marketed as canned food after blanching.

Storage. Celery can be stored in trenches at 10°C or cold storage for 2-3 months at 0°C with 95-98 per cent RH. Isolated storage is necessary as it can absorb other flavours.

Yield. 35-55 t/ha.

23.3. PARSLEY

Parsley *(Petroselinum crispum* Mill) commonly known as Rock Parsley is the most popular garden herb grown on commercial scale in Europe and other countries for culinary and ornamental purposes. In India, it was occasionally grown in kitchen gardens. Garden herbs are now well appreciated throughout the world with the increase of knowledge of their value in the human diet. In India, it was occasionally grown in kitchen gardens. But with its increasing demand in five star hotels, foreigners, and oleoresin or oil extracting industries, the farmers have now taken up it cultivation in the neighbourhood of metropolitan cities and oil extracting units. Cultivators are also getting remunerative prices for some of the European herbs and parsley is one of those as it can also be dried and can be supplied in dried form off-season or can also be exported if we grow standard varieties with judicious use of chemicals or without chemical *i.e.* organically.

Uses. Its fresh leaves, root and seed being used as a spice ingredient in seasoning the soups, stews, souses, garnishing salads and as green bulk for many meat preparations (eaten with trout fish is the delicacy of western people). It is being used more as a spice because of its special aroma and flavour due to the presence of 'Oil of parsley' apiol (Parsley camphor). Fresh leaves mark strong culinary odours and are commonly used for garnishing and seasoning. They are eaten fresh, incorporated in salads and used as an ingredient of soups, stews and souces. The roots are used as a vegetable in soups." Dried leaves and roots are used as condiments. The seeds are used for extraction of parsley oil of commerce. The oil can be tried for a variety of industrial purposes such as making plastics, synthetic rubber, lubricating oil, additives and protective coatings, etc.

Nutritive value. Parsley has a cheerful, uplifting flavour and is very nutritious. It is especially valuable for being rich source of vitamins A, B, C Thiamine, Riboflavin and Niacin and minerals-calcium and iron. The flat leaf type of Italian cultivar are slightly more nutritious and the curly types are more decorative.

Medicinal value. The leaves are also employed to make a sort of tea which is considered to possess antiscorbutic properties. Tea made from seed lowers fever. The herb is reported to possess diuretic, expectorant, carminative, ecbolic, emmenagogue, supposed to be aphrodisiac, antipyretic properties and has long been used for uterine troubles. The juice of the fresh leaves is used as an insecticide. It contains essential oils including apiol and myristicin glycoside apiin, its use should be avoided during pregnancy.

Origin. Parsley is a native of Europe.

Taxonomy. Parsley herb of the *Umbelliferae* family, genus *Petroselimum* and species *crispum* is a hardy, aromatic, biennial or short lived perennial (lasting up to 4 years). Mainly two horticultural types of parsley cultivated for the leave *(con.* var. *crispum)* and for turnip like roots *(con.* var. *radicosum).* But in India, only *P. crispum* type is grown. Other species are *P. sativum* Hoffm., *P. hortense* Hoffm. It produces a rosette of finely divided radical leaves in the first year and a flowering stalk up to 100 cm high in the second year. Leaves 2 or 3 pinnate, ultimate segments cuneate-ovate or sometimes linear oblong incised, dentate or entire, more crisped in cultivated plants, upper cauline leaves often flowers yellow or yellowish green in compound umbels, fruits (commonly known as seeds) 2-3 mm long, crescent shaped, conspicuously ridged, consisting of two mericarps.

Cultivars. Some varieties are being recommended by different seed companies and it seems to be the selections of the following three types :

(*i*) ***Curled leaf types.*** Moss curled, Champion Moss curled, Extra triple curled, Extra curled Dwarf, Paramount, Curlina, Garland, Forest Green.

(*ii*) ***Smooth.*** Italian flat leaf type-Italy Giant, Italian Flat Dark green, Gigante Catalogno, Sweet Italian.

(*iii*) ***Root Parsley.*** Bartowich Long, Hamburg.

A few other varieties are curled leaf, Double Curled and Plain or Single.

It is an old world type grown for fall winter and spring harvest of its white root as well as for the flat parsley leaves for flavouring. Its root has nutty taste for use raw in salads or cooked. The roots are 15-18 cm long. It is a good soup ingredient, especially to give winter soups a fresh flavour, store well like carrot and can over-winter if mulched.

Climate. Parsley flourish well in cool weather and grows vigorously in higher altitudes. As they are usually frost resistant and do not become pithy. But due to repeated freezing the crops for years sometimes they become pithy.

Soil. Parsley grows best in a rich soil deeply worked good moist soil preferably a good loamy soil with lots of nitrogen and organic matter. It can thrive in most kinds of soils and its peculiarity is it grows anywhere and anyhow sometime it grows alone and is not distracted if produces super plant, because it requires lot of space for spreading.

Seed rate. For transplanted crop-250 g and for direct sown 3.250 kg seed of good germination is required per hectare.

Sowing time. Plains — September-November.

Low-hills — October, mid-hills and

Mid-hills — June and August-September.

High-hills — March-April.

In hills — February-June and also in Autumn.

Sowing/transplanting. Both transplanting or sowing directly in the field is practised, being slow in germination it is sometimes sown in green house, hot-beds or specially prepared nursery beds. For transplanting crop, seedlings are raised in nursery beds and seedlings when they are 5-8 cm in length are transplanted in field in evening hours in rows. Although seedlings are thin but are hardy and survive well. If the seeds are soaked in water for a day before sowing hastens germination. Parsley is very slow to germinate (20-30 days or more) and for parsley to come up sometimes short duration crop such as radish is planted in between the rows and is harvested before seedlings are developed. Parsley can also be grown in pots or window boxes in porch or in any type of containers.

Spacing. Seed is sown 6 mm deep in rows 40-45 cm apart with thinning the seedlings to 10 cm apart.

Manure and fertilizer. Dressing with nitrogenous fertilizer promotes rapid growth of seedlings. Apply 15 t FYM and NPK @ 100 : 80 : 40 kg/ha. A special attention is required for crop that is transplanted in the first spring and harvested (by cutting the leaves and stalks) during the first year will also over-winter and for a good spring crop, side dressing is recommended with rich compost or any other nitrogen source when the ground thaws and regrowth just beginning.

Irrigation. It also require plenty of moisture and timely irrigation.

Hoeing and weeding. Parsley requires attention and care in the first operational stages once they are passed it is easy to grow it, with taking care of weeding and hoeing. Good clean cultivation throughout the growing season is important and weeds should be removed timely and only frequent shallow cultivation is recommended.

Harvesting. The leaves are ready for harvest in an about 3 months depending upon the cultivars. The other leaves are periodically cut-off for several weeks and are tied in bunches for marketing. In commercial plantations, a hectare land yields about 2.5 thousand dozen bunches at each cutting and 2-5 cuttings are possible for each planting. Harvesting period can be considerably prolonged by preventing the plants from flowering. For rooted type varieties while root are used as fresh or cut longitudinally for drying. These harvested roots can also be dried by cutting longitudinally to facilitate drying. Leaves are also dried green in shade and kept in airtight bottled for using during winter.

Grading. The leaves along with petiole are tied in uniformly in a bundles for ease in handling in transit and store.

Marketing. The produce should be immediately marketed in fresh form as it is of perishable in nature.

Storage. The produce can be stored for few hours under ordinary conditions, however, at 0°C for few days and 90-95% RH.

Yield. About 12.5 t/ha of leaves can be harvested.

Crop protection (Celery, Parsley)

Diseases/Insect-pests	*Symptoms*	*Control*
Diseases		
Early blight *(Cercospora apii)*	Small concentric rings brownish spots on old leaves and later enlarges.	Seed treatment with hot water at 48°C for 30 minutes. Spray Copper oxychloride @ 0.2%.
Late blight *(Septoria apii-graveolentis* Dor)	Water soaked small circular areas later turn black on the tips and margin of leaves.	Spray Dithane Z-78 0.3% at an interval of 10-15 days.
Damping-off *(Pythium* spp.)	Seedlings colapse topple down and die.	Drenching of nursery beds with formaldehyde (1 : 50) solution.

Yellows *(F. oxisporium f. apii)*	Rotting of crown, petiole and root. Vascular discolouration and check growth of plant.	Grow resistant cultivars. Follow suitable crop rotation.
Bacterial leaf spot *(Pseudomonas apii Jagger)*	Circular reddish spots with pale yellow borders appears on leaves.	Spray Plantosycin @ 100 ppm.
Celery Mosaic	Cause leaf mottling.	Spray Malathion 0.02% to check aphid population.
Insect-pests		
Aphids	Suck sap of the plant.	Spray Malathion @ 0.02%.
Leaf miner and caterpillar	Make tunnels on the leaves and feed on plant parts.	Spray with Nuvan or Disicron @ 0.01% and repeat.
Armyworm, wire worm, cricket	Feed on plant parts.	Spray Endosulphan @1ml/l of water and repeat.
Disorders		
Black Heart	Cause is calcium deficiency, tip burn of young leaves, central stempith tissue rot and turn black.	Foliar spray of calcium chloride @ 0.1%.
Cracked stem	Cause is boron deficiency, lesions and longitudinal cracks seen on the inner and outer surface of the petioles and over the vascular bundles result in dark brown colour of the tissue.	Soil application of borax @ 12 kg/ha.

CHAPTER

24

PERENNIAL VEGETABLES

24.1. ASPARAGUS

It is an important perennial plant which start producing spears in 2nd or 3rd year and continues for 15-20 years under proper management. It is mostly grown in kitchen gardens.

Uses. The soft tender shoots called "spears" are used as salad, vegetables, soup, canned and frozen.

Nutritive value. Asparagus shoots are rich in protein, vitamins A & C and mineral calcium.

Medicinal value. The tender shoots contain a chemical 'asparagine' which is used in the medicine as diuretic.

Origin. It has the probable origin in European region (Mediterranean region).

Taxonomy. Asparagus belongs to the family *Liliaceae,* genus *Asparagus* and species *officinalis.* Roots are numerous, fleshy, grow horizontally inside the soil and serves a storage organs. The crown is made up of roots and rhizomes. The spear (aerial stem) arises from a bud on the rhizome. Spear becomes the flowering plant bearing berries containing seeds. It is a diecious *i.e.* male and female plants are separate, cross-pollination is the rule and on any account no two cultivars shall be grown side by side to maintain the identity of the cultivar.

Cultivars. Marth Washington, Mary Washington, New Jersey Improved, Perfection.

Climate. It is a cool season/temperate crop which thrives over a wide range of temperature (15.5-23.8°C) and fairly tolerant to frost. However, continuous freezing temperatures are harmful.

Soil. It being a perennial crop, requires deep fertile loam soil with good drainage. It is also sensitive to high acidity and alkalinity. A pH range of 6.5-7.5 is found to be optimum.

Seed rate. Propagated by seeds or crowns — 3-4 kg seeds/ha.

Sowing time. Plains — July-November.

Hills — March-May.

Sowing/planting. Asparagus should be planted in a selected place as it will remain for 15-20 or more years. The land should be prepared into better tilth. 20-25 cm deep furrows/ ridges or pits are prepared. The seed or seedlings or crowns (portions of rhizome and aerial shoot separated from one year old plant can be used for planting. Well grown crowns of good size containing large buds are selected to use for planting. They are separated from the mother plant before the buds sprout and planted within a few hours. In sandy soils they are planted deeper (20-25 cm) than clayey soil (15-20 cm). Then the furrows are filled with soil so that the crowns can be covered with soil 2-3 cm above the top of the crown. In case of seedling, after planting they are gently pressed around the base. The seeds can be sown on the sides of the ridges near the bottom.

Spacing. 100-150 × 45-60 cm between plants and rows.

Manure and fertilizer. Apply 30-40 t FYM, 20-30 kg N, 80-100 kg P_2O_5, 50-60 kg K_2O/ha.

Irrigation. The first irrigation is given at the time of planting. The irrigation should be given once in 10-15 days.

Hoeing and weeding. During winter, the frost kills the top growth. This is cut out and added to the soil to increase the organic matter. A very light hoeing is given since the young sprouts which are called 'spear' should not be damaged during hoeing. Under temperate conditions, the crown become dormant during winter. Formation of 'spear' starts in the beginning of the spring. In mild climatic conditions, dormancy of crowns may not be very distinct. A pre-emergence application of weedicide like Bromacil @ 2 kg/ha is recommended.

Blanching. If white asparagus is needed then the spears should be blanched by keeping soil around the plant upto a height of 20-30 cm. When the tip of the spear emerge out from these soil hills. The entire 'spear' should be cut before further growth as they will become green.

Harvesting. The tender shoots arise from the buds on the crowns and come out as aerial shoots called 'spears' 5 = 6 months after planting crown or seedling. Up to one year planting the crown, the 'spears' should not be harvested because this is the active period of growth of root system and rhizome. The production of 'spears' is at the cost of food material stored in the roots during the previous year. So initially the plants should be given sufficient period to prepare and store the food material. The first cutting should be done after two years after planting. In one year, the cutting season should be restricted to a limited period *viz.* 3-4 weeks in the first cutting and 8-12 weeks in the subsequent years of regular harvesting. The well grown 'spears' should be cut with a knife called 'asparagus knife' which has a wide chisel like blade. By holding the tips of the 'spears' in the left hand, the knife is pushed down about 45° angle to the 'spear' to cut it off below the ground surface. The distance below the ground surface should be more when white asparagus is produced and *vice versa* for green asparagus. While cutting, the young adjacent sprouts should not be damaged. Crooked and curved 'spears' should be rejected. After harvest they are made into bunches and carried to the ware house.

Grading. These bunches of 'spears' are graded, trimmed, washed/brushed and packed in crates or cartons.

Marketing. After proper packing, the produce is send to the market. If the produce is to be used to the distant markets or export or the time taken for carrying is more, the position of the 'spears' in the cartons should always be kept upward, this will not allow the 'spears' to get bend.

Storage. The 'spears' can be stored at 0°C with 90 per cent RH for a period of 3-4 weeks. At room temperature the 'spears' become tougher if stored even for a short time. Even during transport while packing in crates, the cut end is kept wet either by placing in a pan of water or a pad of wet moss.

Yield. 3.5-4.5 t/ha.

24.2. GLOBE ARTICHOKE

It is a herbaceous perennial plant and continues to produce the eatable heads up to 8-10 years then new crop need to be planted.

Uses. The immature flower heads (buds) are boiled, cooked and used as vegetable.

Nutritive value. It contains proteins, vitamins and minerals.

Medicinal value. It has manifold medicinal uses.

Origin. Southern Europe and Central Asia are the probable origin.

Taxonomy. It belongs to the family *Compositae,* genus *Cynara* and species *scolymus.* The plant is chiscle like.

Cultivars. Introductions — Purple Globe, Green Globe.

Climate. It is a cool season crop can be grown successfully in areas with a temperature range of 12-18°C. If the temperature goes above 22°C it results in the production of tough buds and tendency to spread. The roots can tolerate and survive freezing weather but the aerial portion of the plant is injured by near freezing temperature. A light frost may not destroy the edible quality of the bud, but produce blistered appearance which will affect the marketability. Freezing temperature prior to harvest (–2-1°C) kill the buds and above ground growths. This will result in delay in harvest from 6-8 weeks.

Soil. Heavy loams or light clays are ideal to grow artichoke. A pH range of 6-7.5 will be best suited.

Seed rate. 1 kg/ha.

Sowing time. Plains — February-March.

High-hills — March-May.

Low-hills — June-July and August-September.

Sowing/planting. The field should be prepared into a better tilth. Beds or furrows should be prepared in the field. The plants are propagated through seed, vegetatively through young off-soots or suckers which are removed from the older plants in November and stored in cool and moist place to prevent drying till February. Sometimes even the old crown is split into several pieces each with a stem. These are planted in rows during February-March when they come out of dormancy and start putting forth new growth. The plants are set at a depth of 15-20 cm.

Spacing. 120 × 45-60 cm between rows and plants.

Manure and fertilizer. Add 15-20 t FYM, 60-100 kg N/ha every year. Half N should be applied during November-December and rest half in July-August.

Irrigation. First irrigation should be given at the time of planting. For the establishment of new crop frequent irrigations are necessary at the early stages. Irrigation is applied in furrows as it is a deep rooted crop and in deep soils, the root system may extend at a depth of 150 cm.

Hoeing and weeding. Should be done as and when required. Since the crop stand for 6-7 years in the field after each harvest the leaves and stems are cut-off several cm below soil level. These leaves and stems are allowed to decompose in the soil so as to increase the organic matter in some cases, the tops are sold for silage to the livestock industry.

Harvesting. The first harvest starts 6-7 months after planting the suckers. The harvest season starts from September-October. A mature plant will produce 12 or more stems and 40-60 edible buds. The harvest continue throughout the winter season. The buds are selected for harvest on the basis of compactness, size and age. Buds which are old and not compact are fibrous and inedible. Each stem has several buds. The terminal one is the most desirable. Each bud is cut along with a portion of the stem with a length of 2.0 × 2.5 cm.

Grading. The immature buds should be graded according to the cultivar, its colour, size and main head or the secondary buds.

Marketing. The produce should be marketed immediately after harvesting.

Storage. The buds can be stored at 0°C and 90-95 per cent RH for a period of 3-4 weeks.

Yield. 10-12 t/ha.

24.3. HORSE RADISH

Horse radish *(Armoracia rusticana)* produces whorl of large rather coarse textured leaves.

Uses. Both the leaves and root are eaten as raw or cooked form.

Nutritive value. It contains protein, vitamins and minerals.

Medicinal value. Medicinal herb.

Origin. It is native to South-eastern Europe.

Cultivars. Bohemian, Maliner Kren.

Climate. It is a hardy, cool season perennial plant growing in wild.

Soil. It grows best in deep, rich in organic matter and moist soils. Yields are reduced and the roots are malformed when grown in shallow, stony or hard soils.

Seed rate. Crown and root cutting.

Sowing time. February-March.

Sowing/planting. It should be frequently planted at the edge of the garden or at a permanent place because of perennial nature. Either crowns divisions or root cuttings are planted. Crown divisions are a piece of root and the crown buds. These are removed from the old plants and planted. Root cuttings are small side roots from the main root, the size of a lead pencil and 15-20 cm long. The part of the cutting that was attached to the main root is considered the top and is planted near the soil surface. Root cuttings should be planted immediately in the well prepared soils. The top of the root cutting should be about 5-6 cm below ground level.

Spacing. 75 × 45-60 cm between rows and plants.

Manure and fertilizer. Organic matter or manure should be applied in the soil before planting. The manure should not be applied in spring.

Irrigation. Horse radish should be irrigated timely to provide enough moisture or from rainfall.

Hoeing and weeding. The field should be kept weed free.

Harvesting. Horse radish may be harvested anytime after a hard frost until the plants begin to grow again. Roots are dug with a shovel or spading fork to pullout from the soil.

Grading. To prepare horse radish, the roots are washed, peeled and cut into small cubes. A blender is filled with half-full with the cubes and a small amount of cold water and crushed ice are added. The roots are ground and add white vinegar which cause the root to turn brown, add one teaspoon of salt per cup of horse radish. For extra hot horse radish, wait three minutes before adding the vinegar. The mixture is stored in tightly capped jars in the refrigerator between uses. In about 6 weeks, the ground horse radish darkens and lose some flavour. When new horse radish should be prepared.

Marketing. Similar to radish.

Storage. Roots may be stored in airtight, black plastic bag in the refrigerator.

Yield. 12-15 t/ha.

24.4. RHUBARB

Rhubarb was called as pie or wine plant.

Uses. Its large thick leaf-stalks or petioles are used for sauces and pies. Rhubarb is a important food used in place of fruit.

Nutritive value. It contains carbohydrates, protein, vitamins and minerals.

Medicinal value. It has manifold medicinal values in human life.

Origin. It is a native of Central Asia probably Siberia.

Taxonomy. It belongs to the buckwheat family, *Polygonaceae,* genus *Rheum, rhaponticum.* There are 25 species belonging to this genera.

Cultivars. ***Green petiole.*** German Wine, Sutton's Seedless, Victoria.

Red petioles. Canada Red, Crimson Wine, McDonald Baby, Valentine.

Climate. It is grown in areas that have cool moist summers and winters that freeze the ground several centimetres.

Soil rate. Seeds are not recommended, as the seedlings vary greatly from the parent plant.

Sowing time. January-March.

Sowing/planting. Rhubarb is a perennial and should be planted at one edge of the garden or a permanent place. Crown from the established plants are planted with the crown bud 5 cm deep in the soil in the well prepared field. Crowns can be purchased or obtained from established plants. Established plants are dug in early spring and split into pieces with one large bud to each section of crown and roots. Vigorous healthy plants should be dug and the crowns planted immediately. To maintain vigorous plants that are not overcrowded and producing small petioles, they should be dug and re-established every 8-10 years after planting.

Spacing. 90 or 120 × 90 cm between rows and plants.

Manure and fertilizer. The plants should be fertilized in spring and mulched with compost or well rotten FYM in late fall. Under conditions of low fertility or overcrowding or with old plants, seeded stalks may form. These should be cut at the base of the plant and discarded rot the energy will go into the roots for the next year's crop.

Irrigation. Plants require abundant water during the growing season.

Hoeing and weeding. The harmful weeds should be removed timely as seen in the field.

Harvesting. Rhubarb produces long leafstalks or petioles from the food stored in its fleshy roots from the previous year. The first year after planting the stalks or petioles should not be picked to allow the roots to enlarge. The second year, the petioles may be harvested for 6 weeks or until they become small, indicating that the food reserve is gone. One-third of the petioles or leafstalks should remain on the plant after each harvest. The stalks are pulled from the plant and the leaf blade is removed. Rhubarb leaves contain soluble oxalic acid, which is toxic and the leaves should not be eaten. Leafstalks or petioles drop frosted plants should not be eaten as the leaf oxalic acid may have moved into the petiole. The stalks are pulled (not cut) and the leaf blades are cut-off.

Grading. The stalks usually are washed before being graded, packed and carried to the markets.

Marketing. Before sending to the distant or local markets, the stalks often are tied in bundles or bunches of 1/2 to 1 kg weight or more for ease in handling the produce in the transit, but in case of shipping or air lifting they are packed in bulk in cartons, crates, boxes lined with paper.

Storage. The stalks can be stored in shade before sending to the market under ordinary conditions for 5-6 days.

Yield. 10-15 t/ha.

Crop protection. Beetles punctures the petioles or leaf stalks leaving black spots. Crown rot develops lesions on the leaves, follow crop rotation for 5 years.

CHAPTER

25

HERBS

25.1. CORIANDER

India is a leading producer of coriander. It is grown almost in every state and home and have export potential too. It is an important subsidiary crop in the black cotton soils of South India and the rich silt loams of Northern India. In India, it is grown in an area of about 334.9 thousand hectares with the annual production of 211.5 thousand tonnes.

Uses. The entire plant of coriander when young is used in preparing chutney and sauces and the leaves for flavouring curries and soups. Mostly the fruits and leaves of coriander are used in the form of condiments in cooked food stuffs, pickling spices, seasoning and important ingredient for salads. The oil of coriander is used in perfumes and also in preparation of curry powder, pickling sauces and for seasoning.

Nutritive value. The fruits and leaves of coriander are found to be rich in vitamin A (carotene), riboflavin (Vitamin-B_2), Niacin (Vitamin-B_3) and Vitamin-C.

Medicinal value. Seeds of coriander are carminative or flavouring agent to cover taste, stomachic, ahprodisiac or correct the gripping qualities of other medicines. The seeds are generally chewed to correct foul breath and lessen the intoxicating effect of liquors and infusion of seeds in combination with caraway and cardamom seeds is useful in flatulence, indigestion, vomiting and intestinal disorders. The roasted seeds are useful in dyspepsia. Their paste is applied to relieve pain in cephalalgia. Coriander water is useful in indigestion and other bowl complaints. The oil is also taken as flavouring agent for spirituous liquors and in cocoa and chocolate industries, medicines and perfumes.

Origin. Coriander is a native of Mediterranean region.

Taxonomy. It belongs to the family *Umbelliferae,* genus *Coriandrum* and species *sativum.* It is an annual herb with small white or pinkish purple flowers borne terminal umbels. The lower leaves are broad with creanatly lobed margins while the upper ones are narrow, finely cut with finer lobes. The fruits are globular and ribbed, yellow brown in colour and when pressed get separated into halves (mericarp) each containing a seed.

Cultivars. Pant Haritima, Swati, Swathi, RCr-41, RCr-20, UD-20, CO-1, CO-2, CO-3, Simmo, S-33, CS-287, Moracan, Gwaliar No. 5365, Gujarat and Coriander-2, Sadhana (CS-4), CS-7, Guj.-l, Guj-2, NP(D)-95, NP(J)-16, NP(J)-214, NP(K)-45, NP(P)-172, IC-3622, S-2- 48, Delhi Local.

Climate. It is grown as *rabi* season crop but severe frost at the time of flowering and seed setting may cause damage. The optimum temperature for normal growth for this crop is 20-28°C. When the temperature goes to 35-40°C the growth is severely affected. Similarly heavy rains also hampers the growth of the crop.

Soil. It can be grown on any soil under irrigated conditions but for a rainfed crop black soils are the best. The soil pH should be 6-7. To some extent it can tolerate alkaline soils.

Seed rate. Spot sowing—Pure crop is 8-10 kg seed and mixed crop 4-5 kg seed/ha.

Broadcast method–20-30 kg/ha (Punjab) and 12-19 kg/ha (South India).

Sowing time. North India plains — September to November.

Eastern India — July-August.

Off-season — August-September.

Hills — March-April.

Sowing/planting. Prepare the land well before sowing and ensure proper drainage. The soil should have sufficient humus. It can be grown as a mixed crop with black gram, wheat, etc. or as a pure crop in gardens year after year. The fruits are split into halves by gentle rubbing them against an iron pan or with a stone/pebble and soaked in water overnight to hasten germination before sowing. Sow 3-4 seeds per hill and the seeds germinate in about 8-10 days. During this period do not allow crust formation otherwise germination is delayed and reduced. Sowing is also done by broadcast method or in rows through drills. Seed treament with Thiram @ 2.5 g/kg of seed should be done to avoid disease attack.

Spacing. The spacing from row to row 25 cm and hill to hill 15 cm is kept.

Manure and fertilizer. Apply 15 t FYM, 20 kg N, 45 kg P_2O_5 and 20 kg of K_2O/ha. Mix complete quantities of FYM at the time of land preparation. Apply half of nitrogen and complete quantities of P_2O_s and K_2O in the soil before sowing.

Irrigation. Keep the soil in optimum moisture condition. Irrigation and after care may be done carefully. Mostly it is raised as rainfed crop. As irrigated crop it needs irrigation at an interval of 8-10 days depending upon moisture in the soil.

Hoeing and weeding. After the germination process is over first hoeing is done. Later on weeds are kept under control.

Harvesting. The green crop gets ready in January-February and seeds mature in May. Harvesting for garnishing purpose, the leaves and stems are nipped carefully so that whole plant may not be uprooted. Nipping should be done when the plants are ten to fifteen days old and 25 cm in height fully grown but tender. Number of cuttings will depend upon the cultivars. Dual pupose cultivars give more numbers of cuttings and quality produce. The crop may be left for bolting after one or two cuttings. This operation may be continued upto the flowering stage and sometimes upto fruiting stage. The crop (seeds) becomes ready for harvest in about 100-120 days. At this stage the fruits are fully mature but still green. Delay in harvest may result in shattering of fruits. Harvesting of the crop is done by pulling out the plant. Keep the plants tied in bundles and dry in the shade. When fully dry, spread the plants on floor and thresh by beating and clean the seeds. Store seeds in a dry place after proper sun drying. Store the dry seeds in gunny bags having paper lining. This saves loss in oil content.

Grading. The harvested leaves are washed and small bundles are tied which ease in handling and selling. These are taken to shade to avoid withering (drying) in direct sun. Proper graded bundles will earn more price in the market.

Marketing. The produce should be packed in baskets, cartons or crates and sometimes in bags with proper ventilation so that the bundles are not damaged. It should be carried immediately to the market in fresh from.

Storage. The produce should be stored in shade and sprinkle water over it to maintain its green colour, flavour and quality.

Yield. The yield of leaves range from 6-12 t/ha. Under irrigated conditions fruit yield of 4-20 t/ha is obtained. In case of mixed crop the fruit yield/ha may vary from 1.5-7 t/ha. The output of volatile oil varies with the variety and ranges from 0.2 to 1.0 per cent of fruit weight. Similarly fatty oil yield may vary from 11-21 per cent.

25.2. CUMIN

In our country it is grown in almost all the states except few like West Bengal and Assam where the agro-ecological situations are not suitable. It is cultivated in semi-arid or arid regions. The cumin is mainly cultivated in Rajasthan and Gujarat which holds important position in terms of area and production and contributes 56 per cent of the total country's production. The spice cumin producing countries are India, Turkey, Iran, Egypt, Pakistan and Syria. However, the competitive contries of India are Turkey and Iran.

In cumin, the quality is based on aroma and brown coloured seed with lustre having at least 3-4 per cent volatile oil content which are free from weeds like zeeri are better for consumption or use.

Area and production. In India, cumin an important_seed spice is grown in an area of 282009 ha with a production of 91361 MT and productivity 324 kg/ha.

Export. The cumin is exported to various markets in UK, USA, Canada, Singapur, Japan, Malaysia, Saudi Arbia and Nepal every year and during 1995-96, cumin was exported to the tune of 3695 MT valuing to Rs. 1734 lakh.

Uses. It is used as powder, beverages, cumin sips, organic cumin, aromatic oil and oleoresin is used as an flavouring, confectionery, beverages and in cosmetics. The green leaves and tender stalks are used as herb like coriander leaves for culinary purposes. The oil is also used in veterinary practices.

Nutritive value. Seed are very rich in an essential oil which varies from 2.5-4.5 per cent.

Medicinal value. It has manifold medicinal uses, as anthelmintic against hookworms and also antiseptic. Seeds are rich source of thymol and protein.

Origin. It is believed to be native of Egypt and Syria, Turkestan and the eastern Mediterranean region (Europe).

Taxonomy. Cumin is a small slender annual herb belonging to the family *Umbelliferae,* genus *Cuminum,* species *cyminum* and grows to a height of 30-40 cm and produces a stem with many branches bearing long, finely divided, deep green leaves and small flowers, white or rose in colour, borne in umbels. The cumin comprises the dried yellowish to greyish brown seeds or fruits which are small, elongated and oval in shape having ridges and light brown in colour.

Cultivars. RZ-19, RS-1, MC-43, S-404, Gujarat Cumin-1, Gujarat Cumin-2.

Climate. Cumin needs dry climatic conditions at the time of seed maturity. The crop flowers normally in February-March and seed (fruit) formation takes simultaneously, therefore during this period, there should be less humidity which allows better quality seed setting and increased yields. More humidity at this stage, invites more infestation of diseases and insect-pests.

Soil. Cumin can be cultivated in almost all types of soils. However, loamy, medium to heavy soils with better fertility level are most suitable. In sandy soils, there is possibility of appearing disease known as ukhata disease.

Seed rate. 10-15 kg of quality seed is sufficient for sowing a hectare of area.

Sowing time. September-October.

Sowing/planting. Soil should be prepared well into a better tilth. The surface of the field should be well levelled, and smooth which may be divided into small beds for ease in germination of small seeds of cumin. The stubbles and remains of the previous crop should be removed. The cumin seed is sown by broadcast method uniformly. To maintain uniformity, the cumin seed being small is sometimes mixed with friable soil or sand before broadcasting. In some places, line sowing is also done. The seed is not sown very deep which delay and affect germination. Immediately after seed sowing, the seed is mixed or covered with a thin layer of soil.

Sowing time. Optimum sowing time is 15-30th November and it may vary from place to place.

Seed treatment. The seed should be treated with Bavistein @ 2-2.25 g/kg of seed before sowing to have better results.

Spacing. 30 × 10-15 cm between rows and plants in Gujarat.

Manure and fertilizer. At the time of land preparation apply 10-15 tonnes/ha of well rotten FYM, 30 kg N and 20 kg P_2O_5/ha. Apply half dose of N and whole quantity of P_2O_5 at the time of land preparation and rest quantity of N into two splits may be top dressed after 40 and 60 days of sowing.

Irrigation. For obtaining better yields, 4-5 irrigation are sufficient depending on rains. A light irrigation soon after sowing helps in better germination and boost the growth in early stages. Sometimes there is crust formation which check the growth and development, in such situations a light irrigation will be helpful to the crop. Thereafter, the crop may be irrigated at an interval of 20-25 days depending on the requirements. The crop at maturity should not be irrigated as it invites diseases and insect-pests.

Hoeing and weeding. The first hoeing and weeding should be done when the plants are 5-6 cm high. Remove all the weeds, unwanted, off-type plants and thin those showing poor growth to maintain optimum spacing for getting better yields. The subsequent intercultural operations be done on appearance of weeds. The weed seeds like zeeri *(Plantago pumilla* W.) and parijan in cumin seed reduces quality and brings less prices Zeeri plant is a serious weed in cumin and cannot be distinguished from the cumin field up to the stage of flowering. Zeeri plant should be removed by hand weeding at flowering for getting higher yields of better quality seed. However, zeeri can be controlled with pre-plant spraying of Fluchloralin @ 0.77 to 1.00 kg/ha. It is reported that the volatile oil contents and test weight of cumin was reduced due to presence of weeds. For controlling other weeds, Basalin (2-2.5 kg/ha) or Stomp F-34 (3.33 kg/ha) dissolved in 750 L of water as pre-emergence application be done.

Harvesting. The cumin crop get matured in 85-100 days depending on the variety and other agro-ecological factors. The maturity of the umbels is indicated by browning of seeds. It should be harvested with sharp sickle in the morning hours to avoid shattering as it is prone to it. After harvesting the crop, it should be collected and spread on the threshing floor or tarpaulin in the open sun for drying in thin layer. The seeds are separated by beating with wooden sticks or now-a-days the modern threshers are/can be used for threshing on commercial scale. The cumin produce is again dried in the sun till it is left minimum moisture content. If the cumin seed is not dried to the minimum moisture level will be infested with fungus during storage.

Grading. The produce should be properly cleaned, graded, packed in the optimum sized standard packs/containers and well labelled.

Marketing. Similar to coriander.

Storage. As in case of coriander.

Yield. Green leaves — 6-8 t/ha.

Seed — 8-10 quintals/ha.

25.3. FENNEL

Fennel a herbaceous plant is widely cultivated throughout the temperate and subtropical regions of the world for its aromatic fruits used as culinary spice. It is known by different names in its different growing regions. In Sanskrit it is known as 'Shatapushpa' and Shataahwa. In India fennel is cultivated mostly as a garden or home yard crop at all the altitudes upto 2000 m.

It is cultivated in the States of Gujarat and Rajasthan with 64% area accounted by the State of Gujarat alone in an area of 17,300 hectares with an annual production of 18,088 tonnes.

Uses. Fennel plant is pleasantly aromatic and is used as a pot herb. The leaves are used in fish sauce and for garnishing leaf stalks are used in salad. Thickened, leaf stalks of Florence fennel are branched and used as vegetable. Dried fruits of fennel have a fragrant odour and a pleasant aromatic taste. They are used for flavoring soups, meal dishes and sauces, bread rolls, pasties and confectionery. They are also used for flavouring liquors and in the manufacture of pickles.

Nutritional value. Fennel fruit contain a volatile oil and fixed oil. They also contain pentosar, pectin, starch, trigonellive and choline. Fruits contain iodine, vitamin A, C thiamine, riboflavin, niacin, and ascorbic acid. Traces of aluminium, barium, lithium, copper, manganese, silicon and titanium.

Medicinal value. Leaves possess diuretic properties, roots are regarded as purgative and have aromatic odour and taste. Fruits are aromatic stimulant and carminative. They are considered useful in diseases of the chest, spleen and kidney.

Origin. Native of Mediterranean region.

Taxonomy. It belongs to the family *Umbelliferae,* genus *Foeniculum* and species *vulgare.* A large annual or biennial or perennial herb, with a thick root stock. Stem 2-4 feet high, hallow cylindrical stem, erect shoot, cylindrical, finely striate, smooth and polished, bright green, solid or nearly so, much branched. Leaves stalked, petiole very long, dilated for the greater part of its length into an open flattened sheath. Umbel long-stalked, large, slender, spreading, curved, often unequal rays, quite without involucers; flowers about 15-20 in an umbel, rather long stalked, not very small. Flower opening and anthesis starts from periphery within umied and umbellets. Dehiscence of anther began at 3.00 a.m. and spreads over period of ten hours. However, it is temperature dependent. Stamens sprining out one after another and shed pollen at an interval of 3 hours. The crop is cross pollinated due to protandry (2n = 22 chromosome).

Cultivars. U.F.-101, UF-1, Co-1, P.F.-35, Sel.-32, K-27, Vr. K-ll, Vr. K-16, Vr. K-52. Pomorie, F-l hybrid , Mutant-1, Mutants- 2, Mutant-3, NN(D)-32, 186 and NP(I)-13, S-7-9, PF-35, Gujarat fennel-1, UF-32, S-7-9, PF-35 and Gujarat fennel-1. Rajasthan Saurabha, LF-32 and LF-35. S-7-9, PF-35 and Gujarat fennel-1.

Climate. Fennel is cultivated mostly as a garden or homeyard crop through out India at all altitudes upto 2000 m. It required a fairly mild climate and is cultivated in cold weather in North India and also to some extent in the hilly regions but susceptible to frost particularly at flowering stage. Prolonged cloudy weather or high humidity at the time of flowering and seed formation increases the chances of aphid infestation and attack of Ramularia blight disease.

Soil. Though fennel is grown in a variety of soils yet it thrives best in rich, well drained loam or black sandy soil containing sufficient lime. However, poorly drained and too much alkaline soils are not fit for fennel crop. In Gujarat, which is the major grower of fennel, the crop is grown in deep black to medium black clayey-loam soil by utilizing the residual moisture. In sandy loam to clayey loam soils, the crop is grown as a transplanted crop under irrigation during *rabi.* In Rajasthan, fennel crop is raised in sandy loam to clayey loam soils by utilizing the residual soil moisture during *rabi* as a cold weather crop and also in friable alluvial and sandy loam soils.

Land preparation. The land should be ploughed 3-4 times in heavy and 2-3 times in lighter soils upto the depth of 15-20 cm to make the soil mellow and friable. After planking, the beds of convenient size are prepared. If soil moisture is low, pre-sowing irrigation should be applied before preparatory tillage. For control of termites and other harbored insects, Endosulfan powder @ 25 kg/ha may be applied to the soil before last ploughing.

Sowing time. North Indian — October-November, Punjab — last week of October, Rajasthan — first week of October and in hill — March April.

For transplanted crop. It is a profitable way of growing fennel crop both in Gujarat and Rajasthan. For this, nursery by sowing seeds in nursery beds, is raised during May-June and seedling of one and half or two months age are transplanted in the main field in August-September at a spacing of 60-80 cm or even upto 1 metre in rows and keeping 40-80 cm spacing between plants within the row. Nursery beds of 3 × 0.5 × 0.15 m size are prepared, seeds are broadcasted by 15th June for *Kharif* fennel while by 15th August for *rabi* fennel.

Seed rate. For direct seed crop — 10-12 kg/ha.

For transplanted crop — 3-4 kg/ha.

Spacing. Irrigated crop — 60 × 40 cm.

Rainfed crop — 45 × 10 cm between rows and plants.

Fennel is also sown by broadcast method particularly where it is cultivated as crop mixed with chillies or Cole crops. Seeds are broadcasted in the field after the seedlings of chillies/Cole crops are established preferably at the time of first weeding and hoeing.

Manure and fertilizers. Apply 10-15 tonnes/ha FYM/Compost may be incorporated in the soil during field preparation and add. 100 kg each of N and P_2O_5 and 40 kg K_2O/ha. Application of N split dose of N (25 kg each) as basal at 60 DAS to fennel increase the yield. Response of fennel to applications of micronutrients like Zn and B along with application of N at 45 kg and P 50 kg from Rajasthan and Bihar have given better results.

Weed management. Fennel is a slow growing crop in the initial growth stages and also grown at a wider spacing. At least 3-4 weeding are required to be done for its proper cultivation. Application of pre and post-emergence Premetryne and Aresin (monolimuron) at 3.0 kg and Afalon (Linuron) at 2.0 kg/ha was found suitable for weed control in fennel. Good weed control with the preplanting application of 0.5 kg/ha Linuron, 4.0 kg/ha Chloroxuron of 1.0-1.5 kg/ha Chlorobromuran gives better results.

25.4. MINT

It is a very popular commercial herb being grown by most of the farmers almost throughout the country almost in every kitchen garden.

Uses. This is a green with very strong pleasant odour in leaves and stems which are mainly used for flavouring foodstuff. It is also used for the preparation of fresh chutney.

Nutritive value. It is a good source, of protein, fat, carbohydrates, vitamins A & B_1 (Thiamine), B_2 (Riboflavin), B_3 (Niacin) and vitamin C and minerals-calcium, phosphorus and iron.

Taxonomy. Mint belongs to the family *Labitae,* genus *Mentha* and species *arvensis* or *longifolia* commonly called *'Jangli podina'*. The other two species are *M. piperita, the* common Pepperment or *Vilayati podina* and *M. spieata* is the common Spearmint.

Cultivars. Himalaya, Kosi.

Climate. It can be grown almost throughout the year under mild climatic conditions but better growth takes place in summer months. In rainy season because of excess water there is more infestation of diseases and insect-pests and the quality of leaves is affected.

Soil and its preparation. Similar to other herb crops.

Planting. 3-4 of suckers are sufficient for planting/ha.

Planting time. Last week of January.

Planting method. Mint suckers are planted in shallow furrows normally 7-10 cm deep. The suckers are cut or chopped into small pieces generally 5-10 cm long and placed in furrows end to end and covered with soil.

Manure and fertilizer. Apply 15-10 t of FYM, 75 kg N, 40 kg P_2O_5 and 30 kg K_2O/ha. The N should be applied in three uniform doses first after 35 days, second after 65 days of planting and third dose should be applied immediately after the first harvest. After each harvest urea is applied @ 10-15 g along with 5 kg FYM m^2 and irrigated.

Irrigation. The mint suckers should be irrigated just after the planting and the subsequent irrigation after every 10-15 days interval.

Hoeing and weeding. As in other herb crops.

Harvesting. The green leaves along with petiole is cut with sharp knife or sickle without disturbing the plant after 40-50 days of planting. Depending on the health of the plant, subsequent several cutting can be taken at an interval of 30 days throughout the year. However, among the different agronomic practices the stage at which crop is to be harvested plays pivotal role in influencing production and quality of produce and oil. To achieve good quality and quantity of oil, green material must be dried two days in shade condition before distillation.

Yield. 3-5 t/ha.

Crop protection (Coriander, cumin, fennel)

Diseases/Insect-pests	*Symptoms*	*Control*
Diseases		
Wilt *(Fusarium oxusporium, f. coriandrii)*	Droop of plant, withering and dieing of leaves.	Grow wilt resistant cultivars-Strain-65 and Strain-83.
Powdery mildew *(Erysiphe poligoni)*	White powdery mass on all aerial parts loose chlorophyll and dry up. No seeding.	Dust sulphur powder @ 10-12 kg/ha after 2 months of sowing and repeat.
Tumur *(Stem gall)* (*Protomyces macrosporus*)	Tumurs or elongated swellings appear on flower stalk, leaves, petioles, green stem and seeds.	Grow resistant cultivars *viz.*, IS-171 Spray Karathane 0.1% and repeat after 15 days. Uproot and burn all infested plants to reduce the incidence of the disease.

Leaf spot	Black lesions on leaves stems peduncles and seeds appears severely infected plants give a blightened appearance.	Spray Bordeaux mixture starting from January onwards or spray suspension of colloidal Sulphur @ 0.25% in water during Feb.-March.
Blight	Angular brown necrosis on the lower surface of older leaves, spreads to stem, peduncle and fruits, covering the whole plant with a fungal growth of ash colour, results in shrivelling and drying up of leaves with blighted appearance.	Spray Bavistin 0.1% or Indofil M-45 0.2-0.3% or copper oxychloride, Blitox or Fytolan or Blue copper immediately after the appearance of the disease symptoms and must be repeated after 10-15 days.
Alternaria blight	Brown spots appear on the tips of leaves of young plants initially on lower buds which turn yellow or brownish and the whole inflorescence dries up resulting in heavy loss of yield.	Spray 800-1000 litres/ha of 0.2-0.3% Diathane M-45 solution of 0.1% Bavistin solution or Blitox/ Copper oxychlori de solution.
Insect-pests		
Aphid	Both nymph and adults suck the sap from leaves, flowers and fruits mainly attacking umbels favours growth of sooty mould.	Manipulation of sowing time. Grow resistant cultivars like RC-7B RC-9 RC-31B, Rumarian. Spray 0.25% Methyl parathion/ Methyl-demetan/Endosulfan or 0.05%. Dichlorous at 30 days interval starting from 30 DAT.
Thrips	Both nymph and adult feed on the leaf sheath and stem which causes drying of the leaves.	Spray 0.2% Carbaryl or 0.05%. Dimethoate/Endosulfan or 0.1% Fenitrothium.
Midge	Developing larvae feeds upon and destroys the embryo and/or endosperm.	Spray Fenvarolate @ 0.01% or Methyl-o-deneton 0.02 5% or Dimethate 0.03%.
Sap sucking bug	Suck the sap from the plant parts.	Spray 0.03% Dithoate or Quinolphos.

CHAPTER

26

MISCELLANEOUS CROPS

26.1. GINGER

Ginger is a principal spice grown in the country in an area of 70,910 ha with an annual production of 2,32,510 tonnes (CPS, 1998). It plays a significant role in earning valuable foreign exchange, besides meeting the entire country's demand. It is cultivated in tropical and sub-tropical parts of the world for its aromatic rhizomes which are used as a spice and medicines. In hilly areas especially Himachal Pradesh, the economy of the farmers depends on this crop. During 1997-98, 28,550 tonnes dried ginger was exported earning a foreign exchange to the tune of ₹ 67.81 crores to the country (Cardamom, Spices Board, 1998).

Uses. Ginger is valued for its spicy properties, extensively used in preparation of different types of condiments, in cooking vegetables, and a number of food products like ginger bread, confectionery, ginger ale, curry powder, certain curried meats, table sauces, in pickling and in the manufacture of certain soft drinks like cordials, ginger cocktail, carbonated drinks, bitters, etc. Add tang and flavour to otherwise insipid food. It also possess anti-oridant properties. It stimulate the appetite and increase the flow of gastric juices and are accordingly called 'adjuncts'; camouflage the unpleasant taste of many dried meats; and increase the rate of perspiration thus producing cooling effect on the body. Ginger is also used for the manufacture of ginger oil, oleoresin, essence and tincture.

Nutritive value. The main constituents of ginger rhizome are water, starch (carbohydrate), oleoresin, fibre, a little steam-volatile oil, fixed (fatty) oils, pungent compounds, resin, proteins, cellulose, pentosans and mineral elements. The pungent principle/essence in ginger is due to gingerols, zingerine, and shogoals which are used for different uses in the country and abroad. Dry ginger contains 1 to 3 per cent volatile oil and 50 per cent starch, fibre content, protein, resins, fixed oils, etc.

Medicinal value. In Ayurvedic medical system, ginger is valued for its manifold medicinal and spicy properties and is useful in gastritis, dyspepsia, flatulence and in cold and cough as an expectorant. It has properties to check cancer and other human maladies. Ginger is stimulant, carminative and stomachic and therefore, extremely valuable in colic, vomiting, spasms and other painful afflections of the stomach and the bowels. Ginger is used in nausea and gripping infusion of it is given in rheumatism. Ginger activate and invigorate resistance mechanism in humans against many diseases. It is used in the preparation of tincture ginger, gongoal, gingerin, digestive tablets, powder ginger and dry ginger. It also has aphrodisiac value. In India, it is a popular tonic given to ladies before and after delivery.

Origin. It is native of South-eastern Asia.

Taxonomy. It belongs to the family *Zingiberaceae,* genus *Zengiber* and species *officinale.* A herbaceous perennial having the underground rhizomes, aerial shoot (pseudo-stem) leaves sheathing the stem, the crop is grown as an annual. The other little cultivated species are Z. *zurumbet* and Z. *casumunar.* The chromosome number 2n = 22.

Cultivars. Rio-de-Janeiro, China, Thinlaidium, Thingpuri, Tura, Poona, Nadia, Maran, Jujijan, Jorhat, Wynad local, Sierra Leone, Uttar Pradesh, Burdwan, Assam, Narasapattam, Mysore, Karakkal, Bajpai, Thodupuzha, Emad, Emad Manjeri, Vengara, Valluvanad, Wynad Manantody, Wynad, Kunnamangalam, Wynad Local and Himachal Pradesh-Him Giri, Kandaghat Selection, Maran, Kerala Local, Local cultivars.

Climate. Ginger is grown from almost the sea-level up to an altitude of 1500 metres. It thrive well under partial shades, though it is also cultivated on a large scale in open areas. It is a warm season crop and needs rains or irrigation during the initial vegetative growth and a dry season is preferred at the later stages of rhizome development. The optimum temperature required for proper growth range from 25-32°C.

Soil. A well drained, friable loam, fertile soil, rich in humus with pH 6.5-7.0 is ideal. The land having sufficiently well distributed rainfall or irrigation and adequate drainage facilities, open, free from insect-pests and diseases is most suitable.

Seed rate. 15-20 q of seed rhizomes are required/ha.

Sowing time. Northern Indian plains — June-July.

Hills — April to June depending upon elevation.

Southern parts — April-May.

Sowing/planting. The soil should be in better tilth and the field is divided into raised (15 cm) beds of any convenient size with a spacing of 30 cm between the beds for drainage or irrigation. Break the fingers prior to sowing in ; such a way that there must be at least 2-3 eyes in each piece weighing 30-50 g preferably use medium sized rhizomes for planting 3-4 cm deep. It is propagated through rhizomes which can be carried easily in living state from one place to other and actually form the seed. The seed ginger is used in bulk and forms 40-45% of the total expenditure.

Spacing. 30 × 20 cm between rows and plants.

Manure and fertilizer. Ginger needs heavy manuring and for raising a good crop, add 40-50 t of FYM, 100 kg N, 50 kg each of P_2O_5 and K_2O/ha, whole of FYM, P_2O_s and K_2O

and half dose of N and added as basal dose and rest N in two equal splits are top dressed after 2 and 4 months of sowing. While top dressing, the fertilizer should be applied in such a way that it do not come in contact with rhizomes or fall on wet leaves.

Crop rotation. Ginger should not be grown on the same piece of land for at least 3-4 years and a suitable crop rotation should be followed.

Mulching. Mulching is done with cow-dung @ 10-15 t/ha or dry leaves @ 5-6 t/ha or green leaves @ 10-12 t/ha is the best substitute for cow-dung mulch, which helps to protect the rhizomes from direct sun or heavy rains, preserve soil moisture, check soil erosion and weeds, generate heat to enhance germination and to obtain uniform growth, besides help in increasing humus in the soil. In Himachal Pradesh, FYM is used as a mulch.

Irrigation. Both irrigated and rainfed crops are raised but preference is given to the former. A light irrigation immediately after sowing helps in for proper germination. The number of irrigation depends upon soil type, nature and stage of crop, evaporation from the surface and rains received during the season. Frequent irrigation after 7-8 days interval in early stages and 12-15 days interval in later stages depending upon situation should be given.

Hoeing and weeding. The field should be timely inter-cultured to keep the field clean.

Harvesting. The maturity of the crop is indicated by yellowing of foliage and their drooping down. Ginger rhizomes get ready for harvesting in November-December. The rhizomes are uprooted carefully by spade without any injury and on large scale, the ginger fields are ploughed with furrow turning plough then the healthy rhizomes are collected. The mother and daughter rhizomes are kept separate as the former are sold and the later are kept for seed after thorough screening or sold fresh.

Curing. The harvested rhizomes are kept under shade in thin layers either in the field under shade or in varandah for 5-6 days. During this period these are freed from soil, roots, stems, etc. The excess moisture is also eliminated and more so if there is some cut, injury etc. get healed up by suberisation.

Grading. The rhizomes prior to selling/storage are graded on the basis of shape, size, number of fingers colour, scales etc. Select only healthy, plumpy rhizomes of uniform size, free from rhizomes rot disease and insect attack.

Marketing. An efficient, proper and reliable marketing system by itself can stimulate production of ginger while lack of it would lessen, subdue and shrink the input of any number of developmental efforts. India has been a traditional supplier of fresh and dried ginger to the domestic and international market. The existing marketing institutions mop up a sizeable share of the consumer's rupee, thus, lowering returns to the producer-sellers. The ginger produce perishable in nature need to be sent to the markets immediately after harvesting through various marketing channels and the price spreads in each channel so that farmers can adopt the most efficient channel for disposing-off their produce resulting in the improvement of their economic condition in the ginger growing areas along with lucrative returns for their fresh and dried ginger produce.

Storage. Ginger can be stored for 4-5 months under ordinary conditions or in pits. One quintal of seed ginger can be conveniently stored in one cubic metre (l × l × l m) pit. In the ginger growing areas the depth and size of storage pit varies and can store up to 50-100 quintals. However, storing is also done in rooms or corners of varandah where the rhizomes are covered with dry grass or gunny bags and plastered with cow dung or soil. The storage spits and the seed rhizomes should be treated with Bavistin (0.05%) and Dithane M-45 (0.3%) Store the seed after proper drying of both storage places and rhizomes. Keep the storage spits open for 3-4 days to evacuate the hot air and put some dry grass and wooden planks and plaster with a thin layer of soil. Take out the seed ginger from the pits at least 20-25 days before sowing.

Yield. The average seed yield ranges from 150 to 220 q/ha.

26.2. TURMERIC

Turmeric is essentially a tropical crop extending from India to Indo-China, East India and parts of China. India is largest producer, consumer and exporter of turmeric in the world. It is mainly cultivated in Andhra Pradesh in the districts — Karimnagar, Nizamabad, Guntur, Warangal, Cuddapah, Krishna, East & West Godavari, Kurnool, and tribal areas of Visakhapatnam and Srikakulam districts. Turmeric is an important commercial spice in Northern Telangana zone of Andhra Pradesh which accounts for 50 per cent area of the State. Nizamabad is the major marketing centre in A.P. with a turnover of more than ₹ 50 crores per year.

Uses. Its underground rhizomes are used as condiment, dye, snuff, drug and in cosmetic preparations. It is also used in ceremonial and religious functions.

Nutritive value. It contains protein, fat, fibre, carbohydrates, vitamin A and minerals. It is rich in essential oils and crystalline colouring matter curcumin.

Medicinal value. It is used as stomachic, tonic and blood purifier, antiperodic alternative, antiparasitic and skin affections. Externally, it is applied to indolent ulcers and its paste with lime forms a remedy for inflammed joints. Rhizome decoction relieve the pain of purulent ophthalmia. Turmeric oil has feeble antisceptic properties. It also acts as carminative, stomachic, appetiser and tonic-sore throat, cough, cold, pharyagitis, laryanigitis and other acute upper respiratory infections.

Origin. It is believed to be a native of Cochin-China and Indonesia.

Taxonomy. Member of family *Zingiberaceae,* genus *Curcuma,* species *longa* or *domestica.* The leaves are broad, lanceolate and bright green. The flowers are pale yellow and borne on dense spikes. The pseudostems are shorter than leaves.

Cultivars. Suguna (PCT-11), Sudarshana (PCT-14) and Local Cultivars. Duggirrali, Kodurtype, Tekurpeta, Armoor, Suganthan, Alleppey and some Clonal Selections-C-1, 2-A, 15-B, IC, 21-A, 3D, Edapalayam (high curcumin), Konni (high oleoresin), Pattani, Rajapore, Karhadi, Chinnandan, Perianadan, Collection No. 325, GL Purana, Daghi, Chaya, Pasupa.

Climate. Turmeric crop requires a warm and humid climate. A temperature range of 30-35°C during germination, 25-30°C during tillering and rhizome initiation and 18-20°C during bulking stage have been found optimum.

Soil. It thrives well under fertile, sandy or clay black or red or alluvial loam soils rich in humus, uniform texture and good drainage facilities. It is very sensitive to water stagnation and alkalinity. Soil pH should be 5.0-7.5.

Seed rate. About 2,500 kg of finger rhizomes are required per hectare.

Sowing time. Last week of May to the end of July.

Seed treatment. Before sowing the seed has to be soaked in 0.3% Dithane M-45 and 0.1% Chloropyrephos for about 30 minutes as a seed treatment measure.

Sowing/planting. Turmeric is propagated from rhizomes. The land is ploughed to bring the soil to fine tilth. Rhizomes are dibbled with a country plough. In loamy soils rhizomes are dibbled at 15 cm apart in the plough furrows spaced 30 cm apart. Land is levelled and flat beds of 3 × 18 m size are prepared, providing necessary channels. In heavy soils, ridge and furrow system is adopted and rhizomes are sown at 15 to 20 cm spacing behind the plough and ridger in the adjacent ridge. Spacing between ridges is kept 45 to 60 cm. In low lying areas and in still black clay soils rhizomes are planted on raised beds of 11.7 m × 0.2 m length with 30 cm spacing. This method gave higher yield than ridge and furrow method.

Spacing. Dwarf/medium-30-45 × 15-20 cm.

Tall cultivars-45-60 × 20-30 cm between plants and rows.

Manure and fertilizer. Turmeric is a heavy feeder and requires heavy manuring. The crop requires 25 t/ha FYM, 300 kg N, 125 kg P_2O_5 and 200 kg of K_2O per hectare in organic and inorganic forms. Nitrogen has to be applied in three or four split doses. Entire phosphorous and FYM should be applied as a basal dose while potassium has to be applied in two or three splits. Fertilizer application should be completed within 120 days from the time of planting.

Irrigation. Fifteen to twenty irrigation are required depending upon the condition and type of the soil.

Mulching. Crop should be mulched immediately after planting with green leaves @ 12-15 t/ha and may be repeated with some quantity of green leaves. Dry leaves and trash is also useful for mulching.

Hoeing and weeding. Weeding is necessary at 60, 90, 120 and 150 days after planting. Earthing-up should be done after every hoeing.

Cropping-systems. Turmeric can be grown as an intercrop in plantations of coconut, forest trees and orchards *viz.,* apple, guava, citrus, etc. In wet lands, it can be rotated rice, sugarcane, banana, or vegetables like onion etc. In garden lands, it is often grown in rotation with rainfed rice, mixed with pigeon pea, maize, yam and minor millets.

Harvesting. The rhizomes are ready for harvesting about 6 to 6½ (short to medium duration cultivars) and 7 to 9 months (long duration cultivars) after planting. Complete drying of leaves and pseudo-stem indicate the maturity of the crop. Leaves are cut close to the ground and fields are irrigated two days before harvest. Underground rhizomes are dug out with pickaxe by manual labour.

Grading. The rhizomes collected and cleaned off soil and roots then subjected to grading of good rhizomes and culling off-types, infested, injured and diseased. The graded produce brings more prices.

Curing. Turmeric rhizomes cleaned, fingers are separated from mother rhizomes which are generally kept as seed material. The harvested rhizomes need to be cured for dry turmeric for the market. Processing involves boiling of rhizomes in sufficient water in a container which is galvanized. If the water is acidic then add sodium bicarbonate to make it slightly alkaline. Stop boiling when typical smell comes out. The boiled rhizomes are practically killed and taken out for drying. These are dried in the sun for 10-15 days till they produce metal like sound. These are then again cleaned and polished mechanically in a drum rotating by hand. The dry product is generally about 20% of the fresh turmeric.

Colouring. In order to get good price of the produce and to attract the buyers colour plays an important role in turmeric trade. The process of colouring the turmeric is very simple in which boiled, dried and half polished turmeric fingers are taken in a basket which is shaken continuously and a prepared emulsion is poured in. Uniformly emulsified fingers are dried in the sun. For 100 kg half polished turmeric the following material would be required. Alum-(0.84 kg), turmeric powder (2.06 kg), caster seed (0.14 kg), sodium bicarbonate (30 g) and concentrated sulphuric acid (30 ml).

Marketing. As in case of ginger.

Storage. For preservation of rhizomes the material is stored by heaping them under the shade of trees or a well ventilated rooms. Heaps are covered vith turmeric leaf and plastered with earth and cow dung mixture. It can be left undisturbed for 2 or 3 months until marketing or processing or retaining for sowing.

Yield. Average yield ranges from 250-350 q/ha depending on the variety and other factors.

Crop protection (Ginger and turmeric)

Diseases/Insect-pests	*Symptoms*	*Control*
Diseases		
Leaf spots	No. of oblong spots appear on the leaves from brown to black. Finally affected leaves wilt and dry.	Use healthy and disease seed. Treat seed before sowing and storage with 0.3% DM-45 & 0.01% Bavistin. Destroy and burn infected leaves.
Leaf blotch	Rectangular spots appear on lower leaves along the veins with pale or yellow and finally reddish-brown colour leading to defoliation.	Spray 0.25 % DM-45 and 0.01% Bavistin 2-3 times. Spray Blitox or Copper sulphate @ 3 g/L of water.
Rhizome rot	Collar region of pseudo-stems becomes soft and water soaked and	Grow resistant cultivars. Treat the rhizomes for 60 minutes before

	plants collapses leading to rhizomes rot.	storage and sowing with 0.25% Dithane M-45 + 0.1% Bavistin + Chloropyrephos 1 ml/L. Spray/ drench with chestnut compound and Agallol 0.1%.
Insects-pests		
Shoot borer	Attack the pseudo-stems and feed on the leaves.	Spray Dimethoate or phosphomides @ 0.05%.
Leaf miners	Suck sap of rhizomes in the field and storage.	Dip the rhizomes in 0.05% Malathion or Dimethoate.

CHAPTER 27

LESSER KNOWN VEGETABLE CROPS

Vegetables are the integral part of our daily diet in all walks of the society. The population of India is increasing at a faster rate (1.8% year) and the vegetable production in India cannot cop with the total requirement of vegetables even if supplemented with lesser known vegetables needed for nutritional security of the developing country like ours. However, the Indian population being vegetarians since ancient times but the per capita consumption is very less as compared to the most advanced countries and the rural population in the past and in hilly area still depended on the use of minor vegetable plants.

Increasing population; urbanisation, industrialisation and large network of roads is regularly decreasing our forest area/hill tops where these crops (trees, bushes, herbs, etc.) were growing in the wild natural habitat has been disturbed and some of the species are not even seen today because of the human's folly. India is fortunate enough to have a diverse agro-climatic conditions available/found throughout the length and breadth of the country which enables to produce both tropical and temperate vegetable plants which includes the wide range of species lesser known but nutritionally superior and are regularly consumed wherever these are available and growing or grown creating variety in their availability. During the last 5-6 decades, there is tremendous increase in the production of important vegetables but the lesser known vegetable crop plants have a special significance, though India is the second largest vegetable producer only next to China with an estimated production of about 80.2 million tonnes from an area of 6.5 million hectares. But very few efforts have been made to evolve new cultivars in minor vegetables and research conducted in this direction is also negligible.

Some of these species not only consumed as vegetable but can be planted in the waste lands, roadsides, railway tracts like kachnar, tamarind, etc., bushes and tender herbs also acts as ornamental material to decorate the surroundings, one or two plants can be planted in kitchen garden to meet daily need, some species can be planted in gardens, home gardens in association with trees/fruit plants to develop natural landscape, check soil erosion and make the atmosphere pollution free. The surplus material can be sold for earning money. It is known fact that the minor vegetables are important food and production, marketing and processing of these vegetable crop plants are important source of national income and nutritional security.

These plants will not only yield valuable vegetable products (tender stem/stalks, leaves, fruits, flowers, flower buds and green seeds) but also help in maintaining ecological balance. Important lesser known vegetable crops are tabulated in Table 27.1.

TABLE 27.1. Botanical name, common name, habit and economic part used of the lesser known vegetable crops

Botanical Name	*Common Name*	*Habit*	*Economic part used*
—	Snap pea	Annual	Pod and seed
Acacia concinna Dc.	Shikakai	Perennial	Tender leaves
Allium ascalonicum	Shallot	Annual	Green bulbs
Allium fistulosum	Welish onion, Cibol	Annual	Leaves
Alternarthera sessilis	Ponnanganni greens	Perennial	Shoot, leaves
Amaranthus gangeticus L.	Lal sag	Annual	Leaves
Amaranthus spinosus L.	Kantallai chauli	Perennial	Leaves
Anthriscus cerefolium	Chervil	Annual	Leaves
Apium graveolens var. *rapaceum*	Celeriac/knob celery	Annual	Roots
Atriplex hortensis	Chakwat or Utach	Annual	Leaves
Azadirachta indica (A) Juss	Neem	Tree	Tender leaves
Barbarea verna	Upland/winter cress	Annual	Leaves
Basella alba L.	Poi or Indian spinach	Annual	Leaves, stem
Bassica latifolia & B. longifolia	Butter tree or Mahua	Tree	Unripe fruits
Bauhinia racemosa	Kachnar	Perennial	Leaves, buds and flowers
Brassica campestris var. *rapiferea*	Swede/sweet turnip	Annual	Root and leaves
Brassica juncea	Mustard	Annual	Leaves
Brassica napus var. *napo-brassica*	Rutabaga	Annual	Root, leaves
Brassica oleracea var. *acephala*	Collards/Karam sag	Annual	Leaves
Canavalia ensiformis or gladiata	Sword bean	Annual	Pods
Cassia tora L.	Fortid cassia takla	Annual	Leaves
Centella asiatica	Vallarai Greens	Annual	Shoot, leaves
Chenopodium album L.	Bathua (Pig weed)	Annual	Leaves

Cicer arietinum	Green gram, Garbanzo	Annual	Green pod leaves
Cichorium endivia L.	Endive	Annual	Chicons
Cichorium intybus L.	Chicoey	Annual	Root, leaves
Clerodendron serratum Moon	Bharang or Bharangi	Annual	Leaves, root
Coleus parviflorus	Chinese potato	Annual	Tuber
Crambe maritima	Sea kale	Perennial	Shoot and leaves
Cucumis milo var. *momordica*	Snap melon	Annual	Fruit
Cynara scolymus	Artichoke	Perennial	Flower bud
Delipta erecta L.	Bhangra or Bhrangraj	Annual	Leaves
Dillenia indica L.	Karambel or Karmal	Annual	Fruit, flower
Fagopyrum tataricum	Buck wheat	Annual	Leaves
Ficus glomerata Roxb	Cluster fig or wild fig	Perennial	Unripe fruits
Helianthus tuberosus	Jerusalem Artichoke	Perennial	Root and buds
Hibiscus	Gogu	Annual	Shoot, feaves
cannabinus/sabdariffa	Water leaf or Kalam sag (Kang kong)	Annual	Tuber, leaves
Ipomoea aquatica			
Lipdium sativum L.	Cress	Annual	Leaves
Malva parviflora. L.	Little Mallow	Annual	Leaves, stem
Medicago denticulata Willd	Jungli Lucerne	Annual	Stem, leaves
Momordica dioca Roxb	Kanta Karkataki	Annual	Unripe fruits
Moringa aleifera L.	Drum stick	Tree	Fruit and flower
Murraya kaenigii	Curry leaf	Bush	Leaf
Nasturtium officinale	Water cress	Annual	Leaves
Oxalis comiculata L.	Khatti buti	Annual	Leaves
Phaseolus acutifolius	Tepary bean	Annual	Pods
Phaseolus coccineus	Scarlet runner or Multiflora bean	Annual	Pods
Physalis pruinosa	Physalis/Husk tomato	Perennial	Flower, fruit
Pisum sativum var. *Macrocarpum*	Edible podded pea	Annual	Pods
Portulaca oleracea L.	Kulfa	Annual	Leaves
Pteridium aqullinum L.	Lingri or lungru	Perennial	Fronds/leaves
Rumex vesicarius	Sorrel	Annual	Leaves
Saropus androgynus	Chakur	Tree	Flowers
Sesbania grandiflora (L.) Pers	Agathi or Jaint	Tree	Leaves, flower, pods
Sauropus androgynus Meeril	Chekurmanis	Shrub	Leaves
Sium sisarum L.	Skirret	Perennial	Roots
Solanum nigrum L.	Black nightshade	Annual	Fruit, leaves
Stellaria aquatica (L.) Cyrill	Chickweed	Annual	Leaves, stem
Stizolobium deeringianum	Velvet bean	Annual	Pods

Talinum triangulare	Ceylon spinach	Annual	Shoot, leaves
Tamarindus indica	Tamarind	Tree	Fruit
Taravacum officinale	Dandelion	Perennial	Leaves
Tetragonia tetragunioides	New Zealand spinach	Annual	Stem, leaves
Tetragopogon porrifolius	Salsify Ayster plant	Biennial	Root
Trianthema portulacastrum L.	Santh or Saranla	Annual	Leaves
Tribulus terrestris L.	Gokkru or Caltrop	Annual	Flower, fruit, leaves
Trigonella polycerata L.	Wild methi	Annual	Leaves, stem
Vigna rudiata	Mung beans	Annual	Bean sprouts
Vigna sinensis var. *Sesquipedalis*	Asparagus bean	Annual	Pods
Zea mays var. *rugusa*	Sweet corn	Annual	Immature cob

BRIEF DESCRIPTION OF LESSER KNOWN VEGETABLE CROPS

Acacia concinna Dc.

Common name: Shikakai: Family: *Minoceae*

The soup and bhaji of the tender leaf tops of this tree are specially good for invalids and the ripe pods of this species after powdering are used for hair washing.

Allium ascalonicum L.

Common name: Shallot: Family: *Amaryllidaceae*

It is an onion like plant originated in western Asia. It can be grown in nearly all parts of the country. It is a hardy plant and can be left in the field over the winter. Shallot produce cluster of bulbs somewhat like garlic. The shallot after harvesting is used like green onion and dry similar to onion bulbs. Dry bulbs can be stored in a well ventilated, cool, dry similar to onion through the winter.

Allium fistulosum L.

Common name: Japanese bunching/Welish onion/Cibol

Family: *Amaryllidaceae*

Normally grown in spring and bulbils are absent in most cultivars. Foliage leaf-bases only and the bulbs are not formed or poorly developed

Alternarthera sessilis

Common name: Ponnanganni greens: Family: *Amaranthaceae*

It is a small perennial herb propagated through soft wood cutting. It is nutritious as well as having medicinal value. The leaves are good source of protein, fat, carbohydrates, vitamins A, B_2, B_3 and C and minerals calcium, phosphorus and iron. The leaves and tender shoots are clipped fried and taken. The first clipping can be harvested 45-50 days after planting.

***Amaranthus gangeticus* L.**

Common name: Lalsag: Family: *Amaranthaceae*

Greenish or dark red tender herb with purple tinted or dark green leaves and shoot used as vegetable which are rich vitamins and minerals.

***Amaranthus spinosus* L.**

Common name: Kantallai chauli: Family: *Amaranthaceae*

It is a spinous perennial herb growing as weed of varying colour from green to purple or red, used as vegetable.

Anthriscum cerafolium

Common name: Chervil: Family: *Umbelliferae*

It is an annual plant grown in hot weather for the curled-leaved cultivars being most popular because of their attractive appearance. It is used for garnishing and flavouring and the foliage is usually harvested usually when young.

Apium graveolens* var. *rapaceum

Common name: Celeriac or knob celery: Family: *Umbelliferae*

It is also called celery root and turnip rooted celery originated from Egypt, parts of Asia and mountains of India. It is a vegetable somewhat resemble to beet and is grown for its enlarged root, which develop at the ground level. The taste is similar to celery but not stringy. It is grown successfully in heavy, moist, well drained soils in areas having mild climate. The roots attain full flavour when fully mature and can be left in the field and covered with mulch and harvest when desired. Roots may also be removed and stored in moist sand in a cool place.

Atriplex hortensis

Common name: Chakwat or Utach

It is also known as mountain spinach. It has somewhat strong flavour than spinach. The leaves become suitable for harvest 4-5 weeks after sowing. In the later stages, the tender leaves can be picked from the branches of the mature plants. It is grown on a smaller scale in Maharashtra and Karnataka during the winter season and in Kashmir during summer.

Barbarea verna

Common name: Winter cress: Family: *Compositae*

It is also called upland or spring cress is a hardy biennial grown as an annual or winter perennial. Crop is raised through seeds in mild climate and the plants are ready for use in 50 days.

***Basella alba* L.**

Common name: Indian Spinach or Poi; Family: *Baellaceae*

Indian spinach is grown throughout India for its tender leaves. There are three types under cultivation *viz.* green basella with dark green round oval leaves, leaves green and stem red and dark green cordate leaves. The first type is the most common and the tender shoot and leaves, leaf stalks and stem are chopped and cooked as vegetable. The tender shoots, fresh or cooked, contain substantial amount of carotene and its juice can remove constipation in children and pregnant women. It has also got some ornamental value. Grows well in sandy loam acidic soils, heavy rainfall, high humid climates with optimum temperature of 25-32°C. Propagated both seed and cuttings.

Bassica latifolia* and *B. longifolia

Common name: Butter tree or Mahua: Family: *Sapotaceae*

B. latifolia is a very common in decidous forests of central India, West Bengal, Konkan, while *B. longifolia* in Penninsula, Karnataka and Burma. Unripe fruits of these trees are used for vegetable purpose.

Bauhinia racemosa

Common name: Kachnar: Family: *Leguminoseae*

It is grown throughout India, Ceylon and tropical Africa. Tender leaves, buds and flowers are used for vegetable purpose.

Brassica campestris* var. *rapiferea

Common name: Swede or sweet turnip: Family: *Cruciferae*

Swede is grown for its enlarged roots and leaves in the temperate areas of Leh and Ladakh of Jammu and Kashmir. The roots are consumed in salad or cooked while tender leaves are used as leaf vegetable. It is quite popular due to its excellent keeping quality even at –30°C temperature. It can be grown at a elevation of 2500-4500 m.a.m.s.l. The plant growth is slightly slower but it produces giant fleshy roots compared to turnip. There is only one variety "Swede Sel-1" identified as the promising and recommended.

Brassica oleracea* var. *acephala

Common name: Collards; Family: *Cruciferae*

It is originated in the British Isles and Western Europe. Collards are a hardy cool season vegetable grown for both spring and fall crops. Collards can be transplanted or directly seeded. It is a non-heading type and forms a large rosette of blue-green leaves which are consumed as a leafy vegetable. Sometimes the whole plant at tender stage is cut-off and used and picking of leaves is also done continuously.

***Brassica napus napus brassica* group**

Common name: Rutabaga or Swede turnip: Family: *Cruciferae*

It was developed from a cross between cabbage and turnip. The roots generally yellow-fleshed and more solid and have a longer storage life. The leaves are smooth and waxy. The tender roots and leaves are consumed as vegetable.

Brassica juncea

Common name: Mustard; Family: *Cruciferae*

Mustard is a native of China and Asia and is used for its tender leaves. It is grown similar to collards or spinach. It is ready to harvest in 40 days and the entire plant may be harvested or young, lower leaves harvested continuously as in collards.

Cassia tora L.

Common name: Fortid cassia takla: Family: *Leguminoseae*

It is growing wild throughout tropical parts of India during *kharif* and *rabi* seasons. Tender leaves of the plant are used as vegetable.

Centella asiatica

Common name: Vallarai greens: Family: *Umbelliferae*

The green is found to improve the memory power of the brain cells. Hence praised very much for its medicinal value and is used in ayurvedic, siddha and homeopathic medicinal preparations. It is also a water loving plant which trails as a vine in the soil surface. Propagation is through offsets and the soil should have more organic matter and moisture always. It cannot tolerate moisture stress.

Chenopodium album L.

Common name: Bathua or Pig weed; Family: *Chenopodaceae*

It is one of the most important winter weeds. In tender stage its leaves are used as greens.

Cicer arietinum L.

Common name: Chick pea: Family: *Papilionaceae*

It is also called Garbanzo bean or gram or Bengal gram, native of the Mediterranean region and is one of the important source of food in India. It is a bush type annual bears pods grown in warm climates and the plant tops and seeds at green stage are consumed as vegetable. Dried plants serves as nutritious fodder. The mature dry pods are shelled and stored in airtight containers.

Cichorium indivia L.

Common name: Endive: Family: *Compositae*

It is also called French Endive, native of Europe and Asia grown like chicory, roots are washed and all the leaves are removed except the center crown bud on top. Roots of medium size are covered and stored in a cool, moist, frost free area. The seeds are sown successive way for continuous salad greens. The blanched leaves along with tender roots called chicons are relished as a salad mostly during winter.

Cichorium intybus L.

Common name: Chicory or Kasani: Family: *Compositae*

It is a native of Europe and Asia and grows best in all types of soils. The seeds are sown successive way for continuous salad greens. After blanching, the leaves along with tender roots called chicons are also relished as a salad. The large sized roots after washing, chopping, roasting are ground into powder and used as a coffee substitute or adulterant.

Clerodendron serratum **Moon**

Common name: Bharang or Bharangi: Family: *Verbenaceae*

It is found growing during *rabi* season as a weed throughout India. Its leaves are used as vegetable and the decoction of root is considered very effective in malarial fever.

Coleus parviflorus

Common name: Chinese potato: Family: *Labiatae*

It is a herbaceous annual native of Africa, spreading or prostate with succulent stem and small tubers rich in carbohydrate. It grows well in a tropical humid climate. The total duration of the crop including nursery 180-190 days and the maturity is indicated by drying of entire plant and harvesting can be done with in 150 days of planting. The yield ranges 18-20 t/ha.

Crambe maritima

Common name: Sea kale: Family: *Cruciferae*

It is a hardy perennial grown for young leaves and shoots. This is not commonly grown in India.

Delipta erecta **L.**

Common name: Bhangra or Bhrangraj: Family: *Compositae*

Its leaves are used as vegetable in Ceylon, Sind and Malaya.

Dillenia indica **L.**

Common name: Karambel or Karmal: Family: *Dilleniaceae*

It is found growing throughout the sub-Himalayan tract and in moist regions of the peninsula during hot weather and *kharif.* The fleshy sepals, surrounding the fruits and also the fruits are used as vegetable.

Fagopyrum tataricum

Common name: Buck wheat: Family: *Polygonaceae*

It is very commonly grown in the hills of Himachal Pradesh. The tender tops are picked periodically for use as greens. In the hills it is sown with the break of the monsoon.

Ficus glomerata **Roxb**

Common name: Cluster fig or wild fig; Family: *Urticaceae*

Its unripe fruits and tender leaves are used as vegetable.

Helianthus tuberosus

Common name: Jerusalem Artichoke: Family: *Compositae*

Jerusalem Artichoke is a native of South America. It is cultivated for its oblong tubers which contains carbohydrate storing in it the insulin which is of great value to the diabetics. It is also a food crop and fed to hogs. It has wide adaptability to a range of soil and climatic conditions.

Hibiscus cannabinus* L/H. *sabdariffa

Common name: Gogu; Family: *Malvaceae*

The tender shoots and leaves are used as greens. Leaves have a slightly acidic taste. Mainly propagated by seed and the tender shoots can be clipped 25-30 days after sowing by which the branches can be induced. The tender leaves and stems are used to prepare chutney.

***Houttuynia cordata* Thumb**

Common name: Jamarda; Family: *Piperaceae*

A perennial herb with creeping root-stocks and herbaceous angular stems, eaten as a vegetable both raw and cooked. It is much relished. It is very common in Naga and Khasi hills.

Ipomoea aquatica

Common name: Water leaf/convolvulus or Kang kong.

Family: *Convolvulaceae*

Water leaf is also known as swamp cabbage or water spinach, the water-leaf is a soft mucilaginous leaves and tender shoots are used as vegetable. It is a trailing vine similar to sweet potato, propagated easily by herbaceous cuttings or seeds. First harvest is ready in 40 days after sowing/planting and subsequent harvest can be continued once in 20 days for atleast 4 months. The crop is ideally suited to areas where water stagnation is a problem and can tolerate saline-alkaline soil and water too. To certain extent it is also drought tolerant. The green yield ranges from 6-7 t/ha.

***Lipdium sativum* L.**

Common name: Cress; Family: *Cruciferae*

Cress is a native of Europe and is called garden cress or pepper grass, a hardy, cool season annual easily grown in kitchen garden or indoors during the winter. Crop is raised through seeds and leaves are harvested when they are 8-12 cm long and consumed at a tender stage.

***Malva parviflora* L.**

Common name: Little Mallow; Family: *Malvaceae*

It is a small, spreading weed found in north-west Himalayas, upper Bengal and Punjab. It is frequently eaten as a pot herb.

***Medicago denticulata* Willd**

Common name: Jungli Lucerne; Family: *Leguminoseae*

It is a common winter weed in the plains and hills. Leaves of the plant in early stages are used for vegetable purpose.

***Momordica dioca* Roxb**

Common name: Kanta Karkotaki; Family: *Cucurbitaceae*

It is found growing throughout India all the year round. Its unripe fruits are used as vegetable.

Moringa aleifera L.

Common name: Drumstick: Family: *Moringae*

Drumstick is an important vegetable in south Indian households and is valued for the distinct and appealing flavour of the fruits. Partially matured fruits, leaves and flowers are used for culinary preparation. It is a perennial tree and recently an annual type have been developed. Drumstick is very nutritious plant susceptible to frost and is propagated by limb cuttings and annual types by seeds. Perennial trees can be retained for 15 years while the annual types can be harvested in 6 months normally in July-September and the fruits are not fibrous.

Murraya koenigi L. (Sprengal)

Common name: Curry leaf: Family: *Rutaceae*

Curry leaf is a spicy leafy vegetable used in our day to day culinary preparation mainly to increase the flavour and taste of food. It is rich in nutritional value and is cultivated on commercial scale. It can be grown in a wide range of soil and climates. It is propagated by seed or seedlings. In the first year, the leaf yield is only 2-4 q/ha which increases in the subsequent years and in 5th year 5 t/ha in three months and 20 t/ha in a year.

Nasturtium officinale

Common name: Water cress: Family: *Cruciferae*

It is a cool season semi-aquatic perennial widely distributed in Europe and western Asia. It grows naturally in clear, cold, shallow slow moving streams, either as a floating plant or rooted to the bottom. Seeds or cuttings are used for raising in containers with holes at the bottom and the plants are pinched for proper branching. The plant is ready for harvest in 60-70 days as a salad or vegetable.

Oxalis corniculata L.

Common name: Khatti buti: Family: *Oxalidaceae*

It is a cosmopolitan weed growing along the banks of streams, channels, lawns, shady and moist situations, etc. throughout warmer parts of India. It is a spreading annual with sour leaves. It is eaten as salad and cooked as a pot herb, particularly at the time of drought. In south India, it is cultivated as vegetable. The curry from fresh leaves improves appetite and digestion of dyspeptic patients.

Physalis pruinosa

Common name: Physalis of Husk tomato: Family: *Solanaceae*

It is also called ground cherry naturally occurring in Western Hemisphere and is a warm season plant grown similar to tomato. The edible fruit is berry enclosed in a thin husk. The husk turns from green to yellow to brown when the fruit is ripe, while the fruit turns from green to yellow. It is eaten fresh or made into jam or sauce.

***Pteridium aqullinum* L.**

Common name: Lingri or lungra: Family: *Polypodiaceae*

This fern is growing in many parts of the Himalayas upto an elevation of 3500 m a.m.s.l. The fronds or unfolded tender leaves of the fern are generally used for vegetable purpose when they are in quite young stage.

Rumex vesicarius

Common name: Sorrel: Family: *Polygonaceae*

It is commonly known as khatta palak and is grown for its sour leaves. When the plants flower, they look very attractive and often are used as an ornamental plant.

***Sauropus androgynus* Meeril**

Common name: Chekurmanis: Family: *Euphorbiaceae*

This is another leafy vegetable which is believed to have been introduced into India from Malaya. It is a small perennial shrub and is considered to be one of the most popular leafy vegetables in Malaya and Java. The crop comes up well in mild humid locations with equable temperature, *viz,* the temperature is neither very high (40°C) nor too low (freezing or near freezing).

***Sesbania grandiflora* L.**

Common name: Agathi or Mar: Family: *Papilionaceae*

It is a perennial tall lanky tree can be grown as a bush also and propagated by seed. Leaves are very nutritious and rich in vitamin and minerals. Harvesting can be done once in a month for 4-5 months. The flowers are also edible and have manifold medicinal utility. The leaves, flowers and pods are used as vegetable. Quick growing soft wooded tree has ornamental, food and fodder value.

***Sium sisarum* L.**

Common name: Skirret: Family: *Umbelliferae*

It is a hardy perennial crop grown as an annual producing numerous swollen roots, forming a bunch from the crown which are greyish white in colour with firm white flesh. It is propagated by seed or off-sets or divisions of the roots. The tender roots have a sweet taste and used similar to salsify.

***Solanum aigrum* L.**

Common name: Black nightshade: Family: *Solanaceae*

It is a nutritious leafy vegetable grown for its tender greens and small ripe fruits used in dried form. It is propagated by seed and through nursery. The tender shoots with well developed leaves get ready in 45-60 days after transplanting and repeated cuttings 2-3/month can be taken and the ripe fruits are collected for next crop.

***Stellaria uquatica* (L.) Cyrill**

Common name: Chickweed: Family: *Carysphyllaceae*

It is an small aquatic weed with white flowers. It is very common on moist and shady situations throughout the Punjab and temperate regions of India. The leaves and tender young stalks are eaten sometimes with fish in Assam. It is also used as vegetable in the Nilgiris also.

Talinum triangulare

Common name: Ceylon spinach: Family: *Portulocaceae*

It is a shade loving plant grown for its tender shoot and leaves cooked as vegetable. Propagation is through herbaceous stem cuttings may be rooted or unrooted. Harvesting can be done once in a month throughout the year yielding 4-6 t/ha greens.

***Tamarindus indica* L.**

Common name: Imli: Family: *Papilionaceae*

This tree is found all over the plains though it is more common in the south. The new twigs of tamarind cooked with grated onion form a tasty vegetable. Leaves and flowers are also used as vegetable during *rabi* and hot weather.

Taravacum officinale

Common name: Dandelion: Family: *Compositae*

It is a native of Europe and Asia, a perennial plant with smooth or jagged, irregular dark green leaves used as greens and in salads. It is a hardy, cool season plant withstand freezing temperature and grows well in fertile well drained soils. Seed is used for its propagation. The leaves at a tender stage are harvested and the root portion is left for next years harvest.

Tetragonia expansa/tetragunioides

Common name: New Zealand spinach: Family: *Azoaceae*

It is a native of New Zealand, Japan and Australia and have spreading habit with much branches grown during summer and prone to frost. Seed germination is very slow and need to soak in warm water before sowing. Leaves and stems are both used.

Tetragopogon porrifolius

Common name: Salsify: Family: *Compositae*

Salsify is often called oyster plant because of the faint oyster-like flavour found in the roots. It is a native of Mediterranean region and distinct from black salsify or Spanish salsify which are common in Europe. It is a hardy biennial grown similar to parsnip but needs 150 days to mature from seed. Roots are harvested and consumed as in salad or vegetable.

***Trianthema portulacastrum* L.**

Common name: Santha or Saranla: Family: *Aizoaceae*

It is a common *kharif* weed distributed almost all over the plains. The leaves are used for vegetable purpose.

***Tribulus terrestris* L.**

Common name: Gokkru or Caltrop: Family: *Zygophyllaceae*

This is a spreading plant growing throughout the year as a weed in wastelands, playgrounds and cultivated fields, producing yellow flowers, spiny fruits and leaves with several small leaflets.

***Trigonella polycerata* L.**

Common name: Wild methi: Family: *Leguminoseae*

It is a common winter weed in north India used for vegetable purpose. It is a trailing trifoliate plant.

Azadirachta indica (A) Juss

Common name: Neem: Family: *Meliaceae*

Its tender leaves are sometimes cooked and eaten.

Vigna rudiata

Common name: Mung bean: Family: *Papilionaceae*

It is a bush type plant cultivated in warm climates and susceptible to cold. It is primarily used for bean sprouts, raw in salads or as cooked vegetable in oriental dishes. The seeds are soaked overnight and then placed in a container that has holes in the bottom for drainage. The container needs to be large enough to allow the beans to expand and swell as they sprout. Keep the container in the dark in a warm place and moistened thrice in summer and twice in winter daily. Thus the beans become ready for use in 5 days in summer and 10 days in winter, usually used when the sprouts are 5-6 cm long. They are stored in a cool humid place until use.

Vigna sinensis* var. *sesquipedalis

Common name: Yard long bean: Family: *Luguminaceae*

There are three types of Southern pea-blackeye pea, cream pea and crowder pea and the yard long bean or asparagus bean is a pole type subspecies of Southern pea. It is a native of middle Asia, both pole and bush types, maturity duration is long and short, respectively. In pole type, the pods are 30-40 cm long and are harvested as green shell or dry peas and can be used like snap bean, green shell or dry beans.